Who's Afraid of Elizabeth Taylor?

By the same author:

Beyond Babel

The Half-Parent

Brenda Maddox

Who's Afraid of Elizabeth Taylor?

M. EVANS AND COMPANY, INC.
NEW YORK, NEW YORK 10017

M. Evans and Company titles are distributed in the United States by the J. B. Lippincott Company, East Washington Square, Philadelphia, PA 19105; and in Canada by McClelland & Stewart Ltd., 25 Hollinger Road, Toronto M4B 3G2, Ontario

Library of Congress Cataloging in Publication Data

Maddox, Brenda.
  Who's afraid of Elizabeth Taylor?

  Filmography: p.
  1. Taylor, Elizabeth Rosemond, 1932-
  2. Moving-pictures actors and actress—United
States—Biography.   I.   Title.
PN2287.T18M3   791.43′028′0924   [B]   77-8798
ISBN 0-87131-243-3

Design by Al Cetta

Manufactured in the United States of America

9 8 7 6 5 4 3 2 1

Thanks are due to the following publishers, magazines, and newspapers for permission to reprint copyrighted material within the text:
  Doubleday and Company, Inc. for Mike Nichols's views on *Who's Afraid of Virginia Woolf?* (pages 192-93). From *The Film Director as Superstar* by Joe Gelmis. Copyright © 1970 by Joe Gelmis. Reprinted by permission of Doubleday and Company, Inc.
  The Economist for an excerpt from Brenda Maddox's review of *Cleopatra* (page 173). © 1963 by *The Economist*. Reprinted by permission.
  Ladies' Home Journal for excerpts from articles by Sara Taylor and Elizabeth Taylor (pages 11, 14, 58-59, 232). © 1954 and 1975 by

For Bronwen

Contents

Preface

Why Elizabeth Taylor? Everybody asks.

Because I wanted to. As a reporter, as a woman, as a moviegoer. What I've written will explain why. Let me simply say that I began with the thought that a female who has been on the world's mind for more than thirty years deserves objective inquiry as much as do elections, schools, atomic energy, or any of the other things reporters write about.

I have not interviewed Elizabeth Taylor. Everybody asks that too. The reason is that she refused—repeatedly, categorically. At first I was mystified. Why should she not be as accessible as any of the other public figures I've talked with? She depends on the public's interest in her; I am not a sensationalist. Besides, what appears in the press does not make her seem exactly Garboesque.

But I was wrong. Elizabeth Taylor is nothing like a senator or an astronaut or the head of AT&T. She has been called a great natural wonder. In fact she is a great natural resource—of which she is the owner. Like an oil well, the asset depletes with time. The owner has absolutely no incentive to share it unless she sees it to her advantage.

About not interviewing Elizabeth Taylor, I'm only half sorry.

Most books about living film stars are authorized. I would not write an authorized book, and who wants to read one? Taylor, I've found out, is particularly choosy about the journalists she consents to see. Just when she was turning down my final appeal, she did let somebody else in the door. I read what he wrote. He sounded grateful. "Then suddenly here she is, magnetically, stunningly beautiful at forty-four, radiating joy at me in the plush Vienna hotel. . . ." It was absolutely right for the woman's magazine that ran it and put her photograph on its cover, with "Gorgeous Glitter Knitting" over one shoulder and "Cooking with Bran" over the other.

Making my own way from London to Hollywood, talking with a great many people who have known or worked with Elizabeth Taylor from the early thirties to the post-Burton years, I have put together a picture of a phenomenon and the world's reaction and overreaction to it. I think I have been able to answer some of the puzzles that her public persona throws out. Why does this beautiful woman, once called the girl who had everything, appear so greedy? Why has she married so often? Why so ill? Why have we all paid so much attention?

The result is not intended as a biography but rather as the story of how a private life became a public myth—and also of how women and sex have changed from the forties to the seventies.

Happily for me, Taylor did not stand in the way of her friends who asked her permission to talk to me. She instructed one merely, "Don't be bitchy" and another, "You'll probably say dreadful things about me, you dirty cow." No fear. Anyone who has a goddess for a friend worships her.

Although I'm not a passionate feminist (for which I feel guilty: Like so many women, I have enjoyed the fruits of the women's movement without the fight), I decided to refer to her as Taylor. "Elizabeth" is too familiar—I don't know her—and "Liz" is worse. Besides, it has been impressed upon me that she is a lady with a powerful temper and that she does not like

"Liz." Her friends enunciate E-li-za-beth carefully, as if she might jump out from behind the couch.

Writing can be solitary but not when the subject is Elizabeth Taylor. Everybody wants to contribute: opinions, dreams, newspaper clippings, memories. My family was a rich source. I'm grateful to my late mother and my mother-in-law, who lived worlds apart and never met but whose views on Taylor were identical; to my father-in-law, A. J. Maddox, my daughters, and to my son, Bruno Maddox, a student of television timetables, who spotted *Courage of Lassie*, which I otherwise would have missed, and to my husband, John Maddox, for accompanying me to old Elizabeth Taylor movies at cult-movie houses in the small hours of the morning. We got home from *Giant* at half past three. I am not grateful to friends in journalism who told me I was wasting my talent; they never said that when I wrote about communications satellites.

Many people in and around the movie industry helped me. Many of their names appear in this book. I am grateful to them and equally to those who asked not to be quoted. I would like to thank the following organizations: American Film Institute, Boston Public Library, British Film Institute, Columbia Pictures Corporation, Dalzell-Hatfield Galleries, Lincoln Center Library for the Performing Arts in New York City, Los Angeles County Art Museum, *Los Angeles Times*, Metro-Goldwyn-Mayer, the Oxford University Dramatic Society, Sotheby Parke Bernet, Starlight Cinema Club, Twentieth Century-Fox, and Wandsworth Public Libraries.

Also I would like to thank, without implying in any way that they share my opinions, Adrian Ball, Enid Bagnold, Nancy Balfour, Pandro S. Berman, Graham Binns, Stephen Birmingham, Dr. and Mrs. Daniel Bleifer, Patricia Bosworth, Frederick Boydell-Barrington, Richard Brooks, Elsie Carper, Thelma Cazalet-Keir, Bosley Crowther, Howard Dietz, Delia Doherty, John Gregory Dunne, Mr. and Mrs. John Finney, Jules Goldstone, David Gordon, Virginia Gordon, Grayson Hall, Lord Harlech, Edith Head, John Heyman, Norma

Heyman, Sheran Cazalet Hornby, Maureen Howard, Robert Rhodes James, Adm. Sir Caspar John, Nora Johnson, Elliott Kastner, Evelyn Keyes, Mr. and Mrs. Brian Lapping, Paul Laskin, David Lewin, Marguerite Littman, Roderick MacFarquhar, David Marks, Sam Marx, Egon Merz, Larry Micchie, Vincente Minnelli, Peter Mitchell, John Morgan, S. J. Perelman, Guy Pilkington, James Powers, Anne Revere, Richard Roud, Nora Sayre, Maura Shaw, Aubrey Singer, George Stevens, Jr., Sir John Terry, Mike Todd, Jr., Betty Vacani, Lady Vaizey, Francis Warner, Paul Weeks, and Brook Williams.

Who's Afraid of Elizabeth Taylor?

1

Downtown

Shortly before 8:30 in the evening of November 10, 1975, Elizabeth Taylor and Richard Burton stepped out of an elevator at the Dorchester Hotel in London and into the small lobby by the jewelry showcases. They had just arrived from Botswana where they had married each other for the second time. During the in-flight movie, the evening papers reported, light from Taylor's thirty-three-carat diamond ring had flashed through the darkness of the first-class cabin. At the Dorchester the crowd that had been gathering in anticipation of seeing the reunited Burtons suddenly clotted. Bodies pressed and surged. Hand-held television cameras teetered dangerously above heads. From the back came a loud orgasmic moan from a woman too short to have seen anything. "Isn't he gorgeous! Isn't she gorgeous!" Burton lowered his head into his bull shoulders and plunged into the private room that hid his party.

Not so his wife. Taylor turned and faced the crowd. She was triumphant and slim in bare black. Smiling, unhurried, she presented her glossy diamond-studded head as if she held it in her hands, like a priest elevating the monstrance at the altar. She rotated it through 180 degrees and back again. It was a very big head. Its features have been known throughout the world

1

for three decades: the high childishly curved forehead, the black circumflex eyebrows, the perfect nose over the MGM mouth, and the eyes blazing blue, abnormally wide and even. The act was that of an old-time movie star, fulfilling her duty to her public, or more primitively, that of a human idol offering itself for worship, protecting itself with its power. Only when it was completed did she too disappear.

I first heard of Elizabeth Taylor on a Saturday morning during the war. The town where I lived with my widowed mother and grandfather was not, strictly speaking, in middle America but rather in the upper right-hand corner, in Massachusetts. There was only one movie theater in the town and it was poised between respectability and sin, on the street that sloped from the green common and the center of town down to the barrooms and the wrong side of the tracks. Around the movie house were stores bearing immigrant names; Balboni sold liquor and penny candy, Gotschalk sold dry goods; Brady kept his diner open late to catch the after-movie crowd, and a succession of Chinese families ran the laundry. Near the common, the elm trees, and the white-spired Congregational church were the stores with what now would be called WASP names—Snow's, Churchill's, Fairbanks's. At the time they seemed simply "good English" names. Their position seemed logical enough; they had got there first.

If we wanted a wider choice of movies, we got into the car and drove to Brockton six miles away. That's what my grandfather did. An Italian grocer and a widower—I grew up in a household of mateless people—he liked to put on *la bella figura* after work and go to the big city where he could enjoy night life without running into his customers. In Brockton there were four theaters: the Brockton and the Colonial on Main Street; on a side street, the Rialto; and on the outskirts of the city, in proletarian Campello, among the shoe factories, Keith's. That the Brockton was part of the Loew's chain, showing only MGM films, and the Keith was named for the Keith-

Albee national movie circuit, we did not know or care. To us what mattered was that the Brockton was the most expensive but had mirrors, thick carpets, and classy movies, that the Colonial was nearly as grand, that the Rialto was rumored to be where Negroes went, so we didn't, and that Keith's, an unglamorous box of gray stucco, gave away dishes. Hideous ones with fluted edges, gold rims, and pink cherry blossoms. It was years before our last "Dish Night" saucer broke.

My mother, who couldn't walk from spinal meningitis, always went to the local movie house on Friday nights. The manager would help her in with her wheelchair and not charge her for her ticket. On one of these Fridays she saw MGM's *Lassie Come Home*. As a widow with an only daughter, her attention was not caught by the dog. At breakfast the next morning she was in a reverie. She told me about "the most beautiful child I have ever seen. About your age. The eyes, such long lashes . . . I can't get her face out of my mind." I decided not to see *Lassie Come Home*. Then came the knife: "And so well spoken."

Before her illness and brief marriage, my mother had been the first in the family to get a college education. She had studied speech and drama, so I was well aware that I mumbled and did not speak up. There was more: the little girl was poised . . . a little lady, and again, unbelievably lovely.

It was clear to me then, sight unseen, that Elizabeth Taylor (whose name I was not to learn until *National Velvet*) was a girl from downtown. Downtown was Protestant, richer, purer. Those of us on the fringes thought we were fiercely loyal (yes, we would fight) to our assorted Irish, Polish, Italian, and Portuguese origins, and to our Roman religion, but in fact, from living in that town, we were Protestants in spirit, with the moral code of John Calvin and the class consciousness of John O'Hara. To be poor was to be bad. Downtown was where the houses looked like Judge Hardy's and the families were as upright. The diction there was better; nobody used a thick dental *t*. Children from downtown did not feel sick when having to eat at a friend's

house. Their big sisters did not "get into trouble." Their
parents ate dinner in the evening, had friends in for cocktails,
and slept in twin beds with a lamp on the table in between.
Everything downtown was so superior that as teen-agers we
even necked in the Protestant cemetery. The scenery was
better.

When I finally did see *Lassie Come Home* years later, on
television, I saw that my guess about my mother's dream child
had been right. On the screen was a little girl playing the
granddaughter of a duke, wearing a powder-blue wool suit as if
it would never need to go to the dry cleaner's. She acted
charming and natural, and even patted a dog, while wearing hat
and gloves (which of course matched her ankle socks). Her
coloring was an intriguing combination: the hair was black
(Passion), the eyes were blue (Class). What's more, she could
ride a horse (Money). The face was full of WASP vitality. Why
shouldn't it trust its instincts? Its salvation was assured, its place
in the world secure.

2

The Cazalet Connection

"I was born in Hampstead."

"No, darling, you were born in Hendon."

"It was Hampstead, Richard."

"Sorry, love, it was Hendon."

Thus did the former Burtons divert their friends. Richard Burton, the working-class boy, was someone else who saw Elizabeth Taylor as a girl from downtown. Teasing Taylor about her birthplace made a good laugh because both were half right. When she was born in London on February 27, 1932 (which makes her five days younger than Senator Edward Kennedy and three days younger than I), her parents were living in a luxurious neo-Georgian house at 8 Wildwood Road, facing Hampstead Heath. The address, though, does not really lie in fashionable Hampstead, but rather in the more bourgeois, predominantly Jewish suburb of Golder's Green, and the birth was registered in the even less chic district of Hendon.

Like everybody else, I always thought of Elizabeth Taylor as English. MGM liked it that way. Its publicity mill ground out the myth long after *National Velvet.* "Elizabeth is as British as they make them" boasted the blurbs for *A Date with Judy* in 1948. For *Julia Misbehaves* the same year, Peter Lawford and

Taylor together were billed as "those two delightful juveniles, as British as their costars Greer Garson and Walter Pidgeon." The London popular press never surrendered ownership: a busty teen-age pinup photo in *The People* maintained: "She's Fifteen, English, and America's White Hope!"

While it is true that Taylor did acquire British nationality because of her birthplace, she was also born a United States citizen. Both her parents were American—very American. They, and their parents before them, came from Arkansas City, Kansas, a sleepy town on the Oklahoma border, a long way from St. Louis, a hundred miles southeast of Dodge City.

In its way, the steep swift climb of Sara and Francis Taylor out of the backwaters of the Middle West to the top of English society was even more remarkable than their daughter's rise from the bottom to the top of the movie industry a generation later. They did it on looks, talent, and charm. Neither graduated from high school—at least not from Arkansas City High School, which Sara Warmbrodt entered in 1911 and Francis Taylor a year later.

Both were extremely good-looking. In London Sara Taylor, with vivacious eyes and bobbed hair, is remembered as "dishy." But it is Francis Taylor who gets the superlatives. One Englishwoman describes him simply as the most handsome man she ever saw: tall, with a leonine head, black hair, which soon went gray, with blue eyes and thick dark lashes. He looked almost Irish, although his origins seem to have been Scottish and English, and he was considered a very smart dresser.

Back in Arkansas City, they say that Elizabeth Taylor gets her looks from her paternal grandmother: Elizabeth Rosemond Taylor. Old Mrs. Taylor, who died during the Depression, is still remembered for her great beauty and dark hair. Her husband, Francis Taylor, was a well-to-do merchant who had come to Arkansas City from Indiana in 1890. The couple were pillars of the Presbyterian Church and the Eastern Star Masonic Lodge, and lived in a brick house which they built at

310 North A Street, and which is still pointed out as the Taylor family home.

About Sara Taylor's origins, Arkansas City is cattier, probably because her father was of German stock without the long middle western roots of her husband's family. Samuel Warmbrodt was an engineer who worked in the Empire Laundry; his wife, Anna, was a musician. A voluble neighbor says, "The Warmbrodts would be what we consider OK, but nothing as fine and refined as the Taylors." She adds, "I've often wished that Elizabeth's father [who died in 1968] had lived long enough to have gotten his parents a nice tombstone, but that is their business. Sara Taylor did bring Elizabeth to Arkansas City for several summers when she was a little girl, but then she went to Hollywood and dropped everyone she ever knew."

Today Arkansas City watches the superstar with awe:

"The Taylors were such a lovely old couple that they would just curl up if they could see their granddaughter today . . . but no one really knows her except what we read."

By the time they married in 1926, Sara and Francis Taylor had each separately shaken off the dust of Arkansas City and made a mark in a more glamorous world. Around the age of sixteen Francis Taylor had left to work with Howard Young, his aunt's husband, an art dealer in St. Louis. He was good at it and developed an expert eye for painting. From St. Louis he moved with Young to New York where Young prospered as a rival to the great Duveen. Sara Warmbrodt made her way independent of family connections. She became a successful actress; she took a new name: Sara Sothern. In the early twenties, she was the drawing card for Edward Everett Horton's repertory group at the old Majestic Theatre in Los Angeles. A play called *The Fool* was her special vehicle and brought her success in New York and Europe. In London, she received an ovation and rave notices of the kind her daughter would work many years to match. Then on a visit to New York, she remet her old schoolmate, Francis Taylor, at a nightclub with his uncle. They married and she never acted again.

Howard Young dispatched the attractive newlyweds to Europe to buy paintings for the American market. For a while the Taylors traveled the capitals and lived, as Elizabeth Taylor was later to do, like affluent nomads in luxury hotels. When their first child, a son, was born in 1929, they settled in London. Francis Taylor opened a gallery in a paneled suite of rooms upstairs at 30 Old Bond Street. His assignment was to get "the good stuff"—the Gainsboroughs, Reynoldses, and Constables, as well as the continental Old Masters, that came into the London art market. He also kept an eye out for English and Scottish portraits, for Howard Young in New York had a steady demand for pictures that might pass as ancestors on American walls.

In London, like many Americans abroad, before and since, the Taylors moved in a higher social circle than they had at home. With their attractiveness and clothes with the right labels, they floated comfortably in the kind of mannered society that made plainer Americans like Henry Adams feel ill at ease. Their progress was helped by their good fortune in being virtually adopted by the wealthy Cazalet family and in particular by Victor Cazalet, a gregarious bachelor, sportsman, and art collector, who was also a Conservative member of Parliament.

Cazalet knew everybody. Short (his nickname was "Teenie") yet sturdily handsome, he exuded and admired charm. He brought the Taylors into a world of politicians, financiers, literati, and royalty, domestic and foreign. Cazalet's sister, Mrs. Thelma Cazalet-Keir, took Sara Taylor to the coronation of George VI; Cazalet's mother, Maud, let little Elizabeth Taylor deliver birthday gift to Queen Mary at Buckingham Palace. Victor Cazalet's Oxford roommate was Prince Paul of Yugoslavia, and the prince's daughter, Princess Elizabeth, later became a friend of Elizabeth Taylor's (until the princess became temporarily the fiancée of Richard Burton after the first Taylor-Burton divorce in 1974).

The friendship between the Cazalets and the Taylors was

built on three mutual passions. One was for fine art. They all particularly admired the work of Augustus John and used to visit the thundering bohemian at his home in Fordingbridge in Hampshire. When John in a terrible temper tore up some of his drawings and threw them into the wastebasket, Francis Taylor quietly rescued them and pasted them back together. Some of them he kept; others went into the Cazalet collection.

Another bond was Christian Science. Both the Taylors and the Cazalets were believers in this fairly isolating religion. In fact, the plot of Sara Taylor's triumph, *The Fool*, turned on faith-healing. The London *Times* called the play "a religious orgy of the type very popular in the United States," and its climax came as the little crippled girl (Sara) threw away her crutches and walked when God revealed himself. For his part, Victor Cazalet was as ardent about his unorthodox faith as he was about every other cause he espoused, from Zionism to the Boy Scout movement. He studied the works of Mary Baker Eddy and preached at Christian Science meetings.

Above all, the two families were bound by the two Taylor children. Both were dazzling even when tiny. They had their father's blue eyes and dark brows and seemed precociously wise, peering out from deep shadows. "I can see them now," says Thelma Cazalet-Keir. "Francis and Sara were absolute charmers. And these two lovely children would come dancing in! My mother and brother absolutely adored them. We all did. We took them straight in. They became a part of us."

So much were the Taylors part of the Cazalets that Victor Cazalet lent them a sixteenth-century cottage on the grounds of his Kent estate. They installed electricity and water and named it "Little Swallows" to complement his house, "Great Swifts." The place was hardly a cottage—it had fourteen rooms with leaded casement windows—and the Taylors used it just at weekends. But it occupied a central place in their concept of themselves as an English family. After they returned to America in 1939, "Little Swallows" came to symbolize a way of life—premovie as well as prewar—that they could never recapture. It was on the Kent estate, on a pony that Victor Cazalet gave her, that Elizabeth Taylor learned to ride.

Sara Taylor was enough of a believer in mind over matter to try to think beautiful thoughts before each of her children was born. This and other details of the birth and raising of Elizabeth Taylor were revealed in a series Mrs. Taylor wrote for *Ladies' Home Journal* in 1954. The gushing essays are vintage fifties— perhaps why they have been scissored out of the bound volumes of the Boston Public Library.

For her firstborn Sara Taylor found that the beautiful- thoughts formula worked. Howard Taylor was a Botticelli child, golden-haired and precocious. But something went wrong with the second, or so it seemed at first. The child was dark and hairy and slow to walk and talk. Mrs. Taylor had to endure the standard commiseration: "Isn't it a pity that she isn't the boy and her brother the girl!"

By the time the girl was two, however, she too was causing people to stop and stare. Still, Howard had the edge. When Sara Taylor went shopping, she used to leave the children in the Bond Street gallery, and Frederick Boydell-Barrington, who worked with Francis Taylor in those years, recalls, "People who came into the gallery would remark on the beauty of the chil- dren. But most that saw the two of them would praise the boy." It was something that the girl obviously noticed.

Very early Elizabeth Taylor exhibited a strong tendency to daydream and to invent selves. When she was about three, she decided to call Victor Cazalet, whom she adored, her god- father. It was not strictly true, as Christian Scientists recoil at the very mention of baptism. Cazalet would have accepted the title purely honorarily. However, he did intervene at a critical stage in her early life as dramatically as if he had stood at the font.

Sara Taylor described the incident in words that scarcely conceal an act of faith-healing. It happened when Elizabeth Taylor had her first serious illness when she was three. Like the many that came later, it was far out of the ordinary. She lay in bed in Hampstead with a temperature of 103 degrees for three full weeks. Her abscessed ears were lanced twice a day. Sara Taylor was not the kind of Christian Scientist, like Jean Harlow's mother, who would not call a doctor, yet she could see that the medical attentions were not doing any good. Finally the child, concerned to see her tired mother get some rest (says Sara Taylor), asked that Victor Cazalet and his mother come up to London to see her. They did, driving ninety miles in thick fog. Then:

> When they arrived, Victor sat on the bed and held her in his arms and talked to her about God. Her great dark eyes searched his face, drinking in every word, *believing* and *understanding*.
>
> A wonderful sense of peace filled the room. I laid my head down on the side of the bed and went to sleep for the first time in three weeks.
>
> When I awakened she was fast asleep! The fever had broken.

Christian Scientists believe that disease will disappear if the idea of health is sent out to supersede it. When the body is cured, it is also purified. It's a belief that is hard on their children, who have trouble distinguishing being ill from being naughty. And so, one can speculate, do major movie studios with a big picture on their hands and a sick star. In 1961 Taylor found that by nearly dying from pneumonia, she was forgiven by Twentieth Century-Fox for bringing *Cleopatra* to a halt and by the public for marrying Eddie Fisher.

If Victor Cazalet was the rich relation the Taylors chose, Howard Young was the one God gave them. Young, who died in 1972, is remembered as a "wealthy man who was not inclined to share it." Like the March family in *Little Women*, who lived in dread of rich Aunt March, the Taylors were dominated by the fact of being dependent upon this rich, hard man. Sara Taylor particularly must have resented it.

Howard Young had also come out of the Middle West, but he

swiftly made himself the embodiment of the American dream. Leaving his home in Belle Center, Ohio, at the age of ten in 1882, without a penny in his pocket, he was worth $400,000 by the time he was eighteen. He made this small fortune in art—in a manner of speaking: Touring the countryside around St. Louis he collected family photographs and transformed them through a chemical process into beautiful portraits set in convex oval frames.

When the panic of 1896 wiped him out, Young began again, moving first into oils, then into oil. He improved on his previous trade by seeking out photographs of deceased members of wealthy families and having them copied by good portrait artists. One day when one of his clients asked him to handle the purchase of some works of art, he found he had become a dealer. When a lucky friendship with a Sinclair of Sinclair Oil led to investment in a gusher well, he suddenly had the capital to deal in Old Masters. Soon the big car industry families of Detroit, the Fishers and the Fords, became his clients and he transferred his base to New York.

It was for this wealthy uncle by marriage who had no children that the Taylors named their son. For their daughter's middle name they chose the family name of Rosemond: Young's wife, Mabel Rosemond Young, and Francis Taylor's mother were sisters. But relations between the two families were not always easy. There was tension about "Aunt Mabel." Also a beauty, she became alcoholic—perhaps because she couldn't handle the transition from Middle West prosperous to New York rich. And there was tension about the running of the Bond Street gallery. Francis Taylor was essentially a shy man and the visits of aggressive Uncle Howard were never welcomed. He would turn up and if Francis Taylor didn't have an instant answer to some question or other, Young would bark, "What am I paying you for?"

A tactful friend of the Taylors says, "Sara and Francis never put on airs because they were related to Howard Young. They retained the truthfulness and honest quality of the American

Midwest." They were poor relations, in other words. But they often traveled with Young, and his homes in Florida, Connecticut, and Wisconsin provided the backdrops for some of his niece's romantic dramas. It seems clear that whatever their other differences, both the Taylors and Howard Young shared an old-fashioned horror of divorce. Young never divorced his wife, even though she was not seen with him for many years. Sara and Francis stuck together, although their marriage went on the rocks during the early days of their daughter's career and they formally separated for a time, and they strongly disapproved of her first divorce from Conrad Hilton, Jr.

When Howard Young died in 1972 he left an estate worth about $20 million. His collection of Impressionist paintings and sculpture alone brought in $1.8 million at auction. None of it went to any of the Taylors, perhaps because by then Elizabeth Taylor's wealth approached his own. Instead Young bestowed most of it on a hospital in rural Woodruff, Wisconsin, on the condition that it be renamed after him. Young was unique among Elizabeth Taylor's relatives in maintaining a separate reputation, and he may have influenced her even as a child to think big. In his obituary, *The New York Times* described him first as a friend of Eisenhower's, second as a major art dealer, and only third as Elizabeth Taylor's great-uncle. (Nicky Hilton, who died in 1969, was not so fortunate. The *Times* labeled him for posterity: "Once wed to Elizabeth Taylor.")

However it was thanks to "Uncle Howard," as they always called him, that the Taylors enjoyed an upper-class standard of living in London. Sara Taylor recounted how, when they found the house of their dreams in Hampstead, "Daddy wrote a check. And it was ours." Theirs also, during their English period, were a cook, some maids, a chauffeur, and a nanny. "Daddy" also brought mother and daughter frocks from Paris. The children went to good private schools—Howard Taylor to the all-boy Arnold House and Elizabeth Taylor to the coeducational Byron House—and they studied dancing with Madame Vacani.

In almost every version of how the Elizabeth Taylor star was born, Madame Vacani's name appears. Invariably the name is misspelled to "Vaccani," for that is how it appeared in the standard reference work, Sara Taylor's *Ladies' Home Journal* reminiscences. But the spelling doesn't matter. The point of the Vacani tale is to illustrate how right from the beginning there was some mystic connection between the two Elizabeths who were to become so well known, and that little Elizabeth Taylor had something akin to royal destiny determining her career. The tale could be called "She Danced for Royalty."

Every year, Madame Vacani (whose real name was Mrs. Rankin—she was only one-quarter Italian) had the pupils of her London dancing school give a benefit recital for charity. Around 1935 or 1936, the occasion was graced by the presence of the then duchess of York, who later became queen in 1938, and her two daughters, Princess Elizabeth and Princess Margaret. Like every other dancing school in the world, the Vacani annual recital included a large free-for-all in which all the tiniest tots were trundled onto the stage in order to justify the tickets that had been sold to doting parents, aunts, and uncles. On this particular occasion, the tinies were dressed as butterflies, angels, and fairies; the program called for them to flutter on, take a bow, and flutter off again.

But the butterfly named Elizabeth Taylor did not exit with the rest. As the curtain was lowered, she held her place. When the curtain went up again, there was the child (beautiful, remember) alone on the stage. The audience began to clap and the little girl circled the stage and came forward to more applause, before frantic hands could clutch her off.

Looking back for the *Journal*, Sara Taylor laughed to see her genes at work. "I gave up my career when I married Daddy and all the king's horses and all the king's men couldn't have made me take it up again. But I knew from that benefit recital that Elizabeth had inherited a certain amount of 'ham.' "

In her own memories, written in 1964, Taylor herself was even more portentous: "It was a marvelous feeling on that stage—the isolation, the hugeness, the feeling of space and no end to space."

When she got to Hollywood, the story took root and made the rounds, suitably enlarged. It made Bosley Crowther's history of MGM, the *International Motion Picture Almanac* ("when three years old, danced before Princesses Elizabeth, Margaret Rose"), and by 1962 the *New York World Telegram* had elevated it to "at three she danced before the King in a command performance at the Hippodrome."

The Vacani school is still there, with sun streaming in through dusty windows on the top floor of an old building near Harrod's. It no longer gives lessons in how to curtsey for presentation at court, but to royal children and others lucky enough to be enrolled, it still teaches the basic unalterable upper-class truths: that manners are important, that little boys, who bow from the waist, are very different from little girls who curtsey, and that even a very tiny child must look people *straight in the eye* when shaking hands and saying how do you do. It is well aware that Elizabeth Taylor must have passed through its hands, but only because it has been reminded often enough. Its own records have no trace, nor of Howard Taylor either. The staff don't deny that she may have participated in some recital or other, but they can't find her name on the program. It would not impress them if they did. Their memories are still too full of the other Elizabeth. Madame Vacani, it seems, "never in her long experience had any pupil quicker at picking up a new step than Princess Elizabeth or one who showed more unflagging vitality and great zeal to learn."

The London art world doesn't retain a clear memory of Francis Taylor either. Some in the trade remember him as a dealer from California; almost all know of Howard Young's galleries in New York. When he was in London Taylor worked quietly on his own. One dealer on Bond Street, Peter Mitchell, says that his father remembered hearing Francis Taylor's name only once—but in circumstances he is unlikely to forget.

"About 1931 or 1932 my father was approached by a runner

named Schmidt who told him that there seemed to be a genuine painting by Frans Hals in a junk shop on the King's Road. My father immediately ran to the spot and saw among piles of old furniture, a Hals, unmistakably genuine. It was unbelievable. The kind of thing you dream about. No need to wonder whether it was painted by a pupil, or in the manner of. . . . But an old boy in a leather apron who was minding the shop wouldn't sell it. He said it was on reserve. The painting, he said, had come in with a load of goods from the flat of a gentleman who had suddenly decided to move to Scotland.

"My father decided that the only thing to do was to wait until the shop owner came back. It was a Friday. He couldn't stay himself, so he hired a detective to keep watch that day and all day Saturday. On Sunday my father stood guard himself, thinking that the owner might turn up. But there was no sign of him. Monday morning my father raced back to his post, and the Hals was gone. The owner had sold it for one hundred pounds and was mystified at my father's story. He said it was against the shop's policy to have any goods on reserve. The purchaser of the Hals must have gotten to the old boy and said, 'I'll see you right.' Later, through the art world grapevine, my father heard that a Francis Taylor had bought it. It must have been worth thirty thousand dollars in those days, when money was real."

"Portrait of a Man" by Frans Hals later became the cornerstone of Elizabeth Taylor's considerable personal collection of great paintings.

In April 1939 the Taylors' English existence came to an end. Victor Cazalet advised them to return to the United States immediately. War seemed possible, although not so inevitable that the London *Times*'s man in Berlin could not report cheerfully that "Herr Hitler's fiftieth birthday was celebrated today in Hitler weather—that is, dry and for the most part warm and sunny." Sara Taylor and the two children sailed alone, with Francis Taylor remaining behind to close up the gallery.

Elizabeth Taylor left behind the memory of a well-mannered, spirited little girl, the kind who loves her horses and her dogs, and is put to bed by a nanny every night at the very tick of six. Certainly the Cazalets never detected a hint or thought of stage careers for either her or her brother. Both children were "utterly unspoiled and natural."

However, with hindsight, it is obvious that she was returning to her parents' native country with some basic questions of identity unresolved: Was she English or American, rich or ordinary, sick or wicked? There were two clear certainties, however, the love of her parents and the importance of beautiful objects.

It was a severe blow to the Taylors, and dreams of returning to England, when in 1943 Victor Cazalet, then Major Cazalet, was killed. He went down in the harbor at Gibraltar in the plane that was carrying General Sikorski, the Polish prime minister in exile, to whom he was attached as liaison officer. The cause of the crash was never settled to the satisfaction of Polish émigrés. A controversial play by Rolf Hochhuth in the 1960s maintained that Winston Churchill had ordered the crash to get rid of Sikorski who was becoming an embarrassment to the British, as they were preparing to give in to the Russian designs for postwar Poland.

Victor Cazalet became the first of a long line of men in Elizabeth Taylor's life to die prematurely. Maybe even as a child she started wondering if perhaps she carried a jinx. In Britain, political memories now tend to dismiss Cazalet as a lightweight; a basic lack of seriousness, it is said, kept him from rising higher in the Conservative party. His memory was recently defended by Dame Rebecca West. If Cazalet seemed shallow and gullible (especially in relation to Nazi Germany), she said, it was because of his Christian Science faith, which taught him to believe the best of everybody, even his enemies. Ironically, Cazalet is less often mentioned as a statesman and philanthropist and more and more as Elizabeth Taylor's godfather. It is in this role that history may ultimately remember him.

Today the Taylors still think of the Cazalets as their English family. Victor Cazalet's niece, Sheran Cazalet Hornby, is one of Elizabeth Taylor's closest personal friends. Taylor often visits her in her flat in London or her house in the country. A sturdy pleasant woman, the wife of a director of the W. H. Smith newsagent chain, her earliest memory is of "going over to the Taylors' and me howling." "Why are we friends now? Because I don't want anything from her. So many have exploited her. And because—I know this sounds strange to say—because we have so much in common. We've known so many of the same people for such a long time. We don't have to explain things to each other." Show business doesn't intrude. "She knows I don't like cleavage. She doesn't wear it here."

So the Cazalet connection held. Its power was even to prove useful in Hollywood.

3

Lassie Comes Home

Exactly two years after the Taylors' return to the United States, Elizabeth Taylor was under contract to Universal Studios at $200 a week. And by the time the war ended, the delicate nanny-reared girl had turned into a child star, as much the property of her studio as of her parents, with a weekly paycheck rising toward $1,000.

How? Sara Taylor, says Hollywood. In recent years as Taylor has become the caricature of the multimarried movie star, Sara has denied the suggestion that she pushed her child to work in the dream factory. In a high girlish voice, she has insisted, "We didn't want her in pictures. We just wanted her to have a normal life."

This claim causes some merriment in Hollywood where Sara is remembered as one of the most determined stage mothers ever to enter a casting director's office. Sam Marx, who is generally credited with discovering Elizabeth Taylor, says: "Her parents moved heaven and earth to get their child into pictures." Jules Goldstone, Taylor's first agent, comments, "Never talk about Liz's *parents*, talk about *Sara*." Francis Taylor was "a lovely, lovely man," but passive.

Whatever fires lay banked in Sara Taylor while the family

enjoyed their heady life in England—another high spot came
when Mrs. Neville Chamberlain had invited them to watch the
Trooping of the Colour from Downing Street—her ambition
seemed to have blazed out once she got home. And the home
she returned to was not New York or Arkansas City but Los
Angeles. Before the war, Sara Taylor had assisted her father in
moving to Pasadena to start a chicken ranch. Los Angeles was
familiar territory to her, because of her early career, and
California's allure to Americans during the Depression needs
no describing. But it may well have been in the back of Sara
Taylor's mind, when she found herself blessed with two spectacular children, that the sprawling state that contained Hollywood, the capital of the movie industry, was not a bad place in
which to establish an American home base.

The three Taylors reached Hollywood just as America's adulation of child stars was at its peak. Of all the creatures in the
dreamworld, the child stars were the most envied. For cute
children everywhere, the routine compliment was that they
ought to be in the movies, and there was hardly a girl child in
the United States whose parents could not detect, in a dimple
or a curl, a hint of Shirley Temple, and if she could hold a tune,
maybe a second Deanna Durbin? But the parental dream didn't
have a chance if the child was not on the spot. While it is true
that even at eight Elizabeth Taylor had looks of the rare kind
that Hollywood marketed and that even if she had been living
in upstate New York or rural Pennsylvania, she probably would
have found her way west—Ava Gardner made it from Smith-
field, North Carolina—she could not possibly have done it
before puberty.

As well as having given up her own career, Sara Taylor
suffered from another frustration. She had been acclaimed as
an actress in the very home of the movies, but had not made it
onto the screen. Once she had come close. She had been
invited to test for the female lead in *Seventh Heaven* with
Charles Farrell, but there were problems with lighting and the
part went to Janet Gaynor. "Sara's face," says her friend Ruth

Hatfield, who runs the Dalzell-Hatfield Galleries in Los Angeles, "was not photogenic. She has Elizabeth's molded forehead but the lower part of her face, instead of narrowing as Elizabeth's does, was broader toward the chin. But Sara was fabulous-looking. And she was a *born* actress, like Mary Pickford. While Elizabeth is a fine actress, she is what I call a *learned* actress, if you know what I mean."

Once in Pasadena waiting for Francis Taylor's return, the family had to adjust to a drastically different standard of living. The children were enrolled in public school. Teased about their English accents, they dropped them. There was no chauffeur: Sara Taylor had to learn to drive, a secondhand Chevrolet. There was no nanny. Mummy became Mother; now in full charge of her children twenty-four hours a day and referring to her husband as Daddy, she worked to install in them the solid American virtues—no elbows on the table, no eating between meals and—for her daughter—no sex without marriage.

The family was reunited in December 1939. Francis Taylor arrived safely from England, with the Frans Hals and crates and crates of pictures by Augustus John. Although John was then virtually unheard of in the United States (and still fetches comparatively low prices), Francis Taylor decided to open a gallery of his own with John as his main stock in trade. Francis Taylor also carried something that was even more valuable: a letter of introduction from Victor Cazalet to the Cazalets' old friend Hedda Hopper.

Hedda Hopper had just passed the turn. Gradually she had sloughed off her first career as a mediocre movie actress and emerged as a Hollywood gossip columnist equal in bitchery and power to Louella Parsons. She obliged the Taylors in two ways. First, she appeared as one of the early customers at Francis Taylor's gallery, when it first opened at the old Château Elysée in Hollywood. (Other celebrities who turned up to buy—the movie world was not full of connoisseurs of fine art in those days—were Douglas Fairbanks, Jr., David Selznick, and Nelson Eddy.) Hedda took home a John study of gypsies' heads, then rewarded the whole family with a mention in her column. She proudly announced "a new find—eight-year-old Elizabeth Taylor, whose mother was Sara Sothern, the lame girl in the play *The Fool*, and whose father, Francis Taylor, has just opened an exhibition of paintings by Augustus John in the Beverly Hills Hotel."

But it was another admirer of Augustus John who engineered Elizabeth Taylor's approach to Universal Studios. Andrea Cowdin, wife, now widow, of Cheever Cowdin, the then chairman of the board of Universal, dismisses Hopper's claim to have discovered Taylor. "I don't know why Sara never spoke up," she says with irritation. Mrs. Cowdin went out to the home the Taylors had chosen in the Pacific Palisades to see how Francis Taylor was getting along; she suspected that the family would find the art trade in Los Angeles rather heavy going. She herself was a patron of Augustus John, who had painted her portrait. A red-haired, wealthy proper Bostonian, she was then a great beauty—and wanted to help both John and Francis Taylor, his West Coast agent, in every way she could. Accordingly, she brought Cheever Cowdin to meet the Taylors and to get a look at their extraordinary offspring. As an elderly woman, Andrea Cowdin is austere and elegant, not the gushing type. Yet she recalls the Elizabeth Taylor of 1940 in terms that would do for the Infant Jesus. "She was the most beautiful child I have ever seen. She did not walk, she danced. She was so merry, so full of love for every living thing, whether it was a person, an animal, or a flower. She had a lovely singing voice, too. I don't know why they never did anything with it. At that time, you didn't know *what* she'd be. But you knew she'd be *something*."

At eight, Elizabeth Taylor was the kind of child who likes to be shown off. She consented, as many little girls will not, to being elaborately dressed and beribboned. Her thick black hair fell in the kind of curls that needed to be worn wound in rags all night and even then she had a passion for fussy accessories: little ruffled pinafores and shiny white pocketbooks. When her parents entertained, she liked to help; if they asked her to sing, she sang. She also submitted to a heavy regime of extracurricular lessons—horseback riding, dancing, and singing.

Cheever Cowdin was duly impressed. Universal knew what pretty girl singers were worth. Deanna Durbin was Universal's own, its chief asset in the 1930s, but at twenty she was over the hill. Cowdin promised an interview with the casting director. What about Botticelli-beautiful Howard Taylor? By this stage he drops out of reminiscences. No more talk of "the two of them." If there is something called star quality, it includes determination, and Howard, as he was later to make clear, had it in reverse. There can be no stage mother without a stage child. Judy Garland's mother, Ethel Gumm, who holds the title as the most ruthless of all in Hollywood's coven of stage mothers, did drag Judy on one-night stands from the age of two. But she also gave her two older daughters the identical punishing treatment. It was "Baby" alone who loved performing before a live audience, and whom the audience loved in return.

Sara Taylor concentrated her energies behind her willing daughter. Suddenly, she found herself with an embarrassment of offers. Before Universal's casting director had auditioned her child, Metro-Goldwyn-Mayer had got a look at her during a music lesson and suggested a seven-year contract at $100 a week. Should Sara Taylor wait for Universal and try to use MGM's offer to whet Universal's appetite? She did, and it paid off. Universal, possibly under pressure from Cheever Cowdin, offered double the money. On the way home from the successful Universal audition, Sara Taylor recalled, her little girl was morose.

" 'What's the matter, Honey?' I asked. '*You* are the one who wanted to be in *pictures.*' "

But the child, it seems, wanted to be in MGM pictures. The bigger studio was nearer home, and the people there had been friendlier to her. Nonetheless, her parents signed her with Universal. They thought, they said, that the smaller studio would be better for a child.

If the Taylors were fighting to keep their daughter out of the coarse clutches of the movie industry, they did not convey their reluctance to Victor Cazalet. At the time, Cazalet was visiting Canada, New York, and Washington with General Sikorski and got the news on the telephone. "Imagine excitement of Taylors" he wrote in his diary on April 16, 1941. "Elizabeth has a contract for 7 years from big Cinema group."

Soon the *Los Angeles Times* carried news of the contract and then Hedda Hopper gave it out, with a plug for Sara Taylor: "If there is anything in heredity, Elizabeth should be a hit!"

Yet Universal was not to be the place where the star was born. Elizabeth Taylor hardly lasted one year there, never mind seven. In that time, all the studio could find for her was three days' work, playing with a brat named Alpha Switzer, in an hour-long film first called *Man or Mouse*, then reissued, with no visible improvement, under the title *There's One Born Every Minute.* After a year on her $200 salary and a great many singing lessons, the studio declined to pick up its option and she was dropped. Universal's verdict: "She doesn't have the face of a kid, her eyes are too old."

If the Taylors had really wanted to keep their daughter, like the girl praying by her bed in the Thurber cartoon, "a normal healthy girl," they could have stopped right there. With their three dogs, they had moved to a modest large house, with no pool, on Elm Drive, one of the leafier streets in Beverly Hills. Francis Taylor had transferred his gallery to small quarters in the basement of the Beverly Hills Hotel, a short walk away, and Taylor, along with her brother, attended the Hawthorne School and played with the neighborhood gang, usually with a chipmunk in her pocket.

Instead Sara Taylor persisted. They went to Hedda Hopper. Her advice was to forget the singing career. Then came the lucky break that is always possible in a one-industry town like Hollywood or Washington where the wheeling and dealing goes on night as well as day. Through a dinner-party conversation, MGM learned that Universal had let the Taylor child go, and the studio made another offer.

Elizabeth, her mother remembers, "sang and danced and *begged* Daddy and me to *please, please* sign a contract with MGM." They did. At the age of ten, she was signed on as a worker at the Rolls-Royce of studios, the huge picture lot in Culver City south of Beverly Hills that was to become her school, her substitute father and—she came to believe—her enemy.

By the time MGM's myth machine had worked it over, the official version of the discovery of Elizabeth Taylor shone with celestial glitter. The studio loved it. It used to pack the story, along with advertisements for Lobby Accessories, into a kit that went to theaters on the Loew's circuit. "Elizabeth Taylor, Metro-Goldwyn-Mayer's lovely teen-age star, currently appearing in ——— at the ——— Theater, claims that her opportunity to act came out of a blue sky. But as a matter of fact, it came out of a black sky."

The sky was black, according to MGM, because of a wartime blackout. The MGM producer, Sam Marx, whose house was on the next street to the Taylors', was an air-raid warden on the same beat with Francis Taylor. As they patrolled, Marx spoke to Francis Taylor about his problem in finding a little girl with an English accent to play Priscilla, the granddaughter of a duke in *Lassie Come Home.* Casually, to help a friend, said MGM, Francis Taylor let slip the fact that he had a daughter about the right age who happened to have a trace of an English accent, and the rest was history.

Sam Marx's version owes less to chance. "We were air-raid wardens, but Beverly Hills was pretty far from the center of the action. What we did was attend meetings. And at every one Francis Taylor took me aside and told me about his beautiful daughter."

However, shooting had begun in September 1942 on *Lassie* and they already had a girl assigned to the part—Maria Flynn, who had played in *Intermezzo* with Ingrid Bergman. "Every-body cut their teeth on that picture," says Marx. "It was known on the lot as the Dog Movie." It was one of his first tries at producing; he had been MGM's story editor under Irving Thalberg. The director was a novice—Fred Wilcox—but a novice with the kind of background that Hollywood respects: His sister was married to Nicholas Schenck, president of Loew's Inc., MGM's parent company, which made her the sister-in-law of Joseph Schenck, president of Twentieth Cen-tury-Fox. Wilcox, in other words, could do what he wanted.

Even though *Lassie* was in the hands of the B (for low budget) unit, Wilcox managed to get permission to film in color, something unheard of for a B movie, and he also man-aged to wangle from Fox the loan of its reigning child star, Roddy McDowall.

As an experiment, they were using a new kind of color film called Monopak, which required only one camera lens instead of three. But Monopak took four days to develop. It was four days after filming began before the first rushes came in. When they did, they showed trouble. Sam Marx remembers: "We saw that Maria was a whole head taller than Roddy," Marx says, "and in those days you couldn't have the girl taller than the boy, you just couldn't do it.

"I had to break the news to Maria. I called her into my office and said, 'This has nothing to do with you, Maria, but you're too tall for Roddy and we can't use you in the picture.' 'Thank you, Mr. Marx' was all she said, and I was totally destroyed. I never saw or heard from her again. Since then when people ask me what a producer does, I tell them that he's the one who has to tell the girl she's not in the picture."

It was then that Marx thought of Francis Taylor's daughter. He telephoned the gallery; Francis Taylor eagerly promised to try to summon his wife and daughter who were visiting her father in Pasadena, at the other end of Los Angeles. It was a Saturday afternoon, Marx remembers, and California law specified that children could not work after six. At quarter to six the two Taylor females arrived at the studio. From here on, he agrees with the authorized version, events were dramatic.

"We had six little girls lined up who had tried out for *Mrs. Miniver*, and as soon as Elizabeth walked in we sent them all home. It was like an eclipse of the sun. She was wearing a blue velvet cape with a kind of glow of purple about it. We sent her right off to Wardrobe—we didn't even bother to wait for the rushes."

In fact, Taylor did demonstrate her acting that day and it was all anybody wanted. She memorized the sample dialogue at a glance and in a perfect cultured accent, poured out her heart to Wilcox, pretending he was Nigel Bruce, the English actor cast as the duke, and to an imaginary dog at her feet.

When *Lassie* was released in 1943, Elizabeth Taylor's career was well and truly launched. It was Lassie's debut as well (Lassie was really a male named Pal) and many years would pass before Taylor outranked Lassie in MGM's hierarchy of stars.

Elizabeth Taylor blossomed out of MGM when Hollywood's Anglophilia was at its height. L. B. Mayer, an immigrant who worried about his ungrammatical speech and Semitic looks, worshiped things English even more than any of us sitting in the dark watching his pictures—so much that his idea of sexiness was Greer Garson. We all had good reason to be pro-British, too, thanks to the Battle of Britain, Winston Churchill, and Edward R. Murrow. The mutual passion reached its climax with *Mrs. Miniver*. The sight of Greer Garson braving the Blitz, her stiff upper lip quivering below the false eyelashes, won eight Academy Awards for MGM, and stirred President Roosevelt as deeply as if it had been a documentary.

English settings were very popular in Hollywood for another reason: even in spite of the war, Britain was the most important market for American films. For Taylor, the consequence was three English parts in a row. *Lassie* was followed immediately by *Jane Eyre* for Fox in which, playing the tubercular Helen Burns to Peggy Ann Garner's Jane, she had her screen hair cut off for the first time (an orphanage punishment), did her first deathbed scene, and got no screen credit. Her name didn't make the cast list in *White Cliffs of Dover* either, another hands-across-the-sea weepie in which she teamed with Mc-Dowall and Peter Lawford. Then came *National Velvet*, which changed everything.

Before *Velvet*, Elizabeth Taylor was just an unusually pretty face among the English multitudes in Hollywood, which included genuine little evacuees like Angela Lansbury, Peter Lawford, and Roddy McDowall. Andrea Cowdin looked after many of them from her home in Bel Air. During the war, Hollywood was very much the end of the line. Once there you couldn't get out, for southern California was an embarkation point for the South Pacific, and the military had priority on all trains, boats, and planes. For the English stuck there, there was little else to do but give parties and make movies.

Another child protégée of Andrea Cowdin's made a successful entry into MGM as Greer Garson's daughter in *Mrs. Miniver.* She was Clare Sanders, an eight-year-old with a sweet face and fair hair. MGM really liked Clare. "She's so goddamned British," a studio executive complimented her mother.

Clare and Elizabeth Taylor used to play together and Sara Taylor was kind to Clare's mother, knowing she must be homesick for England and worried about her husband, a British officer in North Africa. "Little Elizabeth was very sweet," says Mrs. Sanders. "She was a bit precious, though. She didn't *look* English. Sara always kept her very beautifully dressed and her hair was very carefully done. Our children looked like scarecrows beside her. I still remember them tearing like Dead End kids around the block on their roller skates. Sometimes I cry when I see Elizabeth on television—she's so awful now."

Sara, says Mrs. Sanders, "took great care to protect Elizabeth in the beginning. But then it got beyond her."

When the studio offered Clare Sanders a long-term contract, to its astonishment, Mrs. Sanders refused and took her back to

England, right in the middle of the war, on a Portuguese boat. "I had a horror of Clare becoming a child star. They were so artificial and spoiled, not like real children at all."

But Clare Sanders did not enjoy making movies. Once when *Miniver* director William Wyler, who was notorious for his repeated retakes, caught the child yawning, he reproved her: "Clare, you look bored." "I *am* bored," she replied. And at the party to celebrate the end of filming, she asked, "Does this mean I don't have to come back here anymore? Hooray!"

Elizabeth Taylor, at eight, nine, and ten, was not bored. She liked going to the studio early in the morning and being coached and costumed by adults. In spite of all the technicians watching and the infinite tedium that goes into making movies, she somehow had found a world that corresponded to her own dreamworld, and also satisfied her most passionate wish—to please her mother.

At about this time, Francis Taylor took a photograph in the driveway of Elm Drive and sent it to a friend in England so "you can see how Elizabeth is developing." It shows a little girl, small for her age, about ten, with the face of an intelligent, beautiful, much older person—the face, in fact, of the adult Elizabeth Taylor. Beside her stands Sara Taylor, who has changed. No longer the glowing society beauty of her London days, she's a stocky matron, who might be the nanny, with somber dress, sensible lace-up shoes, and proprietorial air.

When she was not filming, Taylor continued at public school. But she was becoming a misfit. She still carries the memory of being laughed at by the class when she said that when she grew up, she wanted to be an actress like her mother. When her movies began to turn up on local screens, her schoolmates were even less tolerant. They called her "Howard's sister, the movie star." Finally—Sara Taylor's recollection—the principal of the school asked that she be taken out because the other children stared at her. The alternative was waiting: the MGM studio school—"a wonderful school." Yet the change left her more isolated with her mother than ever before, for Sara Taylor, like the mothers of all child stars, was required to be with her for every minute that she was at work, and when she got home at the end of the day, she had little time for her friends, her pets, and her father and brother whom she adored.

How tight the family's finances were isn't clear. The Taylors did not look rich, but certainly were not poor. Socioeconomically, they seemed to live in Beverly Hills, as in England, at the bottom of the top. Many years later, when Francis Taylor was in his last illness, Hedda Hopper commented tartly on the pasted-up Augustus John drawings: "That's what the family lived on" when they first came to California, she said. Others assumed that Howard Young remained a benefactor. The gallery never did a roaring trade: Francis Taylor went into semiretirement early, and Elizabeth Taylor herself has said, "I've been self-supporting since I was ten."

Yet if there were economic benefits for the family in their child's career, these would have had to be indirect. By the time Taylor reached the screen, child stars' earnings were protected by the Coogan Law—a piece of Californian legislation that was small consolation to Jackie Coogan who, when he went to retire in 1927 at the age of thirteen, found that his mother and stepfather had spent most of the millions he'd earned. The Coogan Law required the bulk of a movie child's salary to be held in trust.

Every time MGM took up another option on Taylor's contract, bumping her salary up another notch, her parents had to appear in court to swear that she had no dependents and that her savings were being invested for her. But her daughter's career made a job for Sara Taylor herself. She went on MGM's payroll. For being coach and chaperon, she received 10 percent of her daughter's salary (which effectively was deducted from that salary) and went on drawing it, well into the fifties. Like other child stars, therefore, Taylor had some early schooling in the importance of contracts, clauses, and fringe benefits.

If he had been willing, the Taylors would not have objected to Howard Taylor taking up a film career as well. Once, when he was a teen-ager, he wanted money to buy a jalopy, but was getting only twenty-five cents a week allowance. As a source of funds, his parents suggested to him that he might try the movies. Together they brought him to his sister's agent to see what could be done.

As Jules Goldstone recollects, "Howard was very handsome —just as handsome as Elizabeth—and while he wasn't enthusiastic, he didn't say no. So I got him an appointment with Universal. The next week, when the time came, he showed up—and his head was shaved bald. He had gone to a barber. I don't know what Sara said to him when he got home, but that was the end of it. I called Universal and canceled the test."

Howard Taylor may have resented what was being done to his sister, or he may have been jealous. Perhaps if his mother had focused on him from the start, he would have become the movie idol and Elizabeth Taylor what he has become: someone immersed in a large settled family, a totally private person. He may in fact be the first man that Elizabeth Taylor vanquished.

4

Equus

Was it her best film? For me, *National Velvet* was the only time until *Who's Afraid of Virginia Woolf?* when I forgot that it was Elizabeth Taylor on the screen.

National Velvet, which opened at the Radio City Music Hall in New York at Christmas 1944, was to prove a hard act for Elizabeth Taylor to follow. When MGM sent it into general release in the spring of 1945, the war was just coming to an end and everybody was full of impossible dreams of family life. The Brown family seated around the table in *Velvet* was a vision of The Family in some happy preelectrification time, with majestic Anne Revere as the mother, bewildered, authoritarian Donald Crisp as the father, and the teeming brood of children: petulant Angela Lansbury, toothless Butch Jenkins, and prepubescent Taylor. Everything Taylor was to do from then on as an actress and as a woman was measured against the passionate innocence of her Velvet.

Today, like *Mrs. Miniver*, *National Velvet* looks syrupy and pretentious. And like almost every Taylor picture, hindsight loads it with double meanings, lines that work either for the plot or the star. My favorite comes when Velvet faints after winning the Grand National. A doctor opens the blouse of her racing silks. With a straight face that gives no hint of the cleavage to come, he tells the audience, "It's a girl!" At the time, however, the picture was deeply stirring, not only for its family scenes and exhilarating horse race but also for its declaration of the importance of faith.

The faith is fairly pagan, a child's *Equus*. Against reason, a little English girl, Velvet, believes that she will win a horse called The Pi in a village lottery, and she does. Then she believes, convinced by a failed jockey, that she and The Pi can win the Grand National steeplechase at Aintree, the racecourse with the most treacherous jumps in the world. Her mother, a former Channel swimmer, encourages her. She wins. When her sex is discovered, she is disqualified, but she doesn't care. She has fulfilled her dreams.

Some people actually found a philosophy of life in this film. In India a few years ago, I was astonished to hear a man named Chatterjee say that he had seen *National Velvet* in Calcutta when he was ten and "it changed my life." Another Indian told me that picture had the same effect on him. On the spot, he began doing the big mother-daughter scene in the attic: "The mother tells the daughter . . . she gives her the prize money that she, that's the mother, won when she was young, swimming the English Channel . . . so that the daughter can enter the horse in the big race. And the mother tells the girl . . . I've always remembered it . . . 'You must have courage, the courage to follow your dream!' "

The actual words of the script were: "Everyone should have a chance at a breathtaking piece of folly at least once in his life."

The unspoken message is clearer now. Women, unlike men, could expect only one chance—in the brief interval before their sex betrayed them and they had to put aside ambition for marriage. In Enid Bagnold's novel, Ma Brown, when she had swum the Channel, had been a "great burning virgin as close as an oyster and dark as the water at night."

If Elizabeth and Sara Taylor saw any parallel in their own lives with the story of a little girl struggling against superhuman odds to recapture the glory her mother gave up for marriage, they gave no sign. But the critics did notice another resemblance—between *National Velvet* and *Song of Bernadette*, which had made a star of the young Jennifer Jones in 1942. Little Elizabeth Taylor, said one critic, as she imagined how she and her horse, The Pi, could win at Aintree, "emulated the visions and trances of Saint Bernadette before the Blessed Virgin."

In her first major role, Elizabeth Taylor was lucky in her screen mother. Anne Revere played mothers to both Bernadette and Velvet, winning Academy Awards both times. A connoisseur of maternal parts—she played at least eight mothers before the Hollywood blacklist of the McCarthy era cut short her career in 1951—Anne Revere has no respect for the part of Mrs. Brown. "Such a mother never existed," she says. "Ma Soubirous in *Bernadette* was a much better part." As an actress, she could imagine what the feelings of the mother of the young saint were: "She was anguished. She loved this child, yet she had religious faith. She was ashamed of her daughter, and torn. Should she punish her for saying that she'd seen a vision?" In contrast, Velvet's mother was "a caricature."

Few others agreed. Anne Revere was at her best in *National Velvet.* With her flat lips, broad forehead, and speckled complexion, she was homely, wise, passionate, serene. *Time* called her performance "perhaps the best mother ever seen in a moving picture."

But Taylor stole the picture—even from Mickey Rooney who played Mi, the jockey, with a subtle intensity as if he had never heard of Andy Hardy. To Bosley Crowther of *The New York Times*, who from then on was almost always to go overboard for Elizabeth Taylor, "Her face is alive with youthful spirit, her voice has the softness of sweet song and her whole manner in this picture is one of refreshing grace."

In *The Nation*, reviewing *National Velvet* in December 1944, James Agee delivered what may well stand as the ultimate judgment on Taylor's acting abilities. First he had to acknowledge that he found her "rapturously beautiful" and that since he had first seen her on the screen (probably in *Lassie Come Home*) he had been "choked with the peculiar sort of adoration I might have felt if we were both in the same grade of primary school." Then he said: "She has a talent of a sort, in the particular things she can turn on: which are most conspicuously a mock-pastoral kind of simplicity, and two or three speeds of semihysterical emotion." As these qualities were precisely what the picture called for (Agee found it otherwise full of faults: the horse race too blurred, the religious and psychological meanings of the passion for the horse neglected) "and since I think it is the most hopeful business of movies to find the perfect people rather than the perfect artists, I think that she and the picture are wonderful, and I hardly know or care whether she can act or not."

Looking back from 1975, Pauline Kael of *The New Yorker* decided, not bitchily, "The high point in Elizabeth Taylor's acting career came when she was twelve" in what she called "one of the most likable movies of all time." The former *Times* critic, Nora Sayre, goes even further: "I think it was her sexiest role."

For *National Velvet* is primarily a picture about sex. It is a story of a virgin on the brink of puberty, in love with her horse. Not such a startling thought today, when even the neo-Victorian headmistress of my daughter's London girls' day school could lean forward and confide, "My brother who is a gynecologist tells me that the passion that girls of this age have for horses is *quite definitely* sexual!"

It was not a welcome idea to Enid Bagnold, however. In her eighties, still a beauty, still an active author and playwright, she was scathing: "Absolute nonsense! Is that what they're saying? They'll be talking about goats next!" To her, *National Velvet* is the story of "our life here"—the family home at Rottingdean in Sussex. Enid Bagnold was in her thirties, an established writer and freethinker, when she married Sir Roderick Jones, head of Reuter's news agency, and suddenly found herself with a complete new identity, a large country house, and four children who won rosettes in gymkhanas. "I enjoyed it all so wildly that out tipped the book.

"The book came out in 1933 and had an extraordinary success. It happened to hit so many girls with ponies—it was a great piece of luck. We had thirteen ponies at the time, had to get rid of them, couldn't feed them during the war. And we did have a jockey who came to live with us. But he was an older man. When I got wind of what they were doing with my book in Hollywood, making Mi into a kind of husband for Velvet, I asked my old friend H. G. Wells if he thought it would do any good if I went over to Hollywood.

" 'None whatsoever,' he told me. 'I went out there when they were making *The Invisible Man* and they didn't even know I'd written it.'

"When the picture was finished, I was taken to see it by two small gentlemen from MGM—high-ups. As the lights came on, they asked, 'Well? Did you like it?' And I said, 'Not much.' Actually, I hated the whole glossy thing. But I loved Elizabeth Taylor, of course, and have joyfully met her here."

National Velvet went on to become one of MGM's all-time financial successes. It was the second of Taylor's pictures to make *Variety*'s list of films grossing $4 million or more in the United States and Canada (a figure that represents the money returned to the distribution companies after the individual theater owners have taken their share. A rule of thumb is that worldwide grosses are twice those of the United States plus Canada, which are known as domestic.)

The film did not make Enid Bagnold rich. She had sold the rights to Paramount for only $8,000 and moreover had spent the money before realizing that she was liable to American taxes. In the end she had to borrow $2,000 from her husband to meet the bill.

It is just as well that Enid Bagnold had no use for Freudian symbolism, for otherwise she might not have produced her children's classic that is pure juvenile pornography. As Velvet watches without interest as her older sister goes out walking with her boyfriend, the book says, "There are pleasures earlier than love," and goes on to describe them:

> Turning in a flash in the middle of the field she drove him on with her knees. They went at the wall together. Over the grasses, over the tufts and mounds, both knitted in excitement, the horse sprang to the surge of her heart as her eyes gazed between his ears at the blue top of the flint wall. She bent slightly and held him firm and steady, her hands buried in the flying mane firm on the stout muscles of his neck. She urged him no more, there was no need, but sat him still. . . . They cleared the wall together, wildly, ludicrously high, with savage effort and glory, and twice the power and the force that was needed.

Thus the world's first major experience of Elizabeth Taylor was of her locked in passionate embrace with a horse. Many of her public, quite simply, never forgave her for shifting to men.

Time, forties' smart, knew exactly what was on the screen: "an interesting psychological study of hysterical obsession, conversation mania, and preadolescent sexuality." For myself the phenomenon was meaningless, for where I lived horses were not for riding but for pulling junk wagons. But in affluent suburbs around the world, in bedrooms that smelled of leather, little girls began cutting out pictures of Elizabeth Taylor and sticking them up on the wall.

Nancy Hardin, now vice-president of Paramount Pictures, still has her Elizabeth Taylor scrapbook; she brought it with her when she moved from New York to the West Coast. The writer Nora Johnson, daughter of Nunnally Johnson, remembers how Taylor held out hope for the transition ahead: "I saw her as a bridge to the future. I thought to myself, 'It's possible to love horses and look like this.' " Boys were not immune. Wilfred Sheed interrupted himself in the middle of a savage attack on the Burtons in *Esquire* in 1968 to confess that he too had once snipped out a photograph of young Taylor, booted and spurred for the Grand National, and hung it on the wall, with fantasies of marriage.

From the moment she went under contract to MGM, Taylor and her mother had their eyes on the part of Velvet. They knew that MGM had bought the rights from Paramount back in 1937 and that neither company had actually made the picture because they couldn't find anybody to play the girl rider. What's more, getting wise to Hollywood, the Taylor ladies had learned that just being under contract was not enough. You had to get good parts. Jules Goldstone became Taylor's agent and steered her away from the bit parts she'd been playing and into *Velvet*.

For about five years, MGM had been hunting for a Velvet; it was the girl's equivalent of the search for Scarlett O'Hara. Scouts from the studio had scoured riding clubs and summer camps as far away as Canada, where one of those put forward for the part was Shirley Catlin, now Shirley Williams, a leader of the British Labour party. She too had been evacuated to North America because of the war and at her Canadian boarding school, when girls were asked to vote for their candidate for *Velvet*, she was chosen. When she met the MGM scouts, she told them she couldn't ride. "It doesn't matter," they replied. All they cared about was the English accent. In a way, it was a pity she did not get the part, for Shirley Williams, as a politician, has developed a far huskier, more actressy, voice than Elizabeth Taylor has managed.

If riding ability was incidental, so was youth. Both Margaret Sullavan and Katharine Hepburn tested for the part. But the search ended when Goldstone presented Clarence Brown, the director, with Taylor (whom Brown had already directed in *White Cliffs of Dover*). From then on she was Velvet. The studio paid for her riding lessons at the Riviera Country Club and it was there she fell in love with a temperamental thoroughbred called King Charles, and promised him a part in the picture.

Now we come to the third parable in the Elizabeth Taylor

hagiography: "She Grows to Get the Part." Through sheer force
of will, MGM said, she managed to grow three inches in three
months in order to get the part. Taylor herself, in her teen-age
memoirs, is modest: "I just ate a lot, slept a lot, and left the rest
to God. I knew if it was *right* for me to be Velvet, *God* would
make me grow, and *He* did."

Pandro S. Berman, who produced the film, is not inclined to
share credit with divinity. Berman, of whom Myra Brecken-
ridge declared, "MGM without Pandro S. Berman is like the
American flag without stars," did indeed produce a great
number of high-quality hits for MGM, including many with
Elizabeth Taylor. Today in retirement, living in a Beverly-
Hills-model Tara, he is the kind of small, scowling, suntanned
movie chief who looks like Mr. Magoo and makes a female feel
that she is sitting on the Casting Couch. To him *National
Velvet* is a happy memory:

"I loved the story. Most pictures I liked because of the story.
One of the best I had in my life. The quality that came from the
mother, the honesty. The best scene is when the mother and
daughter are in the attic and the mother gives the daughter the
prize money. Preadolescent sexuality? Oh, God! No! It never
entered my mind. Maybe girls, to their minds . . . masturba-
tion . . . I don't know."

For various reasons to do with her later career, Pandro
Berman is not now an admirer of Elizabeth Taylor and he
vigorously debunks the forced-growth story.

"She *had* the part," he says, flapping the other version away.
"She was under contract. We had Mickey Rooney lined up.
I made the decision to wait two years. *I* decided that when
she reached a certain height we'd make the picture. And we
did.

"I wanted to cut her hair off for the picture, but her goddamned father, this stubborn English fella, a compatriot of
yours, well, he said, 'Hell, no, you can't cut her hair.' So we
never cut the hair. She wore a long wig, then a short wig. Her
hair was never touched."

In India, I tell him, there is a man who says that *National Velvet* changed his life.

"That's very nice," says Pandro Berman. "I'm very glad to hear it."

There was no attempt to film in England, nor would there have been even without a war on. Since 1925 when L. B. Mayer had angrily pulled *Ben Hur* home from Italy after millions had gone to waste, and built himself a just-as-good Coliseum at Culver City, Hollywood had hardly bothered with foreign locations. Every conceivable terrain was re-created on the huge empty tracts of land, called the backlots, behind the studios, and if not, somewhere on the crags and coasts of California. Rather than film in New York, MGM made a new Grand Central Station lobby for *The Clock* in 1945 and in the early 1930s when someone pointed out to Irving Thalberg, then production chief, that while moonlight on the water made a very romantic background, Paris, France, was not actually on the ocean, Thalberg said that it did not matter as the audience would not know the difference.

Clarence Brown was a good director for Taylor. Though humorless and sentimental, he worked well with children; he also directed *The Yearling* and *Ah, Wilderness!* But he was not overly concerned with authenticity. "How do you think we've caught the country scenes?" he asked a visitor from London. "Anything like the real thing?" English villages were not that rustic, the visitor said; they had paved roads. Brown laughed. He knew he had made an error, but he couldn't afford to pave a complete road, "I just put the cart ruts on the dry California grass and started shooting." For atmosphere, he stuck daffodils and hydrangeas in the red earth and got out of Wardrobe an assortment of bagpipes and bowler hats for the racing scene.

Brown had everyone worrying about the safety of the horses and riders over the facsimile Aintree jumps. Little Taylor was already known as accident-prone and she was doing the jumps herself. Brown was known as a risk-taker. When he filmed *The*

Trail of '98 for MGM in 1927, at high altitudes in Canada and Alaska six men died. Besides, if any of the horses appeared to be mistreated (and the plot called for them to stumble, fall, and crash into each other, as they do every year in the real Grand National), the Hays Office would judge it cruelty to animals and refuse the all-important seal of approval for distribution in the United States. But all survived. Watching all the jump scenes were two inspectors from the American Humane Society and the only human casualty was a broken collarbone, not the star's.

National Velvet struck the Taylor family like a hurricane. "Elizabeth's fame was so instant," a friend says, "they were totally unprepared for it, and they couldn't stop it." Poor Francis Taylor, says another, "first he lost his daughter, then he lost his wife." Even before *Velvet* was released, Taylor's career had split the family into male and female halves. While mother and daughter moved into a suite at the Riviera Country Club to be near the practice turf, Francis and Howard went to Wisconsin to spend their summer vacation with Uncle Howard. And once she was an instant celebrity and MGM had torn up her old contract and offered a better one, which would take her to 1952, the fan magazines moved in on the house on Elm Drive. All the world was treated to pictures of the little star's bedroom festooned with riding gear and horse effigies. The other rooms were filled with pictures of her, or her and her mother; you wouldn't have known, a magazine later remarked, that there were others in the family at all.

If it occurred to her studio or her parents that thirteen was about the terminal age for childhood, they did not let on. One day during the filming of *Velvet*, someone put a gold star and "Miss Taylor" on her dressing-room door. Horrified, Clarence Brown made them take it off and put "Elizabeth" in its place, just the way royalty insist that servants call little princes and princesses by their first names. She didn't mind, as she wrote a year later, for "he was afraid it might go to my head—or wherever it does go that makes people change—and he wanted me always to stay the same. I knew what he meant because Mummie and I had talked it over before, and I promised him with all my heart that I would never, never change."

From then on, MGM told Elizabeth Taylor what Elizabeth Taylor was like, just as it told the rest of us. Of course, like everybody else, she read the publicity about herself and began seriously to confuse image with reality in a way, to an outside eye, she has never recovered from. Any grittiness in her personality was censored out: ambition, drive, the wish to accumulate goods were just as unmentionable as superficiality or loneliness. Elizabeth Taylor was a girl who was sweet, unaffected, gifted with an almost Franciscan ability to communicate with animals. Yet in Hollywood, nobody, not even a child, gets ahead on ethereality and Elizabeth Taylor was no exception.

In MGM's Life of Childe Elizabeth, the final episode is "The Gift of the Horse." When she turned thirteen in February 1945, with *Velvet* a smash hit, a grateful MGM decided to give her her beloved King Charles, her mount in *Velvet.* When she heard the news, the studio said, she burst into tears, jumped up in the air, and shouted "Jeepers!" three times.

And maybe she did. What the official history omits was that the studio had already given her a horse and that her brother also had a horse. Also the fact that King Charles was a real gift horse: When he was boarded out at the Egon Merz Stables in Malibu, he was found to be lame.

In her teen-age recollections, Taylor relates that she had persuaded her parents to buy the horse, although it was very expensive. So she hung around the office of Benny Thau, the MGM executive in charge of keeping the stars happy, in order that she could ask him herself to let the sale go through. Thau was away. But one day she got a telephone call. Thau had returned and he wanted her to know that she did not need to pay anything—they were giving her King Charles!

Again Pandro Berman remembers it all differently. "All the while we were making the picture, this kid is pestering me to give her the horse. 'Can I have the horse? Can I have the horse?' *I* couldn't give it to her. It wasn't *my* horse. It was L. B. Mayer's horse. So I asked Mayer and he said OK, let her have the horse.

"Now fade out and fade into 1959, when we're doing *Butterfield 8* and she is now Elizabeth, the cold-eyed dame. She says to me, 'Aren't you the guy that gave me the horse after *National Velvet*? And I say, 'Yes, I am afraid that I am.' And she says to me, 'You son of a bitch! I'm still paying for feed for that goddamned horse!' "

5

Coming of Age at Culver City

The only other child star to make the transition to adulthood while remaining continuously in the public eye was Natalie Wood and she never had the same fame. Right from *National Velvet* Taylor was an international celebrity and it hurt her. If she had had acne or had baby fat, she might have achieved a few private years, but luck was against her. She was always a beauty. All her adolescent infatuations were marketed as news, while at the same time her fame limited her actual experience. Today even those who dislike her blame Hollywood. One man, who said he fervently hoped never to have to work with her again, added, "Elizabeth deserves compassion. She's never tasted ordinary life." I can't give his name. Elizabeth Taylor, even today, is not someone that anybody in the movie industry wants as an enemy.

On screen, she made her final appearance as a child in 1946, the year in which more people went to the movies than ever before or since. The film was *Courage of Lassie*, another Technicolor Dog Movie, which still turns up on television. A war story for animal lovers (no human appears for the first twenty minutes), it shows that Lassie was still smarter than most people, especially Germans, and that Elizabeth Taylor had grown since *National Velvet* but was still sweetly tom-

44

boyish, in checked shirt and jeans. From the critics she got her usual compliments: refreshing and natural.

The same year she published a book about her chipmunk. Only diehard Taylor fans remember *Nibbles and Me*, which is a pity, for it is far more interesting than most of her movies at the time. It shows, even at thirteen, the beginning of a compulsion to explain herself to the public—to make her life a myth, in other words. As a self-assignment, it is treacherous. If you succeed (Hemingway tried and failed) how do you get out of it? Judy Garland and Marilyn Monroe took one way out. Greta Garbo and Grace Kelly another. Beyond a doubt, Taylor has succeeded and not tried to escape. Since *Nibbles* she has not only lived in front of flashbulbs but also has resolutely spilled her guts in print until she now has what must be the most public private life in the world. At what cost everybody knows: ordinary men find it hard to live inside the myth with her.

At the time the sheer existence of *Nibbles and Me* made an impression on her fans, some of whom even spent a dollar to buy it. From my vantage point, in J. J. Newberry's five-and-ten, where I furtively read movie magazines while working at the candy counter Friday afternoons and Saturdays (I ate the candy too), I could see that Elizabeth Taylor was as intelligent as she was beautiful. *Nibbles* fitted very neatly into my fantasy of the refined wealthy girl who took time out from her full and orderly private life to make the occasional movie. Of course, I did not read the book—it was about a chipmunk—and besides, Newberry's did not stock it.

I should have. It would have told me far more than *Photoplay*. Recently when I was lent an old copy, inscribed in an exuberant round hand, "To Aunt Mollie [Victor Cazalet's mother] with All my love, Always—From Elizabeth and Nibbles," it was like reading a Victorian children's book about an invalid or an orphan shut away from other children, brimming over with dreams of love and fears of death. *Nibbles* is clearly the work of a pubescent female: the chipmunk is a kind of Frog Prince, a lover in furry disguise.

Oh, he is so cute! He's gone again but not before he kissed me. He stands on my neck with his front feet on my chin and stretches himself so that he can reach my mouth. . . . He is happy with me. He keeps showing me that he is—and can you wonder that I love him so much?

The book was written as an essay for her teacher at the MGM school and the studio, ever-alert, persuaded a New York publishing company, the now-defunct Duell, Sloan and Pearce, to bring it out. MGM advised her (and who knew better what was cute?) to submit the manuscript in her own writing, and she did, with apologies to "Dear Mr. Editor": "I start out writing somewhat like I've been taught in school, then the words start tumbling out so fast I can't keep up with them and my writing goes all *higalty pigalty!*"

What Taylor then goes on to reveal is how very far she was from the all-American experience her mother said she wanted for her. In fact, she never spent a night apart from her mother until her wedding night. While other girls of her age were out at junior high dances, getting into training for the sex war, Taylor was in bed every night at eight o'clock, but not before a half-hour's romp with Mummie (her spelling) and her chipmunk. While she understood that she was on the verge of physical change—being hauled in from the window by her heels was "a little rough on certain developing places"—she accepted being kept as an overgrown child. However, she knew even then that she had the kind of power that few adults ever got their hands on—to make a big company obey her whims, and to make people buy tickets at the box office. From her employers, in this instance, she wanted what she wanted earlier for her horse and later for one of her husbands: a part for her beloved in the picture.

As usual, when the request cost nothing, MGM consented. And then what happened? "After all that beautiful acting on Nibbles's part, they cut his scene right out!" The same fate befell the big scene she had especially written for Eddie Fisher in *Butterfield 8.* Hollywood legend has it that when she saw the cut version, she threw her shoes at the screen.

With her Mummie, Taylor held herself out as having the kind of closeness that magazines were then urging on all American womanhood. No generation gap, no hostility. Mothers and daughters were encouraged to act like sisters, even to wear matching dresses, which came in Mommy size and Girlie size.

The pages of *Nibbles and Me* tremble with loving references to Mummie, worry about her health (Mummie is ill a lot), and respect for her wisdom. When the chipmunk gets lost, Mummie prays to God for guidance, and they find him. And when the pet, inevitably, dies, Taylor seizes the opportunity to explain her spiritual philosophy. It is not too different from what I am told Elizabeth Taylor, although a Jewish convert, believes today. It smacks of Christian Science, which denies death and pain, and for me it answers the most intriguing question that the public Elizabeth Taylor presents. How is it emotionally possible to have so many husbands?

> . . . my heart was broken. Mummie and I went up into the woods and cried it out. We walked and walked—and talked about life. And then I knew just as I knew before, that in reality there is no death . . . I knew that he would always live in my heart—and that another one would come to me . . . not to take his place, but to bring the same sense of love to me, and he did—and I knew him immediately, and I named him Nibbles . . . not Nibbles the second, but just Nibbles—my favorite chipmunk.

Did she write it herself? Of course she did. While the sheer number of genuflections in the text toward powers like Louis B. Mayer, Ida Koverman (his secretary), Hedda Hopper, Louella Parsons, and *Modern Screen* magazine suggest that this schoolgirl essay passed through the MGM PR department on its way east, you only have to read any other of Taylor's later prose to see the consistency of style.*

*See: "We are stuck, like chicken feathers to tar, for lovely always," Chapter 13, page 232.

She writes well, if gushingly. Never afraid of making a fool of herself, she gets real feeling down on the page. At the same time she prettily ignores a lot of what is really going on.

Certainly the publishers believed the book was authentic. Jane Gunther, the widow of John Gunther, who was working at Duell Sloan at the time, carried the proofs of *Nibbles* over to Sara and Elizabeth Taylor who were staying at the Waldorf Astoria. She came away with the memory of a nice child, "rather unattractive—she was miserable with a cold that day," and a difficult mother.

From 1942 to 1950 Elizabeth Taylor received her education at MGM's Little Red Schoolhouse. Just as Mayer was proud that his studio was the home of the child stars, for it fed his patriarchal fantasies, he was proud of the school. His publicity mill churned out boasts that "Many of the screen's greatest stars have answered 'present' at roll calls in this little school" and the accompanying list always included Lana Turner, Mickey Rooney, Judy Garland, and Anne Rutherford.

It was not a bad school. But what the school was best at was meeting the requirements of the Los Angeles Board of Education and Californian law without interfering unduly with the manufacture of motion pictures. Its various teachers were good; they had to be, the way a teacher in a Vermont one-room schoolhouse has to be good. There were never more than twelve pupils at a time, all of different ages, all more interested in their careers and contracts than their books. The law (which had been tightened up since the raw exploitation of child stars in the thirties) required that each pupil have at least three hours of lessons a day, the lessons to be completed before four o'clock. In practice, this often meant that Taylor or others would work the whole morning before the cameras and then, while everybody else was relaxing for lunch, they would sit down, in full costume, for a lesson in history or arithmetic. Or, what was just as bad for learning, the moppets would sit, with a tutor, while thirty or forty adults stood idle, at union rates, and waited for them to finish.

There are still loyalists from the great days of the MGM empire who maintain that the horror stories now in vogue about the child stars are false. Howard Strickling, who headed MGM's West Coast publicity from the twenties to the fifties, is enraged by sensation-seekers. "All they want to know," he says, smarting from some questioning at the American Film Institute, "is did Mr. Mayer ever knock anybody down? If I say anything different, they tell me, 'You're just trying to cover up!' All that about Judy being deliberately hooked on drugs by the studio—that's a lot of applesauce. The studio would have no motive for abusing them like that. The child stars were protected and guarded in every way. They were important pieces of property!"

Emily Torchia, a publicity agent who was at MGM during Elizabeth Taylor's early career, agrees. "Of course, the child stars did not have normal childhoods. They weren't normal, because they were *working.*"

Beyond a doubt, Elizabeth Taylor got kid-glove treatment. She was not starved to keep her slim (as Garland was) nor was she bullied; it was another child star's mother who was credited with telling George Cukor, "Hit her if you want to make her cry." Taylor has said how ignorant she was of the flesh-trading going on. "Evidently that casting couch bit did happen. Of course, I didn't hear about it until years later."

All she was deprived of was her childhood, her sincerity—she hated Mayer, but annually she put on a ruffly party frock and beamed sweetly at him at his birthday party—and any chance of a solid education. To grow up on the MGM 167-acre lot at Culver City, not so much a Disneyland as an industrial site full of hardhats, cables, and forklift trucks, was for her the great leveler, wiping out any middle-class advantage she enjoyed over the waifs, orphans, and showbiz brats like Judy and Lana and Mickey Rooney. Like them, and unlike Grace Kelly and the two Hepburns, Katharine and Audrey whose well-bred screen image she shared, but who reached stardom at college age, Elizabeth Taylor grew up to become a compulsive marrier.

Later on she resented her lack of schooling. It left her unequip-
ped to be little except a movie star, shy and defensive for the
rest of her life among intellectuals and people sure of their
opinions. In actuality, she received most of her education from
the classic female source—the men in her life—and not until
her fifth husband, Richard Burton, did she begin to pick up
what other middle-class American girls were getting from
courses in Great Books. One of Burton's friends, the Oxford
poet Francis Warner, sees Taylor as "hungry for learning."
However, she was never so hungry as to go back for more, not
even to the Actors Studio like Marilyn Monroe.

Between *Courage of Lassie* in 1946 and *Cynthia* in 1947
Taylor grew enormous breasts, very fast. They were not the
kind of attraction that MGM could ignore in a contract player.
Bosoms were big in the forties, thanks to the war, which had not
only separated but caricatured the sexes. Men had to be All
Men. Women had to be female impersonators, like Petty Girls
or Varga Girls, with sticky red mouths and huge erect breasts.
Jane Russell did it best and nobody at the time seemed to notice
that above the drawstring blouse rode a lantern jaw.

In a typical American high school, and mine was nothing else
except typical, a girl with a flat chest could hardly get a date, let
alone reach any of the prizes on the top shelf, like a place on the
cheerleaders' team or a job at the drugstore. The purpose of the
big bust was to attract a date who would ask you to a prom where
you could show it off in a strapless dress. He was not supposed
to touch it.

The lewdest joke I heard in those years came after a high-
school prom that we had all deserted, by prearrangement and
hallowed custom, at about 10:30 P.M. to meet at a roadhouse,
the kind of chickenshed etched in neon that still spells sin in
rural Massachusetts. The comic, seeing a high-school party
come in, in rented tuxedos and goose-pimpled décolletage,
confided over the mike: "I remember my senior prom. . . . It
was so romantic. . . . My girl had a strapless dress . . . and I

had my father's convertible . . . and we had the top down. . . ."

By national consensus, the measure of a real woman was a thirty-five-inch bust; anything smaller was definitely junior miss. Surprising no one, for by then she was being displayed by Metro as the girl who had everything, Taylor blossomed out with a clear size thirty-seven. And just the required shape: full, round, and titless. (The Elizabeth Taylor of today, at her slimmest, still has a forties' bosom. It never looks without a bra and has, as far as the screen audience knows, no nipples.)

It is one of the quirks of history that Elizabeth Taylor reached puberty just as America invented the teen-ager. Mysteriously the Depression had disappeared with the war. Suddenly people had money to buy things they'd never dreamed of owning in the thirties (we threw out the icebox and got a refrigerator in 1946), and they even had spare cash to hand out to their half-grown children. Adolescents were no longer simply low wage-earners, but a cute and separate race called bobby-soxers, with adorable habits like going steady, talking for hours on the telephone, and wearing pennies in loafers. Teen magazines flourished, advising what to buy—*Seventeen* was a *Ladies' Home Journal* for virgins—and offering "tips for teens" on the emotional traumas of adolescence. (What to do if he gives you a corsage that clashes with your evening gown? Leave it in the ladies' room or pin it to your handbag.) The rag trade was beside itself with joy: a newfound land between Girls' and Women's! In my heart, I dreamed of being elected to the Marsha Jordan teen fashion panel of Jordan Marsh's in Boston. (Perhaps even becoming Marsha herself!) But I never told anyone. Jordan's chose its teen advisers only from the inner suburbs of Boston, never from the sticks.

As she passed from thirteen to fourteen, Elizabeth Taylor did have about a year away from the screen, but once she was back, with her new frontage, MGM poured her pictures out at the rate of two and three a year. Two of them were costume dramas. By 1947 she so epitomized the ideal of the well-bred WASP girl that Mrs. Clarence Day, widow of the author, personally asked Warner Brothers to borrow her for the part of Mary, who steals the heart of the eldest son in *Life with Father*. And in 1949, wearing a blond wig and a skintight dress that would have got her arrested in Concord, Massachusetts, she did *Little Women*, playing willful, vain Amy, the compulsive eater who gets her sister's man. *Little Women* was an MGM twenty-fifth-anniversary production and the studio gave it lavish trimmings, including an Art Deco rainbow floating over the March manse at the happy ending. Yet in the shots of the four girls jammed around Marmee (Mary Astor), Taylor is the changeling child. There are three sisters, June Allyson, Margaret O'Brien, and Janet Leigh with normal expressions and ordinary mottled skin tones, but in beside them, jarringly, there is an eery, almost disembodied head: each feature perfect, eyes twice as big as the others, and no visible emotion.

But it was in two absolutely trivial movies about teen-age dating that Elizabeth Taylor became America's Queen Teen. Metro bought the rights to *Cynthia*, which had been a Broadway play under the title of *The Rich Full Life*, especially as a vehicle for "Her First Kiss." In *Cynthia* Taylor played the sickly daughter of doting parents who finally manages to be invited to the prom, and goes heroically—in spite of pouring rain—to be rewarded on the doorstep with a kiss from juvenile actor James Lydon. Taylor wafts, dewily gorgeous, in an off-the-shoulder gown, with her hair swept up and a heart-shaped locket on a velvet ribbon around her throat.

Mike Nichols, who later directed Taylor to an Academy Award in *Who's Afraid of Virginia Woolf?*, has said he fell in love with her after seeing *Cynthia. Life* put her on its cover for the first time. (Elizabeth Taylor holds the *Life* cover record among actors or actresses—thirteen times; her nearest challenger is Marilyn Monroe, with only six.) All around America girls by the hundreds of thousands bought similar gowns, hoping to get kissed like Elizabeth Taylor, never taking in the obvious truth that not only do gowns like that need to be made by MGM, but so too do the miracles of engineering to hold them up. The designer, Frances Bendixson, recalls that *Cynthia* which she saw in Billerica, Massachusetts, "was seminal for me. It took me five years to get over that scene on the doorstep. I bought a strapless dress, it was ridiculous—I had no bust at all—and I covered my walls with pictures of Elizabeth Taylor."

In England *Cynthia* flopped. Perhaps it was the use of the play's original title, or perhaps Francis Taylor's theory was right. He wrote to an English friend that "*Cynthia* was not well received [in London] because our coeducational teen-agers are not understood by the British."

Next came *A Date with Judy* in 1948, Taylor's first and one of her rare musicals. By then she was a voluptuous sight. In a turquoise chiffon and lace gown by Helen Rose, with each full breast sewn into a little chiffon sac of its own, she moved easily into her next stereotype: the spoiled beauty with an eye for the older man. In this case, he was Robert Stack. *A Date with Judy* was based on a radio series and it did have a plot of sorts, which required Carmen Miranda, wearing one of her fruitiest hats, to sing "Cuanda le Gusta" and teach Wallace Beery to rumba. Yet all anybody noticed was Elizabeth Taylor. She had a good scene berating her father for only being interested in the price of AT&T. She looked like a girl who knew what AT&T was, and who wanted more of it for her birthday. She also established herself as the dark powerhouse who could defeat blond competition, especially the whole-meal variety like Jane Powell.

Did I think I looked like her? No. Not exactly. But she was the dark pattern I was working to. I thought of myself as a kind of sixteenth carbon copy. If only my bosom were fuller, and my coloring high instead of pallid, if my cheekbones were present instead of absent and my hair would stay back, then the way out of town, which looked closed except for a hazy door marked "College," would be open and clear. The eyes were a problem, though: I never wanted blue eyes. As for her movies, I made no special effort to see them. My idea of sex on the screen was *A Stolen Life*: Bette Davis and Glenn Ford in a lighthouse in the fog. Nor did I cut out her pictures. My walls, like my day-dreams, were occupied by Bobby Doerr of the Boston Red Sox. What I did was to use the Elizabeth Taylor that appeared in the papers the way pediatricians use height and weight charts. She represented the one hundredth percentile of what girls of my age might expect to achieve in beauty and sexual conquest, which were, of course, inextricably linked. So it was with a kind of physical shock that I read a review of *A Date with Judy* by the middle-aged critic of the *Boston Herald.* Taylor had clearly reached a level of sex appeal that was way out of my teen-age league. "The surprise of *A Date with Judy,*" wrote Alexander Williams, "is Miss Taylor, who has turned into a ravishing beauty. . . . Small wonder that Robert Stack has no difficulty in sidestepping the ogling, minxish wiles of Miss Powell." Down in New York, Otis Guernsey of the *New York Herald Tribune* felt the same vibrations: "The erstwhile star of *National Velvet* and other films has been touched by Metro's magic wand and turned into a real 14-carat, 100-proof siren with a whole new career opening in front of her."

What was totally unappreciated at that time was that she was admired because she was an ideal of beauty—totally atypical. I looked at a picture of her in high heels, wool dress, and pulled-back hair, and mused to my mother, "She looks like a great lady." *Look* confirmed many years later: "In her late teens she had a regal bearing and beauty admired by most of America's teen-agers." She was Queen, not teen at all.

We all thought that she must be about five foot seven. Those early shots out of Metro must have been taken by midgets lying on the ground. Tugging a piece of seaweed at Malibu, she is bent nearly double. No hint of the lack of distance between chest and knees. In a frilly checked strapless bathing suit, she poses sitting on the sand. Shadows conceal the thighs, waist-line, and rump. *American* magazine, which carried this one, lied a little: "Willowy (5 foot 5 inches) and fragile-looking, Elizabeth makes a specialty of portraying the sort of teen-ager too ethereal for bobby sox." Most of her photos concentrated on beautiful head and beautiful shoulders brimming out of beautiful lace or satin.

When did the public realize that Elizabeth Taylor was short? Not until *Cleopatra* perhaps, when the wide screen and cast of thousands inexorably set her in perspective. Her proportions may be the real tragedy of Elizabeth Taylor: that big classic head needs to ride high off the ground, on a long torso and leggy legs. She is in fact a little over five feet tall. Her bust, like her head, belongs on a much taller woman and is probably the main reason why she almost always looks so badly dressed. (Small women with big busts—Princess Margaret is another—never make the best-dressed lists, often make the opposite.) Many years later Burton ungallantly confided to *Playboy* that her chest was too big and her legs too stumpy—the shape of a Welsh village girl, he called it. Perhaps, however, when she was growing up in Hollywood, they simply didn't notice. Even at fourteen, she was taller than some of the movie moguls.

A good child's view of her size was ventured by a four-year-old, the son of the actress Grayson Hall, who appeared with Richard Burton in *Night of the Iguana*. During filming in Mexico, the boy was invited over to the Taylor-Burtons' to play with Liza Todd, then also four. When he got home, the grown-ups guiltily plied him with questions. "Was Liza's Mommy there?" Yes. "What did you think of Liza's Mommy?" "Oh," answered the boy, "she's nice. She's *teeny*."

Just as she was put on a pedestal for aristocratic beauty, Taylor began to show signs of the vulgarity that still irritates and excites the public. She seemed to wear nothing without a low neckline and was always heavily made up. She was always caught with her back arched and chest thrust forward. Her mother couldn't stop her. Emily Torchia remembers, "Elizabeth did go bosomy overnight. Of course, she *would* wear her belts so tight. All the girls then wore very full skirts with lots of petticoats and their waists all cinched up. They all did it—Janie Powell, too. But I remember the day when Elizabeth came into the commissary—an involuntary gasp just went through the room."

Slowly the first trace of scolding began to creep into the fan mags. "Why doesn't someone wise Elizabeth Taylor up? After all, she's only sixteen years old but she dresses like she acts, like she is twenty or thirty. Sally Winter, Trenton, New Jersey." There were also rumors of a gargantuan appetite for food: two steak dinners at one lunchtime during *Little Women*.

For parents, the insult on injury of living with adolescents is having to watch them move into full bloom just as they themselves are going over the hill. It was when Elizabeth Taylor was passing from child to siren that Francis and Sara Taylor formally separated. It made a filmland item in November 1946. "Maybe they loved me too much," Taylor has observed. "They had no life of their own, especially my mother."

To Hollywood eyes, the Taylor separation came as no surprise. The marriage hadn't looked happy. Francis Taylor had moved further and further into the background, while his wife, through their daughter, had reentered show business. Sara Taylor too had undergone the MGM treatment. She lost weight, softened her hairstyle, and lightened its color. And she was vulnerable to the glamour of Hollywood men. She pestered people at MGM to get her an introduction to Clark Gable. She went out with Howard Dietz the songwriter and MGM's publicity chief. And when Taylor spent five months making *Life with Father*, Sara, chaperoning every day, fell in love with the Hungarian director, Michael Curtiz. It was at that point that she separated from her husband.

Four months later, however, the Taylors reconciled. Friends say that they talked her out of divorce. However, Sara Taylor continued to lead a giddy life as a salaried duenna and the two women went to England alone in the summer of 1947, leaving Francis and Howard Taylor once again to make their way to Wisconsin. As the beauty's mother Sara Taylor suffered from the confusion of the operatic chaperon—that some of the attention was meant for her. "Our trip home on the *Queen Mary* was very gay," she later wrote. "We wore some of the pretty clothes we had missed wearing on the trip over."

As her daughter burgeoned, Sara Taylor suffered from the push-me-pull-you dilemma of the typical American mother of that time. She wanted her daughter to remain a virgin, yet she wanted her to attract boys, lots of them, even at fourteen. For quite a while, no boys appeared. As a mother, she did all she could to push her daughter into womanhood. Out went all the horsy paraphernalia in the bedroom; in came chintz and mirrors. Still the phone didn't ring. Brother Howard's friends were no help; they avoided "the movie star." "Who would believe that the most beautiful girl in the world can't get a date?" Sara Taylor moaned at MGM. In desperation, when Taylor really needed an escort—a fan magazine was giving Roddy McDowall a birthday party and wanted the teen stars there, in studio-provided prom gear—MGM obliged with a thirty-five-year-old bachelor from the publicity department.

The first kiss was harder, but Mrs. Taylor also stage-managed that, a few weeks before Taylor got her first kiss before the camera. It was virtually the only female sexual experience that she encountered in private life before acting it on the screen. The kiss was delivered by another young actor, Marshall Thomson, who was prompted to take Taylor out. On the way home (if the *Ladies' Home Journal* history is to be trusted) he committed the required act. As Mrs. Taylor re-created the scene, her daughter ran into her bedroom, "on a pink cloud of wonderment," exclaiming, "Oh, Mother, he *kissed* me."

The kissing on the set was more exciting. During *Julia Misbehaves* in 1948 she fell madly in love with Peter Lawford and had the film crews laughing at her impassioned blushes. At the end of a day's filmed lovemaking, she would go home to daydream solitarily in her room where (mother's rule) she was not supposed to lie on the bed. Is it a surprise that about that time her face went blank? All that childish vivacity totally vanished. Even Louella Parsons noticed.

By 1948 Taylor could walk through any part as a rich man's

daughter. In *Julia Misbehaves* she not only walked but also teed off golf balls, absolutely deadpan, on an expensive carpet in a fake south of France, wearing golf shoes, ankle socks, and a mid-calf-length pleated skirt. The movie was intended to show that Greer Garson really could play comedy. As she really couldn't, it was a flop. But for social historians there are some nice artifacts. At the picture's climax Garson stalks out of a cabin in the middle of the woods in the middle of a raging tempest, to avoid spending the night with her ex-husband, Walter Pidgeon. But her female gear traps her. Her high heels trip her over and her blowing skirt gets drenched with mud. She falls into a bog, and along comes a bear! Finally she has no choice but to go back to the cabin, the fire, and remarriage.

Nonetheless, *Julia Misbehaves* contains one genuinely moving scene. Garson, ostracized by her wealthy husband because she is a music-hall dancer, turns up for the wedding of the beautiful daughter she has not been allowed to see since infancy. She steals into the girl's luxurious bedroom and the girl imperiously whirls around. Garson identifies herself. "Mother!" cries Taylor, flinging herself into Garson's arms, sobbing with joy, and for an instant the picture comes alive. But it falls back dead straightaway as the two women become buddies in stiletto heels.

If she didn't diagnose the cause, Sara Taylor knew the symptoms. Elizabeth Taylor was indifferent to acting. In later years, as she has defended herself, Mrs. Taylor has insisted that she offered her teen-age daughter a chance to "get out"—to go to Beverly Hills High like her brother or to move with the whole family back to "our old life in England." In reply she received a letter, which she likes to quote. It was addressed to "Mom" and read, in part:

> . . . I realize that my whole life is being in motion pictures. For me to quit would be like cutting away the roots of a tree—I'd soon wilt and become dead and useless. . . . I also like to think maybe I have brought a little happiness to a few people—in my way—but

more than anything I would like to have made you happy. But I'm afraid I haven't succeeded very well—I'm not going to stop trying though. . . .

If Elizabeth Taylor at fifteen was contemplating getting out of pictures, no one at Metro knew anything about it. Was there ever any alternative for her? "Not with that mother, not with that education," said one of her mentors. "Elizabeth was very nice, and extremely well mannered but utterly obedient to the career her mother forged for her. Besides, the studio was investing heavily in her buildup. She couldn't have gotten out of her contract, not easily."

Hedda Hopper was still in there pushing. In 1948, in her column syndicated by the *Chicago Tribune-New York Daily News* she made three predictions: (1) Taylor would someday be first lady of the screen. (2) She might not find her real stature until, like other stars, "she leaves the lot which discovered her." (3) She would be another Ingrid Bergman. (An ironic prophecy, for not long after, Bergman lost her crown as Queen of Hollywood for leaving her husband for Roberto Rossellini.)

As one of the fiercest of Hollywood's anti-Communists, Hedda Hopper also took care to protect Taylor from the red scare that was billowing around the movie industry. No one was to think that there was any uncertainty about Elizabeth Taylor's loyalty just because she was of foreign birth. Hopper reported that the girl was eagerly looking forward to the day when she could choose between her two citizenships and take the oath of allegiance to the United States: " 'I feel that I am an American.' Those beautiful eyes glistened as she said, 'I shall be very proud on that day.' "

Jules Goldstone says, "I felt very paternal and very protective toward Liz. I used to tell her she was the nearest thing to royalty we had in this country, that she had the adulation of the world, but I don't think she took it in, in spite of all the fan mail."

What she did seem to take in was that, like a child monarch, she was totally unsuited for ordinary living. Today when she walks into the dining room at the Dorchester in London, the waiters rush up with little dishes of radishes, cucumbers, and spring onions because they know she likes them. It's been like that since she was twelve. She has had to live with the fear that she couldn't exist without every whim and every need catered for (although it is something that at last she seems to be trying to overcome).

By 1948 Taylor was so much the property of MGM that nothing except illness happened to her by accident. The studio knew of Mrs. Taylor's anxieties about having a dateless beauty for a daughter, so they tried to help.

In their choice, they did not let us, the fans, down. Goals for girls were as universal as the laws of physics. Girls were supposed to be sexy. The reward for sexiness was virility. Proof of virility was to be on the football team. A girl's rating was measured by the rank of player she could snare. The backfield was better than the line, the captain of the team was the highest badge of success, a player on the second team was almost worse than nobody at all. (My rank? Right guard, first string.)

Out to the Taylors' beach house at Malibu MGM sent America's most famous football player, Glenn Davis—a halfback and co-captain—and not from any old college but from red, white, and blue West Point.

It was the love story all America had been waiting to read, and nobody told it better than *Life*.

> Even love came without trouble to Elizabeth. One bright Sunday afternoon last July friends brought Lt. Glenn Davis, who had just graduated from West Point, to the Taylor home at Malibu Beach.

For Sara Taylor as for her daughter, it was love at first sight. "When I saw that frank, wonderful face, I thought, 'This is the boy.' I felt such a sense of relief. My worries were over."

6

Virgin

In October 1948 when she was sixteen, MGM shipped Elizabeth Taylor back to England to help the company spend its blocked British earnings on a cold-war thriller called *Conspirator*. Sara Taylor went along too. Francis Taylor would have liked to have accompanied them, but as he wrote to his old gallery assistant, "I don't see how I can, as I am not doing much business right now and it costs such a lot to travel that distance."

Crowds mobbed the two Taylor women everywhere they went. Almost every paper in the world had carried the photograph of her kissing Glenn Davis off to Korea, and the terms of their understanding were public knowledge. She wore his gold football around her neck and wrote to him every day; when he returned in two years, they were going to marry and live on a ranch from which she would run up to Hollywood and make a picture a year. Taylor was then in many ways as beautiful as she would ever become. She weighed only about one hundred pounds, had clear young eyes, very high coloring, feathery blue-black hair, and a delicate smoldering air.

For Sara Taylor, it was her finest hour. The papers recalled her in *The Fool* and photographed the two of them with pseudo-royal tam-o'-shanters on their heads and New Look topcoats swirling around their sling-backed heels as they applied for ration books and watched the Changing of the Guard. If they did look like sisters, Elizabeth was the beauty but Sara was the lively one. Yet their old wartime neighbor Mrs. Sanders who called on them at their hotel could see how Sara was losing control. After watching Elizabeth apply a third coat of lipstick, Sara chided, "You've already done that." Back came the answer: "I always take trouble with my mouth." Helpless, Sara explained, "She's so in love."

There was a third person in their party: white-haired Miss Birdina Anderson, an employee of the Los Angeles Board of Education, which had had to give its consent for the trip. Miss Anderson's job was to administer the daily three-hour dose that would in a little more than a year yield Taylor her high-school diploma.

In *Conspirator*, Taylor was playing her first adult romantic lead and her first married woman. Her screen husband was Robert Taylor, then thirty-seven, playing a Guards officer who, unknown to his young wife, is a secret Communist agent. How the press loved the contrast: the passionate professional clinches, the tutor and the mother in the wings! "Talking to her with a book on social history lying open on the table and her mother resting vigilantly in the little room next door," said *Picture Post*, "it is difficult to decide whether Elizabeth is a star or a high school girl." When her scenes were finished, she would, in an off-the-shoulder cocktail gown, walk through the non-existent fourth wall of the make-believe Belgravia house, step over thick coils of wire, and sit down with Miss Anderson.

She did have thoughts of her own, however. A film director was to hear them many years later from Roddy McDowall, who, as a fellow child star, had told Taylor of his worries about their educations. "How can I concentrate on my education," she replied, "when Robert Taylor keeps sticking his tongue down my throat?"

From that moment, McDowall later told the director, he

realized that Elizabeth Taylor had no chance of being able to touch emotional reality.

Emerging as a full-blown sex goddess at sixteen must have been as terrifying as being handed the controls of a Boeing 747. What was she supposed to do with all that power? There was no thought at all of going to college—although American college students thought of her as one of themselves; in 1948 and 1949 she received more than a thousand requests for campus personal appearances.

As for professional ambition, Taylor had very little. Without any interest in the craft, she had become a top star at the studio that, although sliding into serious financial trouble, was still considered number one. And her beauty had already accomplished all a girl could ask of it: to find her one true love.

During her long career, Taylor has always sought relief from the pressures of moviemaking by inviting friends to join her for lunch on the set. During *Conspirator* she invited Sheran Cazalet (now Mrs. Hornby) out to Elstree and importantly told her to name whomsoever she would like to meet. "I was an overweight schoolgirl then," Mrs. Hornby recalls, "and I was in awe of her as she was then very much the movie star to me. She was ravishing-looking in those days. Anyway, like everyone else, I was madly in love with Michael Wilding. So I said I would like to meet him. She didn't know him, but she asked him to lunch."

It seems to have been then that Taylor began to form the idea that there were bigger catches than football heroes. Wilding was Britain's leading romantic actor, then starring in a series of glossy films about high society that helped to smooth the taste of the new Labour government's welfare state. What's more, Taylor was beginning, as she tested her sexual powers, to exude a kind of aggressiveness that was peculiarly noticeable to older men. Men who danced with her remarked on it; Orson Welles had his eye on her, and Wilding, mildly drawn, wondered aloud why this child was wagging her hips at him.

Her frank sexuality jarred slightly with her public image as a mass media Jane Austen heroine, the young woman of good family awaiting marriage. Back in America for her seventeenth birthday in 1949, she was exhibited by *Life* as an icon of sexual opulence. In a seated portrait by Philippe Halson (who later enshrined Grace Kelly in green chiffon against Grecian columns), she stares out from the page, vacant and voluptuous, her heavy breasts, three-quarters bare, supported by a dull satin gown the color of melted money. While she was still earning titles like Miss Junior America, she looked, in the words of the critic Richard Roud, dipping back into his high-school lexicon, "like a girl who would really put out and I mean really put out."

Her love life then made its move from the gossip columns to the news pages. By March 1949 she was out of love with Glenn Davis and in love with William D. Pawley, Jr., the son of one of Howard Young's millionaire conservative friends from Miami. Unfortunately for her press image, Davis chose that moment to come home from Korea to see her and when his plane arrived in Miami, she simulated joy too well, rushing up the steps to kiss him. In June, her engagement to Pawley was announced. By September that too was off. And the rage of offended public opinion descended.

Was it her fault? Could any seventeen-year-old survive emotionally if her changing loves were announced with press statements like political candidacies? It obviously was not her fault that she fell in love easily or that she couldn't distinguish imagined love from true love. Nobody at that age can. But if she did have an emotional character defect, produced by her odd upbringing, it showed itself in her eagerness to push every romance quickly to marriage. All her life, with brief exceptions, she has found the single state intolerable.

The most noticeable fact about Elizabeth Taylor's early public life is that, while she had the same publicity as royalty, she never had the same protection. No royal child would be allowed to blunder into repeated engagements.

Yet the studio did not provide shelter. It kept her working like a dog, all through these upheavals. Between *Conspirator* and the Pawley engagement, she made *The Big Hangover* with Van Johnson.

And her parents? They were confronted with a passionate girl whom they did not want to have affairs. The only answer was to get her married as quickly as possible. (Some of her acquaintances say that her eagerness to marry was simply to get away from her mother.) However, Taylor's real problem was that Sara Taylor, who had never laid to rest her own conflict between marriage and career, was prodding her daughter in two opposite directions. Insofar as she was willing to consider letting Taylor abandon a promising career, she would do so only for a marriage that held comparable promise.

By that criterion, Glenn Davis, with a dull army career ahead, was not suitable. Pawley looked better, and there was someone who looked even better still.

Howard Hughes wanted to marry Elizabeth Taylor. He was then in his movie phase. As head of RKO Studios, he diverted himself with affairs with glamorous stars, although he was even then a hypochondriac, and grotesquely thin—six feet three inches and 150 pounds in weight—and worried that his hobby might be a drain on his health. Already he was a paranoid recluse. One of his many hideouts was a bungalow in the tropical jungle kept by the Beverly Hills Hotel as a means of hiding the private bungalow on its grounds and it was from a telephone booth in the lobby (Hughes, like a Mafia chief, preferred the anonymity of public phones) that he spotted the young Taylor. Instantly and desperately he determined to have her as a wife. Why? Hughes, according to his longtime associate, Noah Dietrich, had only two subjects of conversation: business and women's breasts. He went after Ava Gardner because, Dietrich told Ava Gardner's biographer, "He was obsessed by big boobies and she *had* big boobies." Taylor had big boobies too and, unlike Ava Gardner, good family connections. Hughes dispatched aides to make a liaison with the senior

Taylors and to buy two paintings from Francis Taylor's gallery.

Surely Sara Taylor would not have allowed her daughter to marry the forty-four-year-old roué with the pencil-line mustache? Someone who witnessed the campaign thought she would have. But her daughter would not oblige. She loathed Howard Hughes. Nonetheless, dutifully, she accompanied Francis and Sara Taylor out to dinner when Hughes summoned, and once went with them, as Hughes's guests, to Reno for the weekend. So far, no movie writer has tried to invent what the conversation among the four might have been that weekend. I long to read it.

However, Taylor did like the look of Bill Pawley. In retrospect, the romance looks like a family rigged thing—it started at Howard Young's birthday party for his grandniece at his home on Star Island, Florida—but Pawley at twenty-eight was not only wealthy but square-jawed, hirsute, and handsome. He made Glenn Davis look like a Boy Scout.

As a founder of the Miami Bachelors Club in 1940, Pawley was by 1948 conspicuously eligible. Although the press always dismissed him as "son of former ambassador to Brazil," he had been a pilot during the war and had a flair for business; he was on his way to making his own millions. As they posed for their engagement photograph in June 1949, he and Taylor made a sultry pair. She by then could have passed for twenty-five— barefoot, sunburned, and with full hair blowing in the wind, low-necked sun dress and gypsy earrings. It was big news: The *New York Herald Tribune* gave it a two-column spread, *Life* a full page. There was a press conference. Pawley did not have much to say, but Mrs. Taylor did. Conflict between marriage and career? "We're going to let it work out." Her daughter did speak up once, to ask the photographers to include in their shots her three-and-one-half-carat diamond ring. "Nice piece of ice," she said. "That's what Bill calls it."

Defensive, Mrs. Taylor denied that her daughter had ever been engaged to Glenn Davis. In doing so, she uttered one of the most intriguing lines ever to come out of movieland. Mrs. Taylor said: "She just wore his gold football like all the girls out there were doing. It was just a perfectly normal part of growing up."

Out there? Who was watching whom? All of us out there were watching Elizabeth Taylor whose mother was making sure that she was just like us? It was the old Hollywood trick— holding out its illusion as the mirror of American reality. L. B. Mayer persuaded himself that his corseted and rouged child workers were typical American kids and that the male response to kissing a girl was to jump up and say Whoopee! Sara Taylor pretended that her beautiful freak on show for what was about to become $1,000 a week was just an ordinary American girl headed for the only thing that could make her happy: marriage and babies.

The trouble was that we believed it, and Elizabeth Taylor believed it.

Actually the Pawley engagement ran into conflict with her movie career almost from the beginning. And even in 1949, as in the next three decades, the career in which she always protested to have little interest won out. Her old producer Sam Marx has an uneasy memory of the Pawley episode. Just when Taylor became engaged to Pawley and was being introduced around the Miami social circuit, Marx was in Miami making *A Lady without a Passport*. It was an adventure drama with Hedy Lamarr trying for a comeback with some assistance from the U.S. Immigration Service. For their share in the film, the immigration people wanted a taste of glamour and they knew that MGM's brightest young star was on nearby Star Island. Marx telephoned Taylor. He asked her if she would come down to the immigration headquarters and have tea. She accepted.

A government car was sent out to escort her in style and with sirens and flashing lights; the car drove up to the Pawley mansion. Marx recalls:

"Pawley came to the door. He was very colorfully dressed,

especially for those times, today it might not be so unusual. I said, 'I'm taking Elizabeth to tea.' 'The hell you are!' he said. 'She's coming fishing with me.' He went to the stairs and called up to her. When she came down, he told her he wanted her to come fishing. And Elizabeth said, 'Mr. Marx gave me my first chance in movies and I told him I would come to tea. And I'm going to tea.'

"I always loved her for that," Sam Marx says. "That afternoon, though, I could see she was quite upset. And when we got back, Pawley wasn't there; he had gone fishing."

After three months the engagement was broken. *The New York Times* reported: "Son of Ex-envoy and Miss Taylor of Films End Betrothal." The rest of the press went wild. Two broken engagements and by then a lengthening string of nationally known escorts, including singer Vic Damone and baseball player Ralph Kiner. They had a new caricature: Fickle Liz. A British paper denounced her as bored, extravagant, and silly, and called on her parents to knock some sense into her so that she would grow up "to be in real life the gracious lady she already looks."

Yet of all the selves that she tried on and cast off, that of Mrs. Pawley is probably the one that would have suited her least. Pawley went on to become richer and more conservative, a leader of the Moral Rearmament movement, who went around giving speeches with lines like "Communism is not the product of poverty but the product of godlessness, bitterness, and immorality." In 1955 the *Miami Herald* was still listing him as one of Florida's most eligible bachelors—handsome, athletic, religious, with six producing oil wells. One girl replied that she needed no reminding: She had carried his picture in her wallet ever since he was engaged to Elizabeth Taylor. Pawley, nonetheless, held out against the husband-hunters and did not marry until 1974, a quarter of a century after the engagement that put him in the papers.

Glenn Davis too has had to live with the fact that he reposes in the collective unconscious as the shy soldier boy who could not get used to flashbulbs in his face as he kissed his girl. Actually, he was less a reluctant cog in MGM's publicity mill than the publicity mill led us to believe. He had wanted to get into movies himself, and the year before the Taylor episode, had made a movie, which was panned. Later he married the tough little starlet Terry Moore who, in tight white angora sweaters, was far from publicity-shy. Divorced from Terry Moore, Davis remarried in 1953, left the army, and became a businessman in Texas. In his modest way, however, he helped to start Taylor's jewel collection. When their romance broke up, he took back his little gold West Point football, but not another ornament he gave her. It turned up in Sara and Francis Taylor's joint will made in 1964: "To our beloved grandchild, Liza Todd, we bequeath . . . the cultured pearl necklace with 69 graduated pearls, given to Elizabeth by Glenn Davis."

In that ferociously puritanical time, no one doubted that Elizabeth Taylor was a virgin. Sex, everybody knew, was something that could be kept in its place if the penalties against it were tough enough. The American army in Germany banned fraternization between American soldiers and German girls, as a solution to what was becoming a problem.

When the first Kinsey report appeared in 1948, arguing that the penalties were not working, that males reached their peak of sexual activity in adolescence, and that rules forbidding premarital intercourse were unrealistic, it was read as pornography.

Kinsey was right; men were more sexually active than people let themselves believe—but women weren't, not then. The second Kinsey report a few years later showed how effective the double standard was. At least three times as many boys as girls under twenty had tried sexual intercourse before marriage. When Elizabeth Taylor was Queen Teen, in other words, it was a time when a few girls were doing very heavy duty for all the rest, and in parked cars across America every night millions of virgins were fighting off the boys they had lured on.

Dating, American-style, was such a desperately serious game that Margaret Mead had to be sent to England during the war to explain why GI's were being misunderstood by English girls. "A really successful date," she told the British, "was when a man asked for everything and a girl gave him nothing, which made him know that she was a fine girl and he was a fine man because he had had the courage to ask and she had had the courage to refuse."

It was all explained to me even more simply one Saturday night by a Harvard sophomore. (I had got to college.) "For a boy," he said, "the object is to get as much as he can on one date, while for a girl, it's to hold back as much as she can in order to get another date."

By her own account, Taylor played by the rules. In her memoir, she says: "When I kicked myself out of the nest and got married, I realized I had been a virgin not only physically but mentally."

It was to play a virgin, the kind of sexy rich girl who knows how to say no and hold out for marriage, that she was picked by George Stevens to play Angela Vickers in *A Place in the Sun.* It was the best part she had been offered since *National Velvet.* She and her mother were flattered that Stevens had asked Metro to loan her to Paramount for the picture, and they should have been. *Conspirator* had flopped, partly because Taylor was so implausible, and her next picture, *The Big Hangover* with Van Johnson and a talking dog, was even worse. It was their eagerness that she seize the opportunity for working with Stevens that led to the final break with Pawley, in September 1949.

George Stevens, a big raw-faced man who looked like a character out of one of his own westerns, was one of the rare Hollywood directors who was both a legend and American-born. He sensed exactly what a sexual time bomb Elizabeth Taylor was. Stevens had a reputation for being a dictatorial director. While some hated him, others loved and accepted his manipulation for what it could produce. Rock Hudson recalls,

"When I got the lead in *Giant*, somebody told me, 'The only way to work with George Stevens is to make yourself into a ball of putty and put yourself into his hands.' " By the time Stevens's long career ended (he died in 1975), megalomania had taken over. *The Greatest Story Ever Told* was a three-hour dud, remembered best for its final shot of John Wayne silhouetted against the Crucifixion, drawling, "Surely this man is the son of Gawd." But in 1949, when *A Place in the Sun* began filming at Lake Tahoe, Nevada, Stevens was in his prime.

And Taylor was perfect putty, with two broken romances and the insults of the world's press ringing in her ears. If she had known at the time Stevens's reasons for choosing her, she might not have been so pleased. Not for her movies. For her photographs. He wanted what she represented to America at that time: "The girl on the candy-box cover, the beautiful girl in the yellow Cadillac that every American boy, some time or other, thinks he can marry."

A Place in the Sun was to be a remake of Theodore Dreiser's *An American Tragedy*. Stevens knew he was treading on dangerous ground. The Dreiser novel, published in 1925, was an explicit condemnation of capitalism and the materialism of the American dream. The first film version, made in 1931, before Roosevelt, came at a time when a second American revolution did not seem impossible. In fact, the first screenplay for it (not used) was commissioned by Paramount from the great Soviet filmmaker, Sergei (*Battleship Potemkin*) Eisenstein, when he was briefly in Hollywood. As it finally emerged, *An American Tragedy*, directed by Josef von Sternberg, gave such a convincing demonstration of how to drown your pregnant girl friend that it was banned in Britain. It's still a good movie to watch, with blond, bland Phillips Eastman as the young man on the make and Sylvia Sidney as the poor girl who stands in the way of his social climb. But it has a jerky cartoon quality. The characters are not developed, for the social situation is expected to tell all.

In 1949, with the Hollywood witch-hunt in full cry, and some of the original Hollywood Ten already serving prison sentences, Stevens was not going to be caught criticizing the American social system. Instead he turned the story into a psychological drama. The cause of the tragedy lies not in the society but in the hero and his uncontrollable passion for a glamorous woman. Refurbishing the story, Stevens altered the names of all the characters; he expanded and made more sympathetic the part of the rich girl, whose twenties' snob name of Sondra Finchley he updated to Angela Vickers. For George Eastman, the modernized Clyde Griffiths, he chose Montgomery Clift. Clift, who had just starred in *The Heiress*, was on his way to becoming a sulky introspective star, carving out a place for himself in stardom halfway between his fellow alumni of the Actors' Studio, Marlon Brando and James Dean. For the cheap blond dummy to collapse before Taylor's expensive brunette, he picked Shelley Winters. Both were infinitely more experienced and subtle players than Taylor was, and both had fought hard to get the parts. Finally Stevens changed the title. The downbeat, subversive *An American Tragedy* became the positive-thinking *A Place in the Sun.*

Yet Stevens's finished movie is as much of a masterpiece as the original, and as savage an indictment of the American way—just because of its concentration on sex instead of economics. *A Place in the Sun* is a black-and-white monument to the enormity of sex in the forties and fifties. Sex is the way to both rise and ruin. Montgomery Clift, being shown by a rich cousin around his uncle's factory where he is to be given a job, is told that there is just one rule: management does not mix with the female employees. Then he is invited out to his uncle's mansion where, in his baggy new tweed suit, a quick vision of Elizabeth Taylor in a cocktail dress is all he needs to tell him he is a social inferior—really low (his mother, played by Anne Revere, is a missionary). He is a man, by Kinsey's definition, without "outlet." He is not supposed to reach for women above or below him.

So he reaches down. Clift picks up Shelley Winters, a worker on the assembly line, and soon they are necking in a convoy of parked cars in a lovers' lane. The police arrive, inexorably: what bigger crime is there?

Long phallic flashlights are thrust into the car to see if anything is unzipped. "They've invented the house," a cop says sarcastically to Clift. "You'd better go to yours." Instead they go to hers. Everything is against her. She is a "good" girl, but poor and lonely. They can't stay outside. It is pouring rain and the top of his convertible won't go up. She tries to resist him but the radio blares out "You came to me right out of nowhere" and it is morning before he leaves.

Then his uncle reinvites him to the big house and Taylor, dazzling, spots him. Rich, bored, she is excited by the vigor of someone from a lower class. Soon they are in love, and he is wearing a tuxedo. They want to get married. Her parents accept the inevitable, and besides, the young man has ambition: He can rise in the business. Just as their engagement is about to be announced, Shelley Winters has some news for her old boyfriend. He waits outside while she goes into the doctor's office under a false married name. The word *abortion* is unspeakable in a motion picture made in 1949, but the doctor says no anyway.

Clift then takes Winters, hideous in a boxy coat, out in a rowboat, intending to drown her. She can't swim, we all have been told. The boat tips over. Was it his fault? The jury decides it was and the judge sentences him to die in the electric chair. But before he does, two women come to say good-bye: Anne Revere, in Salvation Army uniform, doing one of her best mothers ("If you are guilty, then I am guilty"), and Elizabeth Taylor, tremulous and frightened in a little cloche hat, doing her first adult tragic scene.

In her characterization of Angela, Taylor was helped by two of the most important strapless gowns to come out of Hollywood since Rita Hayworth's slinky black in *Gilda* in 1946. The first appears early in the picture, appropriately white.

Angela-Liz is still innocent as she swirls George-Monty around the mansion dance floor to the tune of "Mona Lisa." It's a dress with a tight bodice crowded with white daisies and a skirt of layers of white tulle over silk. It was the first gown that Hollywood's great designer, Edith Head, ever made for Elizabeth Taylor, and she recalls, "When Elizabeth moved, she looked like sunlight moving over water." As soon as the film was released Middle America rushed out to buy copies, confirming that it was a dream dress not meant for a hotel ballroom, but for a sweat-smelling gymnasium decorated with balloons and crepe paper, with the Latin teacher watching enviously from the chaperon's line in her baggy gown made from a Simplicity easy-to-sew pattern.

Edith Head, a tiny paper-dry woman perched among antique sewing machines in her personal bungalow at Universal Studios, has gowned all the stars from Lombard to Minnelli, both in the days when the bosom had to be maximized, like the forties, and in the others, like the present and the thirties, when it had to be minimized. "When Elizabeth Taylor is elegant," she maintains, "there is nobody who can be so elegant. She moves so beautifully." As an example, she cites a scene in Taylor's *Ash Wednesday* (1973) in which Taylor walks into a hotel dining room wearing a dark red gown, by Edith Head, and a single rope of pearls.

If only Edith Head could do Elizabeth Taylor's clothes in private life! She rejects the suggestion like someone told that New York is at the South Pole. She is a *theatrical* designer. Hers are not everyday clothes; they are meant to be photographed, they are larger than life.

Her second *A Place in the Sun* gown could not have been more dramatic if Dreiser had designed it himself. As Taylor pulls Clift out onto the balcony, compelled by the passion that will send him to the electric chair, she wears a gown of jet-black velvet with a vestigial shred of white broderie anglaise edging her breasts. In the dark, away from the glare of the party, they do a scene that can only be described as oral sex—the clever girl's alternative to the troublesome below-the-belt activity of the factory worker. It was one of Stevens's favorite scenes. As Taylor drags Clift along, Stevens had her stare straight at the camera and gasp guiltily: "Are they watching us?" The audience is made into voyeurs.

Years later, Stevens explained to students at the American Film Institute why he'd done it that way. "I tried to create the fact that this wasn't just some meeting and hand-holding and a nice weekend to be in the woods, but a primitive—if you'll accept the superstition—preordained meeting." To get the right nervous effect, he sat up until two o'clock in the morning, trying to get the dialogue spasmodic and overlapping, so that "we get some sense that they're out here for a fractional moment before somebody opens this door and they've got to say it: 'The girl's not guarded by her parents.' " Next morning, according to Stevens, he had the new lines typed up. "And they each got a paper and the little lady says, 'Forgive me, what the hell is this?'

"This is what you're going to say," Stevens told her. The words were, "Tell Mama. Tell Mama all," to be said as she pulled Clift's head toward her, trying to console him. But: "She thought it was outrageous she had to say that. Reasonable too. Jumping into a sophistication that is beyond her sophistication at the time."

Stevens also had tricks played with the camera. He has the two heads jammed together in the kind of close-up that the old squarish small screen encouraged and has the lens go in so close that you can see the fuzz on Taylor's neck and the mole on her right cheek. Jerkily the picture shifts from one face to the other so that half the screen is filled with somebody's hair. Stevens said he had to do it this way. Montgomery Clift got all steamed up in the emotion and "Liz is so dissolving when she's looking at you and falling away for her love object, it could be very disconcerting."

Throughout his career, Stevens was known for getting good performances out of lesser actors. He later got *Shane* out of

Alan Ladd. But in *A Place in the Sun*, he took advantage of the fact that Elizabeth Taylor had hardly been so aroused in real life. On her face, the camera caught the real thing where Clift, a Method actor, had control over his feelings and never confused himself with his creation.

As with her other leading men, she fell in love with Montgomery Clift. Although she had worked in the film world for nearly a decade, she did not recognize sexual ambiguity when she saw it. Homosexuality is still the love that dares not print its name. Clift, in fact, was bisexual. At that time movie magazines contented themselves with describing Clift as a loner and not the marrying kind.

Taylor threw herself at Clift and nothing happened. He was lean and passionate in their love scenes, then indifferent off-camera, retreating with his constant companion, a middle-aged woman who was his dramatic coach. Adeptly, George Stevens played on her physical and emotional frustration. He even scheduled her big farewell scene with Clift just before the film ended and Clift, as everybody knew, was taking himself off to North Carolina to visit blues singer Libby Holman. By then the newspapers had got wind of her passion for him, and while he walked off without a backward glance, the papers were carrying headlines, "Liz Taylor to Wed Montgomery Clift." The episode left her more confused than ever. What good was all that sexiness if she couldn't get the man she wanted?

Why do excessively beautiful women so often choose gays as friends? A homosexual gave me his theory. "It's a relief, in the first place. These terribly good-looking women, somebody's always grabbing at them. But then there's more to it. A homosexual is a challenge. They think to themselves, 'If I can turn *him* on, I must really be something.' "

Later on, Elizabeth Taylor was to learn, along with many celebrated beauties, the value of a Gay Mafia, a traveling claque who look after the details of living, laugh at jokes, and do not touch the goods.

In fact, Taylor got something better than romance from Clift.

He became a lifelong friend until his death in 1966 and stood by her as marriages came and went. He also was the first to instill in her the idea that there was something serious to be learned about the craft of acting. One of her later directors, Richard Brooks, says, "She thought he was God. I think he loved her as much as he loved any woman. It was a tragic situation. It reminds me of *The Sun Also Rises*."

While Elizabeth Taylor's movies continued to mimic her life story, with *A Place in the Sun* the synchronization broke down. Because of the red scare, George Stevens, who was always a slow editor, kept his movie in the editing room for two years; he virtually scissored Anne Revere out of the picture after she was called before the House Un-American Activities Committee. As a result it did not reach the public until Taylor had been married and divorced.

Her improvement did not go unnoticed. For the first time since *National Velvet* she got rave reviews. *The New York Times* called Angela the top effort of her career. The *New York Examiner* declared: "Henceforth she may legitimately call herself an actress as well as a great beauty." The *New York Post* sounded a note of alarm: "As for Miss Taylor, she has only to pass a camera to provide abundant reason for a man to commit murder, or any other crime of violence in her favor."

But many reviews were almost insulting in their praise. *Variety*, for example: "For Miss Taylor, at least, the histrionics are of a quality so far beyond anything she has done previously that Stevens must be credited with a minor miracle." If she was good—and this is an assumption that still dogs her career—it must be because she was playing herself. *Holiday*: "The conceit, artificiality, and awkwardness which mar her playing in most ingenue roles are not only acceptable but essential to her rendition of Miss Rich Bitch of 1951." To *Sight and Sound*, her Angela was perfect casting: "Just the right mixture of ritzy irresponsibility and extravagant adolescent passion."

A Place in the Sun won Academy Awards for George Stevens and Edith Head, none for any of the players. Made in 1949, released in 1951, it bustled Taylor into the fifties (with her forearms already showing a hint of a weight problem) as the virgin temptress, the cock-tease, the girl who could say no at the last minute—in short, the perfect pinup for a generation of youth too preoccupied with sex to be interested in politics.

7
Brides

"They told me she couldn't act," says Vincente Minnelli. "I thought I could get a good performance out of her. What I didn't know was that it would be so easy."

In 1950 Minnelli, director, and Pandro Berman, producer, sent Elizabeth Taylor down the aisle on Spencer Tracy's arm in *Father of the Bride*, opening the decade in which she would marry, off-screen, four times. What Minnelli got onto the screen was the ideal bride: the beautiful virgin, eager for a husband, yet near to tears because she is still half in love with her father. The way that Taylor's own marriages were to depart from this ideal filled the newspapers far beyond the fifties, yet what is now remarkable is that the romantic froth of the film at that time looked like social realism. In the *Times*, Bosley Crowther called it "a honey of a picture of American life."

It certainly was a picture about what Americans *believed* about sex and marriage in the mid-twentieth century. *Father of the Bride* should be put in a time capsule. The story takes place in Hometown, USA, a small watertight universe governed by absolute laws. "Let me tell you about weddings," says Spencer Tracy, slumped in an armchair, and he explains what the laws are. He is supposed to be a comic figure and is (it is one of Tracy's finest performances) because the joke is on him. As father of the bride, he loses his daughter, yet has to pay all the bills.

Yet in the afterglow of women's liberation, he does not look such a victim. In fact, the picture represents the whole ritual of marriage as the handing over of the female from father to husband, for whom she will become a shopper like her mother. Minnelli was pleased by the physical resemblance of Elizabeth Taylor to her screen mother, Joan Bennett. The story shows them identical in interests as well. They buy a tremendous lot, scurrying around in hat and gloves, choosing silver patterns and carrying large oblong boxes. Yet while they have the charge accounts, it is father who has the bank account. They don't have money of their own.

Hovering over the film unspoken is the terror of spinster-hood. In the late thirties, 9 percent of American women of fifty had never been married. Better the caterer, the marquee, the whole costly rigmarole, than no wedding at all. So father acquiesces. His only genuine fear is that he will do something wrong and his nightmare is one of the great moments of the Hollywood screen: Spencer Tracy crawling agonizedly down an aisle made of billowing canvas. But on The Day, of course, it is all right. As he and Taylor advance toward the altar and her wide eyes fasten like lasers on her waiting bridegroom, they look as solemn as if they were going to meet their Maker and it seems just possible that they have never heard the word *divorce.*

Back at MGM, after her loan-out to Paramount for *A Place in the Sun*, Taylor appears as before: vacuous and overdressed. But this only helps her simulate love. In one of those typical American family scenes MGM did so well—dinner in the dining room, waited on by a colored maid—the daughter of the house delivers unfamiliar opinions on adult topics, prefacing each one with "Bradley says . . ." Spouting male ideas can only mean one thing: Spencer and Joan exchange worried glances. Sure enough, when Bradley arrives, with soft hat, topcoat, and briefcase, it is clear that he is the young man from the Junior Chamber of Commerce come to take their baby away. As anxiety engulfs them: Can he support her? Will *his* parents like *them*?, there is not one whiff of suspicion that Bradley will so much as mentally undress the girl until she is his. When the wedding is at last accomplished (they invited the colored maid to the ceremony—a nice gesture), Taylor telephones Tracy from the railroad station. As Bradley waits patiently for his wedding night, she thanks her father for bringing her up. It has all been worth it. Then Spencer and Joan demonstrate that they have not totally forgotten why people get married, by waltzing among the debris before they retire upstairs to their twin beds.

Everything about *Father of the Bride* went so smoothly that the film only took a couple of weeks from start to finish in January 1950. That same month Elizabeth Taylor earned her high-school diploma. She actually collected it by submitting to a little charade that MGM enjoyed—attending a real graduation ceremony of University High School in Los Angeles and sitting in among real students in a white cap and gown. Then like so many of the ordinary American girls that Mrs. Taylor kept her eye on, she went out and that very night accepted a proposal of marriage—for what else was there to do?

On May 5, 1950, Taylor went through her first legal wedding and in June, a delighted MGM released the Minnelli version. Which was the more real is debatable. Both were staged and paid for by the studio. The "real" wedding dress was prettier than the one on the screen and Francis Taylor was just as handsome a father of the bride as Spencer Tracy. But the marriage lasted only eight months while *Father of the Bride* turned out to be one of MGM's all-time hits, a big money-earner, and a classic comedy of manners.

82   *Who's Afraid of Elizabeth Taylor?*

It's been called a forties' comedy in a humorless decade, the fifties. It brought out the best in Vincente Minnelli. As a director, he allowed many of his big musicals to get sentimental and ponderous, but he kept *Father of the Bride* clipping crisply along. Minnelli who looks like a softer version of his daughter, Liza, says that he didn't need to underline the Oedipal theme of the plot. "That scene where Elizabeth says the wedding is off . . . [like everybody in Hollywood, Minnelli treats the fictional names of the characters as irrelevant] and Spencer Tracy goes up to her bedroom and pleads with her . . . suddenly she runs out and down the stairs and she and the fiancé fall into each other's arms, like the river coming into the sea! And Spencer has nowhere to go!"

The performance won Tracy a nomination for the Academy Award. Pandro Berman is still congratulating himself for having the courage to turn down Jack Benny who wanted the part. Benny had offered himself to Dore Schary, who had just become the new head of MGM, when Mayer was ousted in 1951. Schary insisted that Berman give Benny a screen test. For a comedian of Benny's reputation, the test itself was a humiliation and made his ultimate rejection all the harder to take.

"This was a film about a man losing his daughter," Berman has said. "I didn't want a stand-up comic. Jack never spoke to me again. It busted our friendship. But that's showbiz. I had to lose Jack to get the picture."

In both weddings, the grooms were hardly noticed in the bride's dazzling light. But the real husband was more famous than the actor, Don Taylor, who played Bradley. He was Conrad "Nicky" Hilton, Jr., the oldest son of the chairman of the Hilton Hotel Corporation. At twenty-three the Hilton heir had passed through Loyola University and the Ecole Hôtelière in Lausanne, but he seemed to want to be nothing but a playboy. Conrad Hilton, Sr., was glad to see the boy settling down—so glad that before the bride's mother could announce the engagement, as the etiquette books said she should, he blurted out the news himself to Louella Parsons. There were plenty of signs that young Hilton might make an unsuitable husband. Why did Taylor's parents let her marry him? "Are you kidding?" laughed someone who watched it happen. "Sara Taylor couldn't *wait* to get Elizabeth married to Hilton." Anyway, the girl herself was determined. Her parents probably couldn't have stopped her if they had tried.

Whatever their doubts, for the Taylors the Hilton marriage looked like reentry—with a life membership—to the world of the very rich. Soon the social pages and gossip columns were filled with pictures of Hilton and the Taylors entertaining each other at dinners and nightclubs and at the Hilton mansion in Los Angeles. For his part, young Hilton put on his very best behavior. He did not drink or smoke. He brought his fiancée home on time, and he gave her diamond earrings. As the wedding drew near, Hilton unveiled his wedding present—one hundred shares in Hilton hotel stock.

In effect, the real father of the bride was MGM. It paid for everything, including all the clothes: the wedding dress and going-away outfit, the bridesmaids' dresses, the mother of the bride's gown, and a closetful of suits, hats, coats, ball dresses, and "afternoon dresses" ("They can't call 'em cocktail gowns," an MGM aide whispered to the press, "because eighteen-year-old Liz is too young"). How daring would her wedding gown be? Not as revealing as that of Princess Elizabeth, answered the studio, inviting the comparison that has always been so useful to Elizabeth Taylor. (MGM had not neglected to cash in on the other wedding, in 1949: remember *Royal Wedding* with Sara Churchill and Jane Powell?)

Taylor's wedding dress was designed by her old costumer, Helen Rose, and so was the outfit for the bridal night, a white satin negligee trimmed with rose-point lace and a little matching cap, a picture of which was released to the press.

My mother surveyed it on the picture page, facing the funnies, of the *Brockton Enterprise.* "I wonder how long that will stay on," she said tartly. Others since have wondered if it ever came off.

The wedding attracted the kind of crowds that Hollywood had not seen since Jean Harlow's funeral; the police chief of Beverly Hills, C. H. Anderson, went on record as saying he would prefer a gang war to another Taylor-Hilton wedding. It took place at the Roman Catholic Church of the Good Shepherd on Santa Monica Boulevard. (Hilton's Catholicism was the only thing that gave Elizabeth Taylor pause. She put off signing the required promise to bring up her children as Catholics until two weeks before the wedding.) Yet in spite of MGM's careful planning, things had gone wrong.

On the morning of the wedding, the doorbell had rung at the house on Elm Drive, and there stood Bill Pawley, Jr. "I must speak to Elizabeth," he told Sara Taylor. Although she was frightened, she recounted to a friend, she let him pass. He went into Taylor's room and after fifteen minutes, the girl ran out weeping bitterly. She didn't tell her mother what Pawley had said to her. Then when they reached the church, an hour late, the bride tore her veil on the car door and the organ broke down. And as the party came out of the church, there was Bill Pawley standing among the crowds, glaring at them.

None of the strain shows in the photographs. Taylor has always been good in crowds. She smiles confidently, her breasts jutting out like tail fins from MGM's satin-and-seed-pearl construction. "Gift of her studio," *Life* captioned, "it cost $1,200." Hilton looks more nervous, yet manages a thin ferrety smile.

For MGM, it was a family occasion. Emily Torchia remembers, "It was a lovely wedding. We all went. But I don't think her honeymoon was as happy as she had anticipated."

That is an understatement in the best Smiley Face tradition of the studio. Even in double-standard 1950, there were not many brides who left for their honeymoon under such medieval conditions. "Sara had worked so hard to keep the Hollywood sharks off Elizabeth," says Sam Marx, "that she succeeded too well. Elizabeth went into marriage sexually unawakened."

Was any honeymoon in history given more publicity? There

have been plenty more famous newlyweds—Edward VIII and Wallis Simpson, Elizabeth and Philip, Grace and Rainier—but they had the sense, or the advice, to escape to walled châteaus and free-floating yachts. But the young Hiltons, at eighteen and twenty-three, were kept right in the limelight, either because their parents and her studio wanted it, or because they did not know how to avoid it. At the beginning, they did get away for a brief stay at a golf club in Carmel, California, but then it was back to Los Angeles—for Mother's Day. "Elizabeth and I have never been apart on Mother's Day," explained Sara Taylor.

A week's honeymoon had not dispelled her girlish modesty. Sheilah Graham, the columnist, has described how she went along to interview Taylor the day she returned home to Elm Drive to have some wedding photographs retaken. As she felt like a friend of the family, Graham says, she took her four-year-old son with her. However, when Taylor prepared to strip down to her slip, she turned and demanded: "Little boy, will you please leave the room?" The new pictures came out better and Mrs. Taylor sent them over to England for the Cazalets to see.

By the time the Hiltons sailed for Europe on the *Queen Mary*, however, she must have been in a state of shock. The *Father of the Bride* script was not much of a guide for the real world of marriage where people fight about sex and money. Hilton balked, according to one report, at paying her excess luggage charges on their flight east. On the ship (the Windsors had the bridal suite) she was observed walking on the upper deck in the morning—grave, beautiful, and alone.

Reporters were waiting for them when they reached the Hotel Georges V and wrote what they saw. Him: gum-chewing, monosyllabic with a nightclub tan. Her: an expressionless beauty, like, said the *Herald Tribune*, a high-school girl whose friends tell her that she should be in movies. Asked what was in her trunks, she shrugged: "Mother packed them."

On the Continent, the Hiltons were a social prize for the

wealthy middle aged. They appeared to accept virtually everything. Elsa Maxwell got them for a party, the maharajah of Baroda led them to Ascot. MGM got its money's worth too: In Rome, Taylor donned a costume for a bit part in *Quo Vadis* and in London attended the premiere of *Father of the Bride*. But there were arguments and they were not resolved like the river coming into the sea. Instead they produced a spectacle that became part of the Elizabeth Taylor legend. Hilton took to gambling all night. Taylor was too young to be allowed into French casinos. For the first time in her life, she was left alone and she began chain-smoking and losing weight. To be fair to Hilton, he was under enormous strain. "I didn't marry a girl," he said, "I married an institution."

At the end of the summer, when they climbed aboard the *Queen Elizabeth* to return home, they were, not surprisingly, the talk of the ship. Nora Johnson, who was a passenger, was so impressed with what she saw that she turned it into a short story for *McCall's*. "The whole ship," she says, "knew that Elizabeth Taylor was traveling with seventeen trunks—the kind that stood up—and that she had a poodle to match her eyes. She also had a maid and an entourage of about a dozen people. I was traveling first class because I had been visiting my father who was making a movie in Rome and I found myself swept up into the crowd around Taylor. But when I wrote my story, I had to falsify one detail. I had to use a bit of the Monroe image. Because the movie star in my story was dumb, and Taylor was not dumb. She was bright and kept saying amusing things about animals. I know it's hard to believe but it's true.

"She would sit there in the lounge looking beautiful and adorable in tulle strapless dresses. What struck me was both her intelligence and her passivity. People kept telling her that it was time to eat her yogurt or to get some rest, and she obeyed."

Hilton conspicuously neglected his bride. The shipboard reaction was: "How can he?" and "What's wrong with him?" "But if she was eating her heart out with grief and despair, she certainly hid it well. She seemed to be having a good time. 'Nicky, dance with me,' she would say, and he would brush her off. So she'd ask, 'Who will dance with me because Nicky won't?' and, of course, there were dozens of people swooning to dance with her."

Back home the Taylor parents were panic-stricken at what the press was doing to the young couple and at what might be going on. Some of the rumors said that Hilton was worse than indifferent. Conrad Hilton, for his part, was so upset that he had publicity men planting stories with the gossip columnists that the youngsters were as much in love as ever. When the ship reached New York, Sara Taylor telephoned a family friend to try to see her daughter.

"I called Elizabeth at her hotel and she answered," the friend remembers. "Her voice was guarded as if she were being listened to. So I suggested that she might like a change from the hotel and that she might come out and meet me for lunch at a restaurant. I didn't know if she could get away, but she agreed to come. I got there first. It was a steaming hot day. Everybody was sweltering and wearing as little as they possibly could. But when Elizabeth turned up, she was wearing a white blouse buttoned up to the chin and down to the wrist. It had a kind of thin material on the sleeves, and I could see the marks all the way up her arms. I didn't know what to tell Sara."

The marriage ended a few months later, in January 1951, in the divorce court at Santa Monica. The grounds were indifference and mental cruelty. In a tiny voice Taylor told the judge that Hilton had sworn at her mother. Often since she has hinted that only massive self-restraint kept her from telling more. (It wasn't a real marriage, she once told an interviewer.) Because she was then earning $2,000 a week, she did not ask for alimony. "I don't want a prize for failing," she said.

Yet she was allowed to keep her presents, including the Hilton stock, a white mink stole, a Cadillac convertible, and a ring worth $50,000. Moreover, there was a property settlement arranged later between her and Hilton and it was complicated enough to take most of 1951 to be worked out. Was her silence one of the conditions of the final division of assets?

During the divorce proceedings, both her father and her publicity man from MGM, Bill Lyon, were at her side, trying to shield her from photographers. She lit a cigarette while being stared at and the *Los Angeles Times* man observed that her blue suit and white blouse "set off the dark hair and dark complexion not ordinarily associated with deep blue eyes like hers."

The divorce upset *Look.* Maybe we all were responsible. "Can Child Stars Stay Married?" it asked.

When the unfortunate Hilton died in 1969 at the age of forty-two, he had been married twice more—to actress Betsey von Furstenberg, and then to Patricia McClintock by whom he had two sons before separating. He had made his way to the chairmanship of the executive committee of the Hilton International Company and had somehow squared himself with his church, for he received a requiem mass in West Los Angeles.

The flotsam of the Hilton marriage was strewn around Hollywood. The nightdress went back to MGM and in the hands of Taylor's old secretary is the book of wedding presents, listed by number.

If the foundation of the myth of Elizabeth Taylor was the work of MGM, her friends have contributed a lot. That does not mean that what they say is not true. It is because they say the same thing, in the same words, that the story takes on a mythical, repetitive quality, like "Cinderella" or "Snow White." What has fascinated me in hearing it so many times is not only how many people tell it, but that sitting down to talk about Elizabeth Taylor, they open with it. I call it the St. Elizabeth story. It goes like this: "Elizabeth is a highly moral person. She can't go to bed with a man unless he's her husband. Or a lover about to become her husband. At least, not until recently." [a reference to her year with Henry Wynberg].

They want the story known because it corrects what they see as an injustice. Taylor herself has put it out as a kind of defense.

"The morality I learned at home required marriage. I just couldn't have an affair. So I got married all those times, and now I'm accused of being a scarlet woman." Another reason for the story's currency is that Burton used it. "You'd be surprised at the morals of many women stars who are regarded by the public as goody-two-shoes. They leap into bed with any male in grabbing distance. That's what makes me mad when I read stuff hinting that Liz is a scarlet woman because she's been married five times. She's only had five men in her life whereas those goody-two-shoes have lost count."

Against it may be set Hedda Hopper's view, which appeared in her book *The Whole Truth and Nothing But*. About Elizabeth Taylor in the period following her first divorce, Hopper said:

"Before she had a chance to sort out what was happening to her, the parade of suitors began—married men, stars. Did any of them love and try to help her? No. They used her. I'm making no excuses for her, but I'm trying to be objective."

When five years later Mike Todd proposed to Elizabeth Taylor, Todd said, according to Hopper, " 'Elizabeth, I love you, and I'm going to marry you, and from now on you'll know nobody but me.' Only he didn't say 'know.' "

Whatever her private arrangements, Elizabeth Taylor has never had to go publicly without an escort for very long. In 1951 by the time she reached the divorce court, she was keeping company with the director of her next film: *Love Is Better Than Ever*. He was Stanley Donen, now famous for his musicals, especially *Singing in the Rain* and *Seven Brides for Seven Brothers*, then at twenty-six, just starting his climb, with only *On the Town* and *Royal Wedding* behind him. Donen was a landmark for Taylor: he was her first Jew and her first married man. It was from him, she later said, that she got her first interest in Judaism, the religion she later adopted. Today Hollywood people blush curiously when they talk about the episode. "It was just a little romance," or "They *thought* they were in love." MGM was furious about it for it did not want its star tarnished and she was getting "other woman" headlines for the first time, for Donen was not yet divorced from his wife.

When Taylor brought Donen home to meet her parents, she and her mother had a furious argument on the doorstep. Sara Taylor, it is said, was angry at her for not having tried longer to make the Hilton marriage work and Francis Taylor, as usual, backed his wife. It does seem as if the break with her mother hit her harder than the break with Hilton, for she had a real collapse. She checked into the Cedars of Lebanon Hospital, giving the name of Rebecca Jones (a sign, perhaps, that she was trying on Jewishness?). Her illness was variously described as an incipient ulcer, colitis, and flu, and it was the first of her very many major illnesses. Before this time, she had been accident-prone, but not sickly.

Somehow, in spite of these traumas, Taylor kept pace in the production line at MGM. Her screen self leading the way again, she went through a pillowed pregnancy in *Father's Little Dividend*; the script called for natural childbirth, which was all the rage at the time. (Her own children later were born through complicated Cesareans.) Then came her Donen picture, a feeble comedy (retitled, mysteriously, for Britain, *The Light Fantastic*). It was dismal, both in its own right—Taylor, in white tutu and pumps, played a small-town dancing teacher—and as another example of Hollywood's abject surrender to McCarthyism. The leading man was Larry Parks, the popular star of *The Jolson Story* and *Jolson Sings Again*. But before *Love Is Better Than Ever* was released, Parks was summoned before the House Un-American Activities Committee. That finished his film career. Embarrassed, MGM did not let the picture out for more than a year and Parks appeared on the screen only twice more in his life, in 1955 and 1963.

The turn of events left Taylor homeless. At first she moved in with her agent, Jules Goldstone, a genial lawyer. He and his wife were terrified at how vulnerable the girl was. She had no idea of how food got onto a plate, let alone how to fend off men.

So Goldstone went out and found a Sara substitute, Peggy Rutledge, who had been secretary to Bob Hope's wife.

Peggy Rutledge remembers her first meeting with her new employer: "Elizabeth arrived late. She was going with Stanley Donen at the time and it was quite serious. Elizabeth is always late, but it's not her fault. She takes a long time to get dressed, she answers the phone, she can't find her bra. Anyway, she looked at me and said, 'What shall we talk about?' 'Let's talk about what I can do for you,' I suggested, so she said, 'All right, find me an apartment.'

"I went out and found two. She saw the first one and took it. It was on Wilshire Boulevard—Tony Curtis and Janet Leigh were downstairs—and I moved in with her. I wasn't married. I've never been married."

For Taylor, it was her first experience of anything remotely resembling ordinary adult life and of how important money was. She paid all the bills, but was in many respects a baby. She was literally on a diet of baby food. She amused herself with friends like Montgomery Clift and Roddy McDowall, who, she later said, "made me feel loved but weren't always trying to get serious." Occasionally she would try to cook in the small kitchen, but a disaster, like spilling bacon fat all over the place, would bring the experiment to an end. All the while the studio was trying to look in, to give advice, worrying what was happening to its property. Peggy Rutledge remembers:

"Somebody at Metro said to me, 'You've got to clean up her language. Out of that beautiful face comes this language.' I don't know where she got the habit of swearing—I think from Stanley Donen, or maybe Montgomery Clift—he swore a lot. But I couldn't." (Years later, Richard Burton claimed to have cured Taylor of her Hollywood vocabulary. "Haven't I, darling?" he asked in front of a reporter. "You bet your ass," she confirmed.)

The break with Sara Taylor was not so absolute that she was not allowed to visit, but she irritated her daughter and, according to Peggy Rutledge, everybody else. "Sara would say,

'Oh my angel' and 'Oh darling, you are so beautiful.' Nobody wants to hear that. Elizabeth would say, 'Mother's coming to dinner, please stay.' "

One of the ironies of Elizabeth Taylor's long reign as a public beauty is that when her face was at its physical peak, she had nothing to put on it, and as she acquired emotional depth, she began to get fat. To her credit, in 1951, she at least knew she was a cipher.

On a magazine cover one day she noticed the face of her neighbor, her screen sister in *Little Women,* Janet Leigh. "How beautiful she is!" Taylor exclaimed enviously. "Now Elizabeth," said Peggy Rutledge, "there's many more beautiful in Hollywood than Janet. But her beauty is not just in the face; it comes from something inside. You know, there *is* somebody in Hollywood who they say is just an empty beauty. . . ."

Who? Elizabeth demanded to know. Peggy Rutledge could not remember (she insists with a straight face). Then, after about half an hour: "Elizabeth! That name I was trying to think of: it's *you!*"

The child-queen shrieked. "I should throw you right out of that window!"

"But I told her, 'Now Elizabeth, when I met you, it's true. I thought you had no personality. But you've *grown* in the past three months. You're beginning to show lots of character.' "

Taylor moaned, unconvinced. "If I was run over right now on Wilshire Boulevard, and my face was ruined, would anybody be interested in me for myself?"

Nineteen fifty-one—her year of no husband—was also the last full year of Taylor's seven-year contract with MGM. Should she sign with the studio again? Hollywood was not what it had been in 1945. The old studio system was collapsing as the movie industry was hit with two hammer blows worse even than the Communist witch-hunt. One was television, which was sweeping over America. There was a new factory town in Pennsylvania that was reported to have fifteen thousand television sets and no movie house at all. The other was the consent decree that the Justice Department had wrung from the industry. The big production companies were going to be forced to divest themselves of the distribution companies that sent out their pictures and that owned the movie theaters. For the studios, in other words, the days of the guaranteed audience were over. They needed to make fewer, more competitive pictures. Among the majors, MGM was in a peculiarly weak position. Profits had dropped and the studio had not pulled in an Academy Award for years—the reasons why the parent company, Loew's Inc., had finally expelled L. B. Mayer and put in Dore Schary.

Elizabeth Taylor was a rising star. Could she not advance her career as a free-lance actress, now that the studio could no longer be her father-protector? The big stars were rushing for independence. James Stewart had led the way in 1946, when he got Universal to give him a percentage of the profits on *Winchester 71* and made millions. Stars who succeeded as independents could not only reap a share of the profits but could choose their own pictures and write off a big chunk of their expenses as business deductions. And Taylor was bitter toward MGM. It kept casting her in tripe, as if she had never made *A Place in the Sun.*

No doubt about it, Metro wanted her to stay. Dore Schary regarded Elizabeth Taylor as an investment that had yet to yield its return. His attitude comes through nicely in Lillian Ross's celebrated satire, *Picture,* about MGM's internecine struggle as Schary made one of his beloved "message" pictures, *The Red Badge of Courage.* Lillian Ross was present in the Waldorf Astoria the day that Schary received a visit from Elizabeth Taylor and Jules Goldstone.

> Schary asked her whether she wanted a drink. She asked for a gin and tonic. "Take sherry," said Goldstone. "Gin and tonic," said Miss Taylor. "Give the girl anything she wants," Schary said exuberantly.

The trouble was that Miss Taylor did not know what she wanted. She was making, as her options had been taken up, about $2,000 a week. "She was so in love with clothes," says Goldstone, "that frequently when I had Metro ready seriously to reconsider increases for her, she would go in and ask for some of the clothes she wore in a recent picture. That would satisfy her. That frequently occurred."

Taylor's business dilemma did not escape the eagle eye of Howard Hughes. "He was still desperately in love with her," says Goldstone. "He would have given all his millions to marry Liz." In a renewed frenzy to capture her after her divorce, Hughes came up with the idea of an independent company, built around her. He went so far as to set it up. It was called Walden Productions (for a street in Beverly Hills, not for a lake in Massachusetts) and through it Hughes intended to finance Taylor in six films. Because she was still legally a minor, 60 percent of the shares were in Francis Taylor's name, the rest in Goldstone's.

Goldstone recalls that Hughes went wild any time Taylor's name was linked with that of other men. Did Hughes, as rumor had it, ring up the gossip columnists to say that they were homosexuals or Communists? "Worse than that," says Goldstone, lips still sealed. Yet Hughes never attempted to make himself a more attractive suitor. One day when Goldstone was waiting to have lunch with him at the Hillcrest Country Club, across from the Twentieth Century-Fox studio, Hughes drove up, unshaven, in a battered old Chevrolet. The parking attendant shooed him away. Goldstone says he ran up to intervene with the only excuse he could think of. " 'It's my gardener,' I said."

To be sure that his conversations about Taylor's possible deals were not tapped, Hughes had a special telephone installed in Goldstone's office to which only he, Howard Hughes, would know the number.

All Hughes's maneuvering was in vain. In the spring of 1951 MGM sent Elizabeth Taylor back to England to make *Ivanhoe* (and to get her away from Stanley Donen). As soon as she arrived, Michael Wilding telephoned. Instantly Donen was out and Wilding was in. Howard Hughes and Walden Productions were forgotten. Taylor never signed Hughes's contract and the private telephone in Goldstone's office rang only once. It was a wrong number.

Even as a divorced woman, Taylor was treated by the studio as a valuable idiot. She responded by trying to sneak around their rules while getting her whims indulged. Peggy Rutledge was sent with her to England. On the way, their flight was grounded in New York; she dispatched Peggy out to buy hot fudge sundaes (against her diet) and special chocolates (which she counted to make sure that Rutledge had not eaten any). She telephoned furtively to Stanley Donen to tell him how much she loved him. By then she was such a celebrity that a BOAC executive came and sat in the living room of Uncle Howard's suite at the St. Regis while she slept to make sure she didn't miss the plane.

Once they reached London, she found out that her secretary was supposed to write reports back to Goldstone and MGM every other day. "Stop it!" she ordered. Then she set her sights on Michael Wilding.

In the movie itself, Taylor had very little interest. She memorized her lines a day's worth at a time, as the studio car took her out to Elstree at six o'clock in the morning. But she's always been a quick study: she could do it. She was playing Rebecca the Jewess, daughter of Isaac, who loses Ivanhoe (Robert Taylor) to the blond blue-eyed Rowena (an aged-looking Joan Fontaine). The part probably fed her growing identification with the persecuted Jews, but if so nothing showed up on the screen. Her face is so blank as to be slack-jawed. Was this the face that married Nicky Hilton? It looks unused, as if it did not know how to be a bitch. In despair, the English director, Richard Thorpe, went to the producer—Pandro Berman once again. "Don't waste time trying to get a performance out of her," said Berman, not wanting the shooting to run over schedule. "I told him, just do the best you can. And when we got her back we got her to speak every line again. The whole thing was dubbed here in Hollywood."

Even after two tries, some of her lines are masterpieces of monotone. "I was taught healing by Miriam of Manassas" is the one that sticks in my mind. One critic wrote that he would always cherish the memory of Elizabeth Taylor going to the stake with the expression of a girl who has been stood up on a date.

But *Ivanhoe* only made Elizabeth Taylor more desirable to MGM. The picture, a rousing swashbuckler, with good Technicolor jousting scenes, was nominated for Best Picture of 1952 and supplied the studio, and the actress, with another entry on *Variety*'s list of all-time box-office hits.

During that year, Taylor proposed to Michael Wilding. She admits it. He admits it. Why did he accept? His answer, for everywhere he was asked to explain the twenty-year difference in their ages, was courtly: "Elizabeth wants to be married to someone who will love and protect her and that someone, by some heaven-sent luck, turns out to be me."

It's easy to see why she was drawn to him. Michael Wilding was the leading romantic actor in a British film industry that still had some pretense of being independent. Tall, with sandy hair, a wide forehead, and narrow chin, he exuded a middle-aged boyishness: a cross between Bing Crosby and George VI. Obviously, for her, he carried overtones of Victor Cazalet. He was polite, whimsically witty, and insouciant; he could order in French, and he was entirely unpretentious: qualities conspicuously absent in the Hollywood male. He succeeded in films, he said, "because I never tried to act." He didn't, it's true, but he had a way of bending toward his leading lady (usually Anna Neagle) and peering intently into her eyes, like a well-bred man trying to conceal an erection, that was very effective in romantic scenes.

Yet to those who saw the two of them at close range, Wilding looked far from eager. At a small dinner party, he said wistfully that all he really wanted to do was to retire to the country and to paint. "I hate acting," he said, looking directly at Taylor, "and I hate actresses." She burst into tears and fled upstairs. "But," says one of the dinner guests, "she got him to marry her anyway and they had those two *terrifying* boys."

Possibly Wilding's distaste for actresses was feigned. He later had a very happy marriage to an actress, Margaret Leighton, who died in 1975 (although during it he did retire to the country and become a painter). Possibly also he wanted to try his luck in Hollywood. In spite of his fame he had not had a real hit since *Maytime in Mayfair* with Anna Neagle in 1949 and an attempt to become a producer-director had failed. Some of the press speculated that he wanted to emigrate to emulate his friend, Stewart Granger, who had just settled in Hollywood with a child-wife, Jean Simmons. It is also conceivable that he was genuinely in love with Taylor. She was spectacular—an internationally recognized prize—and she mothered him. A Hollywood friend says, "Whenever I ask myself why she'd want to marry men like Wilding and Fisher, I'd think: Why! She *mothered* them—like her animals. She had a strong personality even then, although she had some weak spots."

That strength is the most plausible explanation of all. She had made up her mind. What Elizabeth Taylor wants, she usually gets.

From all sides the couple were advised against marrying. Peggy Rutledge told them bluntly the difference in their ages was too great. Louella Parsons telephoned to ask Taylor: "Do you think you'll really be happy?" Sam Marx, making the rounds in Manhattan one evening when the Wilding engagement was announced, had doubts of his own.

"I saw Elizabeth at the St. Regis. She and Montgomery Clift were together, slugging vodka, by the way. I joined them and the atmosphere was very tense. Later that evening I saw Elizabeth with Wilding. He looked *so* bored. And later that same night I was in '21' and I saw Wilding with Marlene

Dietrich. And he was so alive. The difference was astonishing. I wondered then what Elizabeth was getting into."

Surrounded by middle-aged people—Anna Neagle, her bridesmaid, was forty-eight—she married Wilding at Caxton Hall Registry Office in London in February 1952, just before her twentieth birthday. As usual, crowds mobbed them, or her, and Taylor, poised in another Helen Rose wedding outfit (gray this time) delivered herself of some of her finest nuptial *urbe et orbi* statements: "I am glad to be British again," "Michael is just a child at heart," and "I only want to be with Michael and be his wife and have a baby right away." Wilding's remarks were less ringing. He was "weary . . . too weary to smile" and he worried to the press about how his British $60 currency allowance was going to cover the honeymoon. The Taylor parents did not attend. Sara Taylor told the United Press that Francis Taylor was forced to stay in Hollywood for business reasons.

Taylor signed again with Metro. The bait was irresistible: $5,000 a week for seven years, a three-year contract for Michael Wilding, and a promise to keep her mother on the payroll. Neither emotionally nor financially was she ready for her own production company, a step that Marilyn Monroe, a far weaker personality, took a few years later. To follow her to Hollywood Michael Wilding had to sever a long professional association with his old friend and producer, Herbert Wilcox, Anna Neagle's husband. It cost him dearly; even at the beginning before leaving he had to face the tax demands of the British inland revenue for about $100,000.

At that time the typical star's contract with a studio calculated salary on a weekly basis. One purpose was to dazzle the public: $5,000 a week—wow! Another was to dazzle the star. The salary was paid only over a forty-week year. What's more, the studio retained the right, which it almost invariably exercised, to lay off the star for any three months it chose—the time to be selected to suit the studio, which wanted to release the star's pictures to the public at measured intervals. During the enforced vacation, the star could not make pictures for anybody else.

Taylor soon found that after paying her staff and her income tax in the 90 percent bracket, there was not a lot left over.

When the Wildings arrived back in what the papers called "slump town," they declared they would live modestly in her old Wilshire Boulevard apartment. But Taylor had achieved her wish to get pregnant right away. Instead, they bought an architect-designed hilltop house on Summit Drive, at a cost of $75,000. Wilding was quoted in the British press as saying it was "too bloody expensive." How to pay for it?

One way was to collect her Coogan money. Wearing a white satin maternity smock and tight black skirt, accompanied by Wilding in a yachting cap, Taylor went to the Los Angeles County Court to collect her childhood savings held in reserve. They amounted to $46,000—not enough. To bridge the gap she could not turn to her parents, so she turned to MGM. Would they lend her the money? By her account, she went down on her knees before a nameless executive of the studio. He scoffed at her, pulled out a wallet "choked with hundreds and thousands," and made her feel that she was one of the cattle. "I got the money only on the condition that I would make an exhausting tour—pregnant, mind you, to promote a picture. I vowed then and there that I would never have to ask anybody for anything again."

Like most of Taylor's anecdotes, it leaves a lot unsaid. Why didn't she ask Uncle Howard? If she hated MGM, she must have resented her millionaire uncle even more. And if she really didn't approve of touring in the gravid state, why did she pregnantly follow Mike Todd around, publicizing *Around the World in 80 Days*, a few years later? Someone who was at Metro says: "Chalk up some of that account as rampant imagination."

Yet there was nothing imaginary about the Wildings' shortage of cash. Wilding, who was only making one fifth of his wife's salary, turned down the first film they offered him, the part of a playboy in *Latin Lovers*. The studio put him on suspension—that is, off salary. That fact made the title of her next film ironic—*The Girl Who Had Everything*—the label under which MGM was still marketing her. The picture was a remake of *A Free Soul* in which in 1931 Clark Gable had made himself a star by slapping Norma Shearer. In the 1952 version, Fernando Lamas did the slapping, Andre Previn did the music, and the picture sank with scarcely a ripple and as soon as Taylor finished her publicity tour, MGM put her too on suspension. While she had planned her pregnancy, she had not planned on returning to a studio that was making swinging economies. Nicholas Schenck, president of Loew's Inc., had come out from New York and was forcing Metro to cut back on everything, even to cancel new uniforms for bellboys. MGM was still geared up for the old picture-a-week past: Loaded with contract workers, not only stars but also writers, directors, and electricians, it employed a staff of four thousand to make twenty-nine pictures a year. With her old idols and costars departing almost daily—Spencer Tracy, Mickey Rooney, Jane Powell, Greer Garson, Clark Gable, and Esther Williams, all were let go—Taylor might have felt lucky to have been kept on. But she did not. She never forgave the studio for refusing to pay her $5,000 a week during the period when she was unphotographable.

And she was unphotographable. During her pregnancy, she luxuriated in wild overeating. Bigger and bigger she grew until by the time the baby was born in January 1953, her weight had increased to 150 pounds and she was left with a lifelong, and only intermittently successful, battle to regain her youthful shape.

Life on Summit Drive was not quite up to *Family Circle* standards. A woman columnist who got a look inside wrote about the dessert eaten with iced-tea spoons and the woven grass wallpaper shredded by cat claws. It was true. While Taylor adored motherhood, she remained a beauty who could not be without her beasts. At that point she kept four or five cats, four dogs, and a duck. They all had free run of the house and would sit, with the adults, on the king-size bed watching television. As an animal lover, Taylor has never been the same type as the other Elizabeth, who is governessy, leading her corgis firmly on leads well away from her face, and who mixes up their dog biscuits every day in silver salvers brought in by her retainers. Taylor is more of a cuddling, indulgent pet-lover; Peggy Rutledge and a friend, Virginia Streeter, who often sat with the Wildings' babies and dogs, recalled that "Elizabeth wanted the pets around all the time, but she didn't want to do anything with them. They would run all over the place. It got so bad that the smell was worse inside than out." One day, wanting yet another dog, Taylor begged Peggy Rutledge to keep the animal at her house, "because Michael's forbidden me to have any more pets." And on one memorable evening, while the Wildings were out, one of the little dogs ate a box of chocolates and was sick all over the thick white rug. Rutledge and Streeter cleaned it up. It took them until four o'clock in the morning.

Why would anybody do a favor like that? Does Elizabeth Taylor command a kind of slavish obedience from her friends? It seems that she does, but she does it unconsciously. Rutledge and Streeter say, "You'd do it for a friend. And she was a friend." Yet it is a service that those around her find themselves performing again and again. At the Dorchester in London the staff cheerfully clean the carpets after a visit by the Taylor menagerie; nothing is added to the bill. And Raymond Vignale, the French secretary who was with the Burtons for many years, has revealed fondly how he came to work with them for five weeks, and stayed ten years, in spite of "les chiens qui pissaient partout."

Married to Wilding, Elizabeth Taylor began to have ailments of the elderly. In Copenhagen where they visited in 1953, she had—at twenty-one—what the press called a heart attack. The headlines—"Liz Taylor Able to Stroll after Illness"—made her sound like an aged head of state. In 1954 she had to wear a cast on her leg from an injury she could not recall, and in 1955 she was on crutches from sciatica. Childbirth for her was a surgical excursion to death's door: She was bedridden for two months after her first. Her most awesome injury came when a steel splinter was flung into her eye by a wind machine; she was hospitalized for days and there was a chance that she would be left with a withered eye. In between were sandwiched bouts of flu and appendicitis.

In no way was Elizabeth Taylor Queen of Metro, let alone of Hollywood. She was beautiful but dull. At the box office she was good but not best. Her fans went to see how she looked, in violet, in yellow, in the jungle (*Elephant Walk*, 1954), in a white wig (*Beau Brummell*, 1954), with dark leading men (Vittorio Gassman, *Rhapsody*, 1952), and fair (Van Johnson, *The Last Time I Saw Paris*, 1954). Always she was rich.

In *Rhapsody* she played a wealthy girl with a passion for musicians. That was enough for Bosley Crowther, who was carried aloft: "Her wind-blown black hair frames her features like an ebony aureole and her large eyes and red lips glisten warmly in the close-ups on the softly lighted screen. Any gent who would go for music with this radiant—and rich—Miss Taylor at hand is not a red-blooded American." A serious charge—to which the British critic Alan Brien would have had to plead guilty. In *Rhapsody* he saw Taylor as the kind of girl who can only play her father's cash register.

The Last Time I Saw Paris was based on a Scott Fitzgerald short story and Taylor played a kind of dark Zelda, a discontented beautiful girl married to an unsuccessful American writer. Richard Brooks, who directed, thought she was very exciting in the part but that the picture was ruined by the miscasting of Van Johnson as the Fitzgerald character. Michael Wilding had been considered, so had Montgomery Clift. But the studio had Van Johnson under contract. Brooks says, "And they said, 'He's in it.' In those days a director had no say. They just told you the cast. Van was good, very facile, but you just couldn't believe that either one of these two people was desperately in love with the other." The critics agreed. One asked, "Can a man with freckles have troubles?"

These pictures are now historical curios for art movie houses or the late night shows on the UHF channels—all except *Elephant Walk* in which she was loaned to Paramount, after Vivien Leigh had a nervous breakdown, and which, thanks to the rampaging herd and Edith Head's dresses, was a very great success on the international market. Taylor certainly had no Englishness left. In *Beau Brummell*, shown in London at the 1954 Royal Film Performance, the local critics found her accent so American as to be incomprehensible. And she didn't get the parts she wanted. Jean Simmons got the lead in *Young Bess* because—even MGM did not need to be told—Taylor's voice was too shrill.

Anyway, blondes were in season. The Queen of Hollywood was Grace Kelly. Her success was instant and seemingly unstoppable. Starting with *High Noon* in 1952, every one of her movies was a hit, most grossing over $5 million on the domestic market alone, and she did it, getting an Academy Award as well, with a flat chest and a square jaw that had to be very carefully photographed. Hitchcock adored her cool brand of sexual elegance. It is not surprising that he never worked with Elizabeth Taylor. He seems as revolted by brunettes as he is by eggs.

"I am not a believer in the sexy type," Hitchcock has said. "I think it should be discovered in a woman. If you take the Englishwoman, North German, or Nordic types, you know they all look like schoolteachers, but I gather that they are murder in bed."

There was a market for stars with raw sex appeal, but there were others to provide that. Twentieth Century-Fox had begun its big build-up of Marilyn Monroe and for swarthy animality, Metro had Ava Gardner.

The fifties were a conformist time for women. It was unthinkable to pursue a career without having marriage and babies as well. Sylvia Plath, the poet, another fifties' career girl, worked on *Mademoiselle* and aggressively threw herself into the role of housewife, breast-feeder, and apfelkuchen-maker while trying at the same time not to write poems better than her husband, Ted Hughes. The preoccupation with marriage even extended to the stars. The dream of a fair woman was not only to become a famous movie star but also to attract a glittering husband who would then lend her his identity like an overcoat. Thus we had the spectacle of Marilyn Monroe, the wife, at the New York Yankees spring training camp and on the New York-Columbia-Connecticut literary circuit. Grace Kelly was the apotheosis of the ideal. At the height of her screen fame, she gave up her career, produced a child nine months and four days after the wedding, and from then on devoted herself to her family and her husband's business. According to Grace Kelly's biographer, Kelly was (much like Elizabeth Taylor) a child with an intense fantasy life. Yet she was able more comfortably to live in the myth she chose to make of her life because she was willing to swap big-league illusion for little-league royalty.

While Grace was on the Hollywood throne, Elizabeth Taylor was nobody's sex symbol. "Liz Taylor Can't Even Be Naughty!" wailed a reviewer. What she could be (as she may again have become) was a woman's woman. Women strove to look like her. Her impact was as strong in Britain as in the United States, and a *Picture Post* writer marveled in 1954:

> Every morning Elizabeth Taylor punches my tube ticket. At lunch Elizabeth Taylor serves me with a drink. In the afternoon, Elizabeth Taylor comes to my office to model for a story. . . . If imitation is the sincerest form of flattery, Elizabeth Taylor is the most flattered girl in the world—apart from being amongst the most beautiful. Not since the war, when every girl one saw was Veronica Lake, have the girls of this country striven so hard to look alike.

It was then that Mrs. Taylor sold her gushing series to the *Ladies' Home Journal*, proud that Elizabeth Taylor had solved the problem that confounded so many other girls—how to combine marriage and a career. Said Mrs. Taylor, looking at her daughter and new grandson, "Now she knows why she was born."

Taylor threw herself into the little mother part well. Photographs always seemed to show her clutching a baby as she got on and off planes. America's florists in 1953 voted her Mother of the Year. She maintained her flair for issuing quotes suitable for her image of the moment. The one I remember was: "To me the most beautiful smells in the world are babies and bacon."

The reality was pretty far from what appeared in the press, as events soon would make clear. But no one wanted to know. The world was still living by Lives of the Stars. As late as February 1956, *Collier's* published an accolade, which it did not know was an epitaph, for the homebody Liz. It conceded that she neither cooked nor sewed nor cleaned nor grew vegetables, the way all other good young wives out there were doing.

"But still, at the same time, she is many of the things the girl next door should be. She is a wise and conscientious mother, a devoted wife, a person of dignity, humor, and abundant common sense. . . . When she works, she works hard. When she relaxes, she does so completely . . . making up to her sons for the days she must spend away from them.

"It takes intelligence and ambition to lead two such full lives. She has both. She is a success as a woman—despite her success as a star. And this, in Hollywood, circa 1956, is an impressive achievement."

8

A Touch of Scarlett

The wide screen was the movies' answer to television and among the major studios, MGM was slow with its answer. While some of the others set off in hot pursuit of the right technical process to fill the new vast expanse, MGM hoped that the gimmick, like television itself, would go away. No such luck. The stunning success of *This Is Cinerama* in 1952, with a curving screen six times wider than ordinary, showed that width was around to stay. For a while, it even seemed to Cinerama's credit that it made people feel physically sick while watching the roller-coaster ride. The three-dimensional process (3-D) looked good too. However, both quickly lost their charm. Cinerama had irritating seams and 3-D required special glasses to be worn—not much fun, especially if you happened to be wearing glasses already. A long train of other "visions" and "ramas" followed, but by 1953 Twentieth Century-Fox had emerged the clear winner with CinemaScope. Fox's *The Robe*, starring the young Richard Burton in a purple toga, became the first wide-screen commercial success and MGM resignedly leased the process for itself.

Because of her pregnancies, because of her studio's conservatism, and because she was not their top property, Elizabeth Taylor had to wait longer than Grace or Marilyn for the blockbuster that would spread her charms over the new postcard-shaped screen. The wide screen presented a lot of new problems for plots; the human figure tended to get lost in all that landscape. MGM finally hit the right story formula with *Bad Day at Black Rock* in 1954, in which looming mountains and bleached desert actually helped to underline Spencer Tracy's isolation as the one-armed good man in an evil town.

Taylor finally got her chance when George Stevens gave her Texas. In 1955 he asked Metro to loan her to Warner Brothers to play the female lead in *Giant*, the epic he was going to make out of Edna Ferber's best-selling novel about a Texas millionaire family as the source of their wealth changes over three generations from cattle to oil. Stevens, wrestling with the social and psychological meanings of the American landscape, had already come out with *Shane* in 1953.

Once again, especially after the kind of drivel she'd been making, Taylor was delighted to be picked by Stevens, even though she believed that he had really wanted Grace Kelly for the part of Leslie Benedict, the Maryland girl who marries a rancher and learns to love Texas. Rock Hudson, who had the male lead, says, however, that Stevens gave him the choice.

As a director, Stevens's tactics were unchanged. He used every ruse he could think of to turn an actor into the character he wanted. It was part of his plan to cast the part of Bick Benedict, the owner of the million-acre Reata Ranch, before any of the others. To general amazement, he picked Rock Hudson. Although a fixture in the box-office top ten, Hudson was considered just a muscleman. "I was chosen over everybody else in town," says Hudson, looking back to the best part he has ever had. "Gary Cooper wanted it, everybody wanted that part. George did all his direction of me before the filming began. By the time we went on location, he had me feeling so rich and arrogant that I didn't have to act." On the Warner Brothers lot, as stagehands constructed the Charles Addams-Gothic mansion that looms up out of the Texas dust as Bick and his bride return from their wedding, Stevens asked Hudson, "What color is the house?"

" 'How should I know?' I told him. George said, 'It's *your* house. *You* live in it. What *color* is it?' So I said, 'Tan with brown trim.' " Rock Hudson makes his hands into a megaphone. " 'Paint it tan with brown trim.' And they did and then they took it apart, piece by piece and shipped it to Texas." In the same spirit, Stevens asked Hudson whether he wanted Grace Kelly or Elizabeth Taylor for a leading lady. "I said Elizabeth Taylor, because she had such an incredible beauty. But I had a feeling that if I'd said Grace Kelly, George had the reason ready to obstruct it."

Stevens himself selected the third leading player: James Dean. Dean's reputation as Hollywood's bad boy was well established, although his powers as an actor were just beginning to be realized. When work began on *Giant*, Dean's *East of Eden* had just come out, while the film that would make him most famous after his death, *Rebel without a Cause*, had not yet been released. Dean loved the part of Jett Rink, the surly ranch hand. It suited him (although Stevens had considered Richard Burton). Rink is the subversive, the poor boy who spoils Bick Benedict's absolute power over his world. Rink, who inherits a small plot of land from Benedict's sister, turns it, in front of Benedict's enraged eyes, into an oil field and a fortune. Then, after lusting silently after Benedict's wife (Taylor) for years, he starts to court their daughter.

Dean saw himself halfway between Montgomery Clift and Marlon Brando, and like them, was a true believer in The Method. At night he would wrest his concept of a scene out of his unconscious and come in character to work in the morning. As soon as he got to Marfa, Texas, on location, Dean affected cowboy dress. In jeans, silver-buckled belt, and ten-gallon hat, he would lounge on the railing with the local cowboys and was furious when photographers picked him out of the bunch.

Nobody got along with Dean on the set—except Elizabeth Taylor—and she didn't make contact with him until the picture was half done. She has an affinity for strays. Besides, they had two things in common: their youth—she was twenty-three, he was twenty-four—and neither of them liked George Stevens. Stevens had no use for Dean's psychological warming-up exercises: He liked to prepare his actors himself. And he never let Dean forget his third-place status. Dean was furious. To Hedda Hopper (whom he shrewdly made one of his protectors in Hollywood, one of the few people he never insulted) Dean spluttered, "Stevens has been horrible. I sat there for three days, made up and ready to work at nine o'clock every morning. By six o'clock I hadn't had a scene or rehearsal. I sat there like a bump on a log watching that big lumpy Rock Hudson make love to Liz Taylor."

Once they got down to work, Taylor forgot all about what Stevens had done for her in *A Place in the Sun.* She was emotional pulp again. Only about four months past from her second messy Cesarean, in the state in which other women indulge in depression or letting themselves go, she handed her second son to a nurse, allowed herself to be laced into sexy riding skirts and mannish blouses, and went off for several months in Texas. Her postpartum mood, combined with the everyday paranoia of the star, made her feel that Stevens was deliberately trying to humiliate her. In her autobiography, *Elizabeth Taylor: An Informal Memoir*, a slender volume that appeared in 1964, she devotes five whole pages to telling why she was right and Stevens was wrong on one memorable day in the spring of 1955.

It happened when they filmed the scene in *Giant* in which Taylor-Leslie had fled back to Maryland because she can't stand Texas and her husband's macho bullying. While she is at home, her sister gets married and she is matron of honor. During the wedding, her husband, Rock-Bick Benedict, arrives from Texas, repentant. With ten-gallon hat in hand, he steals into the back of the room. Wordlessly, husband and wife gaze at each other. As the words of the marriage service boom out, they remarry each other with their eyes. At that moment *Giant*, which has been teetering on the edge of soap opera, falls in.

In Taylor's recollection, she had to play the scene in a state of Stevens-induced distress.

That day after lunch, she waited in her dressing room, but the call to return to the set never came. Finally she emerged to see what was wrong. She found the lights switched off, extras standing idle, and George Stevens slouched over, his head on his fist. Then Stevens spoke: "Just who the hell do you think you are to keep these people waiting? Just how far do you think you can go? Just how much do you think you can get away with?"

Taylor explained. She had had her lunch, repaired her makeup, and had her dress ironed. Stevens persisted: "I suppose you think that your makeup is more important than those people's makeup. I suppose you think your costume is more important than their costumes. Well, I have news for you. It isn't." For support Taylor turned to the assistant director and the truth comes out: the person assigned to call her had not done so! Does Stevens apologize? Never. Then, recalls Taylor, "I had to go and act before all the extras. I was quivering and in the scene I was supposed to cry. Now I've always wondered whether he did all that deliberately for the sake of the scene."

The same episode is lodged in Rock Hudson's memory, but with a different tinge.

"We began filming interiors in Hollywood, before we went to Texas," he recalls, looking reflectively down at his fifties-style thick white socks and hand-sewn loafers. "Elizabeth and I had never worked together before and she thought it would be a good idea if we got better acquainted. So she kindly invited me, and my then fiancée, up to have dinner with her and

Michael. Well, we drank and drank and we got smashed. We didn't stop until about four o'clock in the morning, and the women had a six o'clock call for Makeup and I had to be there at seven. You know, we were really drunk." He laughs. "Well, hungover like that, both of us, we did the scene where I go back to her sister's wedding, and we're reconciled. And we had even the wardrobe ladies crying. What acting! And it was our hangovers."

After months on location, James Dean finished his work in the film before the others. He left Texas and went back to California. On September 30, 1955, he slammed his racing Porsche into the side of a Ford that was turning left at the intersection of routes 466 and 41, and died instantly. Long before *Giant* was released in October 1956, he was a cult figure from beyond the grave.

Dean's death hit Elizabeth Taylor very hard. "George was not very kind to her," Hudson admits. "Elizabeth is very extreme in her likes and dislikes. If she likes, she loves. If she doesn't like, she loathes. And she has a temper, an incredible temper which she loses at any injustice. George forced her to come to work after Dean's death. He hadn't finished the film. And she could not stop crying. Remember that scene in my office? She kept sobbing and sobbing, so he photographed me over the back of her head. But she let him have it."

One way she may have let him have it was by collapsing. Stomach pains diagnosed as a twisted colon sent her to the hospital for two weeks.

Rock Hudson is a rarity among movie stars, a nice guy, one who doesn't mind talking about a star other than himself, and he likes Elizabeth Taylor very much. "She took great delight in breaking me up, getting me giggling," he says.

"Another thing about Elizabeth, she's absolutely delighted when she gets a present. Whether it's a diamond tiara or cherry chocolates, she's like a child at Christmas. It's not overacting. It's genuine, a great quality."

One of the Dean legends that has sprung up concerns

Elizabeth Taylor and *Giant.* I heard it from my hairdresser. It probably originated in David Dalton's biography of Dean, where it is told by Dennis Hopper, who played Benedict's son in *Giant.*

If this story is true, it shows that James Dean had more honesty and self-awareness than he's been given credit for. For it has him admitting that he was afraid of Elizabeth Taylor. And fear of her is a basic ingredient of the Taylor myth, fear of her fame, of the private associations she inspires, terror of the dark depths, of the power of the abnormal eyes. Hopper said that in his first scene with Taylor, the big movie star, "Jimmy was really fuckin' nervous.

"They did take after take, and it just wasn't going right. He was really getting fucked up. Really nervous. Suddenly he walked away from the set toward the football field where all those people were standing. He wasn't relating to them or anything. He just walked over, he stood there, unzipped his pants, pulled out his cock, and took a piss. Then he put his cock back, zipped up his pants, walked back to the set, and said, 'OK, shoot.' And they did the scene in one take."

It was The Method in action: "I figured if I could piss in front of those two thousand people, man, I could be cool. I figured if I could do that, I could get in front of that camera and do just anything, anything at all."

Today Elizabeth Taylor insists she has absolutely no knowledge of the incident. Rock Hudson doubts that it ever took place: "On a set . . . you would have heard." Norma Heyman, one of Taylor's best friends, was so upset after hearing it on television during a program commemorating the twentieth anniversary of James Dean's death, that she asked Taylor why she didn't speak out and deny it. Taylor's reply was interesting: "They're too private to me, Jimmy and Monty. I just want to leave them in peace, up there where they are."

So James Dean joined the list of Elizabeth Taylor's lost men. Someone who observed her in 1973 after Laurence Harvey, another of her close friends and costar, died of cancer just as the two of them had finished *Night Watch*, said, "Elizabeth has a bad feeling. So many men die on her."

Up there where he is, if he can see how Stevens left him for posterity, Jimmy must be grateful. The most memorable scene in *Giant* is that of Dean, in black silhouette, stomping exultantly over his acres of land, drenched in oil as his first gusher comes over him. And his final scene, as the aging and drunk Jett Rink, with receding hairline, dark glasses, and thin mustache, is brilliant proof—and the only proof that exists—that James Dean could play anything except a tormented adolescent. Dead or alive, James Dean stole *Giant* and always will. When I saw it, the house was filled with James Deans in ducktails and nail studs, who burst into rapturous applause every time their god appeared on the screen.

Yet Taylor and Hudson both were very good, in spite of the powder in their hair that called attention to their youth when they were supposed to be grandparents. (Stevens also made Hudson wear a fifty-pound belt to help him simulate age.) Taylor is gorgeous, almost green-eyed in *Giant.* Stevens achieved his miracle again and he tones down her overblown beauty. Often he sets her off-center and submerged in groups and shows her thin, nervous, and fussing. He gets onto the screen the maternal strain in her personality that may be her most powerful and enduring sexual message. "Give him to me," she says, reaching out for a Mexican woman's baby with the confident air of a woman who knows she is good with babies.

As with *A Place in the Sun*, many connected with *Giant* were nominated for Academy Awards (Stevens, Dean, Hudson, Mercedes McCambridge—not Elizabeth Taylor), but only George Stevens won. The director's attention to detail had been so meticulous that he even had the Benedict mansion repeatedly redecorated to show the changing decades, from gloomy Edwardian to beige ghastly good taste. Yet *Giant* is a tedious triumph, full of set pieces: the roundup, the hero's return, suppression of women, hatred of the Mexican.

For Taylor, however, it was the turning point in her career. It grossed $7 million in its first year and began for her the unbroken string of box-office successes probably unmatched by any other star. *Giant* brought Elizabeth Taylor's face to the cover of *Life* for the first time since *Cynthia* in 1947. Her ability to portray a character aging from eighteen to fifty was noticed with admiration and respect. *Giant*, said the London *Times*, revealed "a long sustained achievement by Elizabeth Taylor which is an astonishing revelation of unsuspected gifts."

By the time *Giant* was finished, the Wildings' marriage had deteriorated from dull to dead. It was one of those marriages that seems to have been made only to produce babies. Once the second was born, it fell apart. Socially, the Wildings had led a quiet life. They played poker with Peggy Rutledge and Virginia Streeter or had friends in to dinner—the Stewart Grangers, the Bogarts, and particularly Montgomery Clift who got on well with Michael Wilding and had moved to a house near theirs. Any illusion that Elizabeth was the child-wife faded when anybody compared their careers. She was the breadwinner and the star. In spite of her two pregnancies, she was steadily at work, in leading roles. Wilding had little or nothing to do. The move to Hollywood had been, professionally, a disaster. While his immigrant friends Stewart Granger and James Mason were making good in Hollywood, Wilding had made only three dreary pictures for Metro: *The Egyptian, The Glass Slipper*, and *Zarak.* "Oh, Michael Wilding, what have they done to you?" wailed the London *Daily Express*, seeing him dressed up as pharaoh, with black wig and gold headband. "Come home at once," it pleaded. "There's a suit of tails—and a carnation—plus a warm welcome—awaiting you on the dockside." Wilding did not go home. After Metro failed to pick up his options, he tried to make his way with independent productions. He formed a company called Summit Films and tried to get his wife to join. But Metro refused to loan her out and she was unenthusiastic. Wilding, left watching his wife's star ascend, did not walk into the sea at Malibu, but eventually tried what some actors might consider a fate worse than death: He became an agent.

Giant was the first of Elizabeth Taylor's films conceived as a second *Gone with the Wind. Cleopatra* was the third, and in between came *Raintree County*, which tried hardest of the three. It was to be a Civil War epic, based on Ross Lockridge's 1,100-page novel, and it marked the first time that MGM pulled out all the stops for Taylor. Dore Schary announced that it would have a budget of $5 million—the most ever spent on any picture made entirely within the United States. All her previous best work and big pictures had been done on loan to other studios. It was to be her first southern role, her first mad scene, and her second film costarring with Montgomery Clift.

Clift at that time was at the peak of his career, thanks to *From Here to Eternity*. However, his friends recognized that he was just as self-destructive as James Dean: killing himself merely took longer. One night before *Raintree County* began, he and actor Kevin McCarthy had been dining at the Wildings'. They left early in separate cars, twisting down the narrow canyon road. Then came a crash so loud it was heard back up at the house.

Taylor, for whom the accident was a major trauma, placed the time at 10:30 P.M. Police reports gave it as 12:30 A.M. but agreed with her that there were no signs of drinking. Everybody at the Wildings' pelted down the hill. One of the guests was Rock Hudson: "Monty had wrapped himself around a telephone pole. We got there and he was spitting teeth, oozing blood. Elizabeth held his head in her lap. She mothered him. 'Monty, we can't move you until the doctor comes,' she said, but it didn't matter what she said because he was in shock. It took forever for the doctor to come . . . forever! And when he did, he was immediately followed by the photographers. Elizabeth prevented the photographers from taking Monty's picture by the foulest language I have ever heard. She *shocked* them out of taking it. 'You son of a bitch!' she said, 'I'll kick you in the nuts!' ["Pardon my French," Hudson interrupts politely.] The photographers were startled. 'Miss Taylor! You shouldn't be talking like that!' they said. And then six of us formed a line—all *stars*—to hide Monty and we said to the photographers [Hudson bares his teeth in a death's head grin], 'Take a picture of us! We'll smile!' "

Clift recovered, that time. His jaw was broken in four places. The shooting of *Raintree* had to be postponed two months while his face healed. He never recovered his earlier good looks, or his confidence. Shortly after, he took an overdose of sleeping pills and twice during the making of *Raintree* he was found at night wandering the streets of Danville, Kentucky, nude.

While Clift convalesced, Taylor passed the time learning to speak with a southern accent. Her coach was a young woman about her own age, Marguerite Littman, now the wife of an executive of the British Steel Corporation. A writer herself who had never lost her deep New Orleans drawl, she'd blundered into work as an accent coach, "as a favor to Tennessee," tutoring Barbara Bel Geddes for *Cat on a Hot Tin Roof* on Broadway. She finds it very boring, she says, so she charges a tremendous amount. Along with Elizabeth Taylor, she has a long string of credible southerns to her credit, including Carroll Baker, Lee Remick, and Claire Bloom.

Her recipe, given in a London house furnished like a Tennessee Williams set, with climbing orchids, snakeskin upholstery, and an army of stuffed tortoises, sounds easy. "I don't try to build the accent into every word. If actors spoke real southern, the film would be too long and monotonous. It would never end. I just teach them to change a few words and pronunciations and leave the rest of their accent alone. Make the *e* sound like *i*," she says. "Hit the verb, slur the pronouns, drop the *g*'s in the *ings*, and come down on the first part of a word *hard*. Chair is CHAY-uh—and take a long time to add the end syllable. Drag out and dramatize the adjectives. If something is ugly, make it UGG-li . . ." (Presumably as in, "Why can't you get ugly, Brick?"—big line in *Cat on a Hot Tin Roof.*) "And raise your voice at the end and you get a . . . sort of . . . ten-ta-tive questionin' quality . . . ?"

On location for *Raintree County* Elizabeth Taylor displayed an appetite worthy of Scarlett O'Hara. Always she has loved coarse peasant foods and wherever she is, she finds the local variety: chili con carne in California, sausages and mashed potatoes in London. "She used to love corn on the cob with lashings of butter," says Mrs. Littman who accompanied her to Kentucky. "If possible, she used to like to get away from the set for lunch. Otherwise, if we ate there, an assistant director would wander over and look into her plate to see what she was eating. But she could lose more weight between a Friday and a Tuesday than anybody I ever met." Like Scarlett too, Taylor occasionally was laced up too tightly. Once she fainted. The problem was diagnosed as hyperventilation and, according to *Time*, added $45,000 to the film's cost. (Actuaries decided, said *Time*, that if Clark Gable was the best insurance risk in films, Elizabeth Taylor was the worst.)

Elizabeth Taylor slid into southernness with a sense of dis-covery and delight. Her southern accent "took," she told her coach, "like a vaccination." (Years later, when she was married to Richard Burton, she used a similar medical metaphor to describe her Welshness. On a live BBC television show, she announced that she was "Welsh by injection." The BBC were not amused.

Yet Mrs. Littman felt that Taylor, besides being a good mimic, had the right qualifications for a belle. "Like most southern women, she has a high, sort of tentative voice, and an air of being absolutely dependent on a man, of having a man at the center of existence. Given that, she's a rock."

Richard Brooks, who later directed Taylor in *Cat on a Hot Tin Roof*, is even more emphatic. He sees her as the quintes-sential Tennessee Williams heroine, and counts the reasons: "First, she's a beauty. Then, she's a combination of child and bitch. Third, she wants to love passionately, and to be loved. And . . ." Brooks holds up a finger for a dramatic pause. "She's hiding something."

Raintree County, released in October 1956, was a flop, but not because of Taylor. As a southern belle, who retreats into insanity because (why else?) of fantasies about Nigra blood, she was generously praised as the only good thing in it. This picture along with the fantastically successful *Cat on a Hot Tin Roof* and *Suddenly Last Summer* established Taylor as a player of sultry hot-weather females full of passion that might at any moment spill over into madness.

Mock-southernness was one of the many qualities which, curiously, Taylor began to acquire in common with Marilyn Monroe. Both were WASP Californians who took Jewish husbands and became converts to Judaism. Of Monroe, Norman Mailer said, "You could go into another southern town and find twelve of her." Of Taylor, Andy Warhol wrote, "I have lots of southern themes in my paintings. Flowers and Liz Taylor and bananas, which all the monkeys down there eat."

When Taylor left Los Angeles for Kentucky, she was hiding something, but like most of her secrets, it was shared with the world's press. Her next husband was going to be Mike Todd.

Around the World
in Twenty-One Months

Dames who want diamonds, furs, and paintings
make guys work harder to *get* 'em.
                                        Mike Todd

The phenomenon that the world now knows as Elizabeth
Taylor is the work of Mike Todd. In the brief time they had
together before his plane crashed in a thunderstorm over New
Mexico in 1958, Todd, the master showman, changed Taylor
from a dull movie beauty into an international celebrity whose
sybaritic life and loves are a running news story, and into the
archetypal star goddess who takes her public with her to the
very brink of death. Norma Heyman admits, "I first became
enchanted with Elizabeth Taylor when she married Mike
Todd. Of course one hadn't been unaware of the impact she had
on people, but it was Todd who fascinated me. I knew that the

woman who married Mike Todd must be truly fantastic." Rock Hudson agrees. "When we were making *Giant*, Elizabeth was a big star, but she was not news. Not like now. People weren't coming onto the set and fighting to get a look at her. She led a quiet life with Michael and their two boys."

The transformation wrought by Todd was total. He woke Taylor up sexually, professionally, and financially. He changed her religion, although not deliberately; she didn't formally convert to Judaism until after he died. He taught her, and she was an apt pupil, to enjoy ostentation. He gave her her first Rolls-Royce.

And he did it all as a business expense of *Around the World in 80 Days*. That is not to imply that all his rapturous statements —"What we've got is so great and so right it scares me"— weren't sincere. It is just that Todd did nothing unless it was to his financial advantage, that he routinely paid for extravagances with borrowed money, and that in a lifetime of gambling, *Around the World in 80 Days* was his greatest gamble.

As she has searched for a man to complete her life, Elizabeth Taylor has alternated between weak and strong men and in Mike Todd she found a man who did not think it excessive when people called him "Todd Almighty."

Mike Todd was even older than Michael Wilding. Born Avrumele Goldbogen in 1907 in Minneapolis, he moved at twelve with his family to Chicago when his father found a post as a rabbi with a poor congregation. Chicago was the place where Todd made and lost his first fortune (in construction) and where he married, at twenty, his first wife, Bertha. All his life Chicago was to remain for him the essence of Big Town and he has a monument there today: the Mike Todd Theater, which Elizabeth Taylor owns, along with one other, the Cinestage, both bought from the Mike Todd Company in 1971.

In 1934 (when Elizabeth Taylor was two), after the Depression had disposed of his second fortune (construction, Los Angeles), Todd entered show business and stayed. It was the

1. *Elizabeth, Sara, and Howard Taylor in London*

2. *Elizabeth and Sara Taylor in Beverly Hills*

3. *With Glenn Davis at 1949 Academy Awards*
4. *Named "Smo-o-o [for smoother] Girl of 1949"*
   by the boys of Sigma Chi at Northwestern University
5. *The graduate congratulated by her mother*
6. *Mr. and Mrs. Conrad Nicholson Hilton, Jr., May 6, 1950*

7

7. *In 1951, announcing her intention to divorce Hilton*
8. *Francis and Sara Taylor after Wilding wedding*
9. *Mike Todd with wife and stepsons*
10. *The Todds with month-old Liza*

11. *Todds and Fishers at Ascot*
12. *Taylor, with the Fishers, at Las Vegas, in her first public appearance after Todd's death*
13. *Just married: 1959*
14. *Taylor, Liza Todd, and Eddie Fisher at Los Angeles court on reported adoption day*

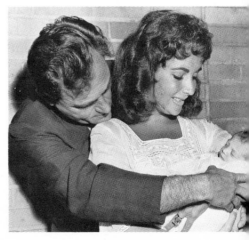

11

12

13

14

16

17

18. *Taylor announces her engagement to John Warner*

year of Chicago's Century of Progress Exposition, and he came up with the perfect symbol: the Flame Dance, an artistic strip-tease. Todd's hand on a gas jet produced a flame that burned the gossamer wings of a dancer and left her looking nude. His flair for showmanship took him to the 1939-40 New York World's Fair. By the time it ended Mike Todd was a household word. He came up with five hit shows, blazing "Mike Todd Presents" above their titles. The war years he spent producing a dizzy succession of hits and flops. *The Hot Mikado* and *Hamlet*, with Maurice Evans, were two of the hits and Todd allowed himself readily to be patronized by Damon Runyon, Walter Winchell, and Lloyd Lewis of the *Chicago Daily News*. They printed his quips (he told one of his favorites to President Truman—"I've often been broke but I've never been poor") and they sold him to America as the prototype of the lovable Broadway con man.

In reality, says S. J. Perelman, who wrote the screenplay for *Around the World in 80 Days*, "Todd wasn't funny."

Todd did have a knack of getting people to back his ideas with money—particularly women. He was a one-woman man, but for a long time was unable to marry the various women of his choice because Bertha Todd refused to divorce him. She made a vow to remain Mrs. Michael Todd until she died, which she did, under mysterious circumstances, in 1947. One of Todd's backers was Gypsy Rose Lee. He had engineered her emergence as an intellectual, respectable striptease, under the title of "The Best Undressed Woman in America," and when she became rich, from shrewd investments, she loaned him $25,000 to get *Star and Garter* over a pre-Broadway crisis. Miss Lee was rewarded with a good profit. Not so lucky was Joan Blondell, who eventually became the second Mrs. Todd. She lent Todd her life's savings and in 1948, ten weeks after they were married, he went bankrupt—$1.1 million in debt.

From then, until the day he met Elizabeth Taylor in 1956, Todd's life was one long attempt to throw off the cloud over his reputation and to regain his razzle-dazzle. There were two clouds, really. The bankruptcy proceedings, which had dragged on and on, had turned nasty when the trustee in charge of the case accused him of concealing assets and transferring them to his son, Mike Todd, Jr. Todd recovered from this scandal only when a New York University professor of law advised him to stop fighting the charge, to withdraw the plea to be discharged of his debts, and to try to pay back his creditors. Then there was the manner of his wife's death. Bertha Todd, after a fight with Todd in Los Angeles fierce enough to make the *New York Daily News* (he supposedly was demanding a divorce), was taken to the hospital with an injured hand—cut, she said, slicing an orange. A few hours later she was dead. At first the coroner refused to issue a verdict on the cause of death and Hollywood buzzed with rumors. Eventually Todd was absolved of any blame. The ruling was that Bertha Todd had died from the effect of anesthetic, but he was hurt by the scandal regardless.

As he cast about for new ways to revive his fortunes by entertaining the public, Todd hit upon the very medium that rejuvenated Elizabeth Taylor's career: the wide screen. He saw the possibilities right from the start. He mocked the conservatism of the old movie moguls: "The Big Numbers don't care. They created a one-generation business and they don't care what happens to it after they're gone."

His excitement began the day he first saw an experimental showing of the Cinerama process and after a frenzy of wheeling and dealing, with help from Toots Shor, he launched himself in a partnership with Lowell Thomas, the broadcaster. *This Is Cinerama* was a sensation; but Todd perceived it was useless for anything but a travelogue and with three cameras projecting the separate pictures, would never mesh into a single unbroken image.

Todd went out to find something better. He had to. Boardroom politics had pushed him right out of Cinerama;

Lowell Thomas and assorted financial interests forced him to sell his stock for $300,000. He decided to try again—by coming up with his own wide screen process. He went to the American Optical Company. "I want a Cinerama with everything to come out of one hole," he said, and he wanted it in six months.

He got it, Cinerama without the seams. The invention was named Todd-AO (the letters stand for American Optical) and was an oddity. It was a process that required a big nine-inch lens called a Big Eye and employed sixty-five-millimeter film that produced prints so big they could only be shown by special projectors artificially cooled.

But Todd-AO re-created Cinerama's physical sensations with a crystal clarity of focus that would satisfy the National Geographic. The process was good enough to persuade Richard Rodgers and Oscar Hammerstein to have it for the filming of *Oklahoma!*, in 1955.

Unbelievably, Todd was soon pushed out of the Todd-AO corporation as well. He was, said his biographer, Art Cohn, "only half-smart when it came to finances." But his publicity sense was the greatest since Ziegfeld's. A poll at the time showed Todd, with Mark Hellinger and Cecil B. DeMille, as one of the most famous producers in the world—and he had never made a movie. He had not even had a hit show since *Up in Central Park* in 1945.

For all these reasons, Todd was unusually motivated, even by his standards, to make a hit out of *Around the World in 80 Days*. He had next to no money and it was to be his most expensive production ever. To produce it, he formed his own company, the Michael Todd Company, and scraped up the financial backing from wherever he could.

Todd had bought the screen rights to the old Jules Verne novel from Sir Alexander Korda precisely because he felt it had all the right ingredients for Todd-AO: exotic locations and a good story full of suspense. It would give him a chance to slot in lots of famous faces. Todd, who was as miserly as he was extravagant, liked to boast about his "cameo shots"; the term itself was his own ingenious invention. What it meant was that he got big names cheap. In *Around the World* he packed in Frank Sinatra, Marlene Dietrich (an old flame), Fernandel, John Gielgud, and Charles Boyer, among others. Noël Coward said he was hooked "at a mediocre lunch." Instead of authentic foreign backgrounds, he used Hollywood mock-ups whenever possible, borrowing the backlots of half a dozen studios, and when forced to send a camera crew abroad, he sent them, according to Perelman, equipped with shaved heads and begging bowls.

"The finances of *Around the World in 80 Days*," Perelman wrote in *Vinegar Puss*, "were as impenetrable as the Mato Grosso. All I knew is that my pittance was extracted only by deep surgery. Week after week, it took cajolery, pleas, and threats of legal action to collect one's salary. All the while, of course, our impresario lived like the Medici, running up awesome bills that he waved away airily on presentation."

Perelman's pittance was $29,000, less 10 percent for his agent. Even though he won the Academy Award for his screenplay, he refused to accept Todd's invitation to prepare the script for his next project, *Don Quixote*, at a more generous fee.

The film's backers included the Columbia Broadcasting System, Paramount Pictures, Lorraine Manville (Tommy's sister), Lucey, the owner of Hollywood's Lucey's Restaurant, and anyone else who could be persuaded to come in. Once shooting had to stop because Todd couldn't meet a payroll and at the very end, he only scraped together enough to finance the final big ship-burning scene in the Catalina Channel by borrowing money hours before it was to begin. Only then did he embark on his next venture. He called it Project Liz.

The woman in his life at that time was Evelyn Keyes, the blond actress who had played Ruby Keeler in *The Jolson Story*. Frank, witty, self-mocking, Evelyn Keyes pleased Todd by telling him off and suffering silently when he humiliated her. She psychoanalyzed him, teasing him for his anti-intellectualism and persecution complex. (When I interviewed her, she analyzed me. "Say," she said, interrupting herself, "I get it. I bet you think you *look* like Elizabeth Taylor!" She squinted painfully at me and tipped her head from side to side. "Yes. . . . I think I can see it . . . in a way.")

Evelyn Keyes has no patience with young reporters who accept literally the old Hollywood euphemisms they read in the files. "They keep referring to me as Mike Todd's good friend," she says. "I have to tell them, 'Look. We were more than good friends. I was *living with him.'* " Keyes, who has married Charles Vidor, John Huston, and Artie Shaw ("I'm a terrible cliché. I've married fathers"), accompanied Todd to Russia. He got her a visa in a day—no small feat in 1956. Keyes also shared in the planning for the distribution of *Around the World*. This was a big job: Not only was the picture going out as a "road show"—a big film with intermission and reserved seats—but theaters had to be especially and expensively equipped for Todd-AO.

His discovery of Elizabeth Taylor was well documented. Todd hired a yacht to take a party out to watch his maritime bonfire. Included in the party were the Michael Wildings (he with yachting cap, she in pink toreador pants and blue sweater), Kevin McCarthy, the Hollywood agent Kurt Frings and his wife, Ketti, and Art Cohn, Todd's biographer. At that time, Taylor has recorded, she and Wilding were living like brother and sister. Todd was the kind of man who could sense a vacuum. Not long after, he and Keyes invited the Wildings to a small dinner for Edward R. Murrow, and soon Evelyn Keyes found herself dispatched on a long trip to South America and Europe to arrange for *Around the World* showings.

She enjoyed her trip. "After all, I'd learned at the feet of the master." Making long-distance telephone calls with each hand—"I used to tell Mike that if he had three hands, he'd use three telephones"—chartering planes, giving orders, she reached Paris before she got the news from Todd over the telephone: "I'm in love with Elizabeth."

"Elizabeth who?" Keyes asked. It was probably the last time that anybody in the movies asked that question.

Unlike Debbie Reynolds two years later, Evelyn Keyes was not and is not bitter. In the first place, she had no children. Nor any illusions about the power of beauty. "Look, in this town [Hollywood], *everybody's* gorgeous. *Everybody's* spoiled. *Everybody* can pick and choose. Mike just figured he'd had this and now he'd have that. And he liked to see his name in the papers. He knew how famous she was.

"I liked Elizabeth," she continued. "I didn't resent her. If I resented anything about her, it was that she was movie royalty. She started at the top. The rest of us had to work hard to be movie stars." Evelyn Keyes's first big part was Suellen, Scarlett's sister in *Gone with the Wind*.

So Evelyn Keyes made a polite exit from Todd's life, taking with her a 5 percent share of the Michael Todd Company, which she later sold for $100,000.

With Elizabeth Taylor, Mike Todd was not interested in being just good friends. He wanted marriage. His movie was good, he knew it. He was ready for a rebirth; with Taylor, he insisted on the whole *Father of the Bride* scenario. He was so scrupulous about propriety that when Michael Wilding formally issued a separation statement to the press, it contained the words: "Elizabeth and Mike Todd did not see one another alone until we were separated, and I wish to say that Todd's conduct in this whole thing has been above reproach."

In Taylor's account, too, the proposal was out of Louisa May Alcott. All in the same breath (in the office of Bennie Thau at MGM) Todd declared his love and told her that she was going to marry him. She assented with curious passivity, "like a mongoose mesmerized by a cobra."

It was this scene that Hedda Hopper later ventured to amplify, with " 'from now on, you'll know nobody but me.' Only he didn't say 'know.' "

At forty-eight, Todd was aging, short, with a rattrap of a mouth and an eternal cigar. Taylor had matured into a voluptuous satiny beauty that made men buckle at the knees. They were not beauty and the beast, however. "They were not an incongruous couple," says Perelman, "because they were both so showbiz. They engaged a lot in a kind of arguing banter that was very hard on their hearers, but there is no doubt he was very fond of her."

Marina Vaizey, art critic of the London *Sunday Times* remembers seeing them one day in Provincetown. "There was a buzz coming down the street. People were staring before they knew that it was Elizabeth Taylor. It was an extraordinary physical phenomenon, that's the only way to describe it . . . these incredible blue eyes, raking the horizon." Taylor didn't look short, she added, because Todd was so short.

For their first weekend trip together, Todd took Taylor to Atlantic City, the home of Monopoly, but their first formal public appearance as a couple, when they announced their engagement was—no surprise—at the premiere of *Around the World in 80 Days*. Todd had staged it well. The filming of *Raintree County* had ended the day before. Conveniently, he was able to sail into the greatest night of his life with arguably the world's most beautiful woman on his arm. "Meet Miss Lizzie Schwarzkopf," he joked, but it was no joke. With Todd she began to look Jewish. There is a saying, "When you're in love, everyone looks Jewish," and it was a kind of rich contented opulence that Todd brought out in her. In rubies and Grecian velvet, she queened it over the occasion, dispensing some of her most heartfelt "my man" statements. Utterly dismissing his predictions that she would get the Academy Award for *Raintree County*, she told everybody to concentrate on *his* picture.

From then on the movie and the myth were entwined. Publicity for one was publicity for the other. Her engagement ring from Todd was her first real rock: a thirty-carat diamond, an inch and a half across, and the press happily carried Todd's

boast that it cost him $92,000 and represented only the begin-
ning. He gave her a present every day, a big one on Saturdays
because he had met her on a Saturday. At every opening of the
movie he gave her another major jewel. It all fed what she must
have always conceived of as the use of beauty—to be indulged,
gather wealth, and never ever be left alone. During this whole
transition from Michael to Mike, Elizabeth Taylor was never
manless for a day, in the public's eye at least.

If it makes a strange contrast, Todd eluding his creditors and
employees while showering Taylor with expensive gifts, there
is no evidence that she asked the womanly question: who's
paying for all this? She would have been laughed off and it
would have been uncharacteristic of her. All her life she has
accepted gifts as homage.

Taylor's assessment of their two movies was accurate. She
knew that *Raintree County* was not going to fulfill MGM's
hopes—although it did bring her, for the first time, a nomination for an Academy Award. In contrast, *Around the World in
80 Days* was lavishly praised—ludicrously so, in retrospect.
"Mike Todd's picture makes this a better world!" exclaimed the
Associated Press. In London, the *Daily Mirror* wanted him
knighted. The *Saturday Review* wondered: "Is it a film? Is it
entertainment?" but advised going to see it anyway.

Shortly after, Taylor sued Michael Wilding for divorce—her
complaint was "extreme mental cruelty." Then she collapsed
with three crushed disks in her spine and was admitted to
Columbia-Presbyterian Hospital where she had a five-hour
operation. The disks were removed and a new construction
made of bits of bone was grafted in their place. Of all her
illnesses over the years, except the pneumonia that nearly
killed her in London in 1961, this was the big one. She was
advised not to undertake any more pregnancies.

Why is Elizabeth Taylor ill so often? In the fifties it was
fashionable to explain illness, especially among the young and
apparently healthy, as psychosomatic. George Stevens took
this view of Taylor's back; Todd sarcastically offered to send

him X rays of Taylor's spine. Today people are less fierce about snapping "psychosomatic" at anything lacking a neat diagnosis. There appear to be lots of overlapping reasons, physical as well as emotional, why Taylor should have suffered from what a doctor who has treated her and other stars calls "a chaos, a symphony of illness."

Stars, he maintains, are a curious combination of strength and frailty. They will push themselves to finish a film—or even go to a party—way past the point where lesser mortals would go to bed with some antibiotic. They say, "I can't be sick until Thursday" and then they collapse, sicker than ordinary. Then too, like athletes, movie stars represent commercial investments. Insurance companies take an intense interest in how ill they are for how many days. As a result, they are overdoctored. No ailment escapes attention. Nor—in the case of a super-celebrity like Elizabeth Taylor—does it escape the press. On every street there is somebody who is ill as often as Elizabeth Taylor, just as there are families that have as many tragedies as the Kennedys, especially if they are big families—but it doesn't cause a ripple.

With Taylor, psychological element must play a part. For anybody with Christian Scientist upbringing, illness stirs up anxiety, and for anybody constantly in the public eye, illness offers an opportunity to escape from the strain. Nonetheless, the doctor in question states categorically that Taylor's illnesses have had fundamental medical causes, and that she has suffered an extraordinary degree of pain. Back pain, especially. As with John Kennedy, the hair and the eyes and the toothy smile show up in the photographs and the backache does not, but it is there.

As much as he gave her, did Todd ever appreciate what jewelry symbolized to Taylor? When she came out of the anesthetic after her spinal operation, the first thing she said was, "Where's my diamond ring?" Todd laughed and told reporters. "That really killed the doctors and nurses," he said. What the rocks seem to mean is, first of all, security—she comes from a family of collectors, after all—but more than that: magic charms to ward off envy. Someone who has been stared at all her life needs some eyes to glare back.

Even as he indulged Taylor, Todd pursued his own self-interest. One of the most widely circulated Todd anecdotes tells how he brought Taylor an armful of great paintings to brighten her drab green hospital room. They included a Renoir, a Pissarro, a Van Gogh, a Monet, and . . . "Portrait of a Man" by Frans Hals.

Did he buy the family treasure and present it to his fiancée as a way of ingratiating himself with the Taylors? Or did he merely carry in what she already owned? Todd certainly had some dealings with Howard Young, for Mike Todd, Jr., later recounted that his father accidentally punched a hole in the Van Gogh with a pencil taking it up in the hospital elevator. "Fortunately Elizabeth's uncle was in the art business and patched it up." Either way, Todd added mileage to his reputation as the philistine with an eye for culture. It was Mike Todd and not his wife who got the publicity a year later when the whole batch was sent to the Los Angeles County Art Museum. (He probably had in mind a good tax deduction during his big-earning year as well.) "Todd Presents Museum with Rare Paintings" exclaimed the *Los Angeles Times*. It reported that they were worth $300,000 and on indefinite loan. The museum's own records, however, indicated that the paintings were the property of Mrs. Elizabeth Taylor Todd, not Mr. Todd. One year later she took them all back.

Todd was not above trying to save a penny on his extravagances, either. He had invited Peggy Rutledge and Virginia Streeter to come to New York after closing up the Wilding house in Beverly Hills. There was a lot to do in New York, looking after the boys, helping Taylor in the hospital, organizing the next wedding. "One day when Elizabeth was still in the hospital," says Virginia Streeter, "Mike gave her some diamond earrings, and he told her how much he paid for them. I knew he was exaggerating because I had heard him on the phone. So when he went out, I told her the truth. I said, 'Come on, Elizabeth, let's have a look.' We got out the glass and she screwed it to her eye and she could see the carbon flaws in the diamonds. When Todd came back, she shrieked at him! She made him take them back."

Peggy Rutledge's assignment was to bring her a present a day. "I used to do most of her shopping and I knew the kind of things she liked, nightgowns and lace. I did a lot at Bergdorf's. The boxes were so big we couldn't go on the subway." One day Peggy Rutledge asked Mike Todd if she could have a limousine, and he blew up. "Don't ever let me hear you ask for a car again!" he stormed. "You should *demand* it!"

Old guard and new did not get along. For a while Todd tried. He gave the two women a check on the condition that they spend all the money in one day. But soon there were arguments and Rutledge and Streeter found themselves out of the entourage. Now living in Los Angeles, they still correspond with "Michael," whom they adore, and restrain themselves when speaking of "Mike": "a man you could love but not like." They have never seen Elizabeth Taylor again.

Nineteen fifty-seven was the year of the Todds. They got married in Acapulco on February 3. It was her first Jewish wedding, her third Helen Rose wedding dress. Michael Wilding, settling down into his new role as brother, made the arrangements. Todd's best friend, Eddie Fisher, sang a wedding serenade. Fisher's wife, Debbie Reynolds, was a bridesmaid. Taylor could hardly walk. Cantinflas, the Mexican comic star of *Around the World in 80 Days*, helped Todd lift her up and set her down. Fireworks blazed out their initials in the sky and whenever Todd left her side, she screamed "Mike!" in a high-pitched voice. It will make a great scene when they come to make the movie.

Sara and Francis Taylor were there this time. As their daughter began her career of multiple marriages, they were mute and loyal. They had lost her for a long period and by this time had accepted that their life's work was now to protect her and to provide a refuge from celebrity. Francis Taylor was virtually retired. In 1956, he had sent Augustus John a bank draft for a little over $1,600, to cover ten years' sales. "I closed up the gallery in the Beverly Hills Hotel," he wrote, "and since have not been very active in these parts."

Of all Taylor's husbands, Mike Todd was probably the most alien to the Taylors, but they would never have allowed themselves to say so. An English friend says, with some amusement, "Whatever man it was, Francis and Sara would always insist that this time it was just the perfect match for Elizabeth."

In March 1957 *Around the World in 80 Days* beat *Giant* for the Academy Award as Best Picture of the Year and it collected four other awards as well. That same month Todd announced his wife's pregnancy and with her and her two boys began a European tour to publicize his movie. If she felt exploited, she never let on.

By then their fights were part of their legend. As they flew in to Louisville for the premiere of *Raintree County*, a rumor swept the waiting crowds that they'd had a fight on the plane. Some today say Todd used to hit her. Taylor has always laughed off the famous photograph of the two of them snarling at each other at London Airport: she elegant in white dress and white cloche hat sitting on a suitcase, Todd with his face contorted like an angry dog and his fist extended in an unmistakable gesture. "We have more fun fighting than most people do making love," she said. But that quip did not erase the suspicion that such elemental anger revealed in public meant uglier scenes in private, and in later years, Taylor made merry quotes about Richard Burton "clouting her around the earhole" and her crashing plates on his head.

But the man who can rein in the troublesome filly is a favorite stock character and this element led to Todd's instant and enormous popularity as Mr. Elizabeth Taylor. My aunt told me, "If she has a headache, and he's playing poker, he just tells

her to sit there and she has to wait until he's ready to go home."
An Englishwoman smiles happily and says, "He stood for no
bloody nonsense. He broke her in. He made her obey." Todd
himself fostered the story. "Look, this gal's been looking for
trouble all her life," he said. "Now she's found somebody who
can give it to her."

Even now, many say that Taylor was never happier. Her lyric
cry to the press was: "Why did I have to wait until I was
twenty-five for this to happen to me?" At last she had an escape
from MGM and she responded with total dependency. Todd
would tell her to pack and she never knew whether she was
going to New York or to China, whether she would be away a
night or a couple of months. Todd chose her clothes and never
has she worn such elegant lines and such simple colors. He
even tried to keep her slim. At a party at Tyrone Power's in New
York, Nora Sayre listened while Taylor talked of nothing but
dieting. She and Todd were both on diets. Suddenly she burst
out, "Mike's eating again! I know it!" She ran into the next room
and sure enough, there was Todd with a chicken leg. "I'm going
to eat this"—he waved it gaily—"and you too!"

Todd's finest hour came at the Battersea Fun Fair in London
in July 1957. He rented the whole amusement park for a
celebration to follow the London opening of *Around the World
in 80 Days*. At the theater, he pushed Taylor in ahead of
royalty, shouting, "Stand back, everybody. My wife's pregnant!" When they all came out he had rows of red London buses
waiting to take them to the party. It was just the combination
Todd loved: low life for high society, and his guests obligingly
got into the spirit. Laurence Olivier and Vivien Leigh rode the
Rotor, the duchess of Marlborough ate a hamburger out of a
paper napkin. It rained, of course, but Todd was ready for it.
He handed out umbrellas and plastic raincoats (Aly Khan got a
ladies' white one). Taylor dutifully stayed up until the small
hours of the morning, resplendent in a coral pink Dior maternity gown, although she admitted to discomfort as the baby
kicked against her newly made spine.

With Elizabeth Taylor, as with many politicians, what she says is not so important as what she does. What she was saying all during those months was, "I don't want to be a movie star, I just want to be a wife and mother." What she was doing was working.

In August, she had her third Cesarean, early out of necessity. The baby, a girl, did not breathe for fifteen minutes, but then was declared well, and named Liza Todd. Todd cooed to the press that compared to his new daughter, "her mother looks like Frankenstein" and soon the pictures were available—some of the loveliest ever taken of Elizabeth Taylor, lying back with the baby on her shoulder and even Todd looking gentle, leaning over them. They made the front page of the *New York Daily News, Life* magazine, and other family albums. Six weeks later Taylor was on her feet again, touring with Todd. In October they gave a party at Madison Square Garden that was as much a flop as the London one had been a success (witnessed by the nation, for Todd sold television rights to CBS). Then they embarked on the kind of world tour that would break an ox— Japan, Australia, Russia—publicizing his picture. And in December she was back in the hospital again, to have her appendix out.

"You've got to admit," said a hopeful MGM aide, "that these are the royalty of America." But royalty would not dare to court such a bad press. In Sydney, Australia, they were ninety minutes late for a news conference and when they showed up, announced that they were too tired to give it. At an official lunch in New South Wales, Todd leaned across the prime minister to kiss his wife. Todd boasted of their ostentation, of champagne buckets labeled "His and Liz." "We got that on our towels and everything." And royalty cannot get away with leaving new babies that long. Princess Margaret was roasted in the London popular press for going to the Caribbean for three weeks after her daughter was born.

Under Todd's tutelage, Taylor raised herself to a silent movie queen level of extravagance and greediness. When they visited

Moscow, she wrote a column for International News Service in which she said, "I was told the Georgians and most Russians are very hospitable. If you admire something they give it to you." So she went and admired the Russian crown jewels. "I stood there and admired and admired them—but nothing happened. I saw the jewels that the czars kept for their horses. That made me wish I were a horse."

In terms of her own personal development, Todd had somewhat the same effect as Sara Taylor had earlier: he both babied her and pushed her forward. Once when she telephoned him in London from the south of France, he said, "Look, sweetheart, I'm gonna get me a plane and come and get you, 'cause I don't want you to come here alone." At the same time he did not let her be dependent in the one way she really seemed to want—to give up acting and retreat to private life. She boasted that Todd would buy her out of her MGM contract. Instead, in February 1958, he propelled her back to work.

The film was *Cat on a Hot Tin Roof*, a Tennessee Williams hit play from Broadway, and he promised her that it would be the right vehicle for the talent she had showed in *Raintree County*. Pandro Berman, ever-present, remembers, "We got Mike to get her to do it. You had to go to Mike if you wanted anything. She was plastic in his hands. She had no thoughts of her own in those days." She agreed, announcing that it would definitely be her last picture—that, plus *Don Quixote*, Todd's next production, in which she had promised to star.

Todd also used his influence to make sure the picture was a good one. MGM, having paid Tennessee Williams $600,000 for the screen rights, wanted nonetheless to "bring in" the picture, in Hollywood's hallowed phrase, for about $1 million. Technicolor was out, therefore: It would have doubled the cost. (Taylor, remember, was no expense; she was still on straight salary.) Richard Brooks, who directed *Cat*, remembers with great pleasure what happened when Todd came to pick up his wife after the first day's work. It was about five o'clock when Todd ran into Brooks and greeted him:

"What's the matter, kid?"

"Aw, it's starting in a bad way. They're making it in black and white."

"And you think that's stupid?"

"Yeah. Here they are, supposed to be a wealthy family in the South and here's one of the most beautiful women in the world, and it's going to be in black and white."

"How long will you be here?"

"Until six."

Exit Todd, upstairs. About twenty minutes to six, down came the three big guns of MGM—Eddie Mannix, Bennie Thau, and Laurence Weingarten, the producer. They walked over to Brooks and demanded: "Why don't you make it in color?"

For her leading man, Taylor had drawn yet another Stanislavskian, Paul Newman. A cerebral actor, Newman thrives on rehearsal—something Taylor avoids if she can help it. After they had gone through a few listless run-throughs, according to Brooks, "Paul comes to me and says, 'What's going to happen? There's nothing there.' 'Paul,' I said. 'She doesn't work that way. You watch. When we're ready to go, she'll be *there!*' And when we filmed, she came on like Gangbusters!"

A month later Todd was dead. He died attempting what many people would not, especially in 1958—to fly from Los Angeles to New York for the weekend in a small chartered plane. Taylor was supposed to have gone along, but was kept home with a bad cold and a fever. Todd had to go. He was being named showman of the year by the Friars' Club. The plane did not get past New Mexico before ice on the wings brought it down.

There was no way in which she could have a private grief. Brooks remembers Dick Hanley, who had been Todd's secretary, telephoning him. "You'd better come over here. She's screaming like a maniac." Brooks went, and she shouted at him, as she had at the whole parade of movie people flocking to her rented house: "You son of a bitch! I suppose you've just come to find out when I'm going back to work!"

Never before had Elizabeth Taylor been a tragic figure. Now she emerged as the survivor of a tragedy that began to look preordained. The very name with which Todd had chosen to rename himself hints, in German, at death. (He switched to Todd from Goldbogen when his own father died.) He had tempted fate by naming his little rented plane, "The Lucky Liz." All his Runyonesque quips suddenly took on prophetic tone: "I'm so happy it scares me."

And if he had lived? Would the world have been spared the soap operas that followed? Maybe. Maybe she would have retired and become a hausfrau. One friend of the family who thinks otherwise says, "It could not have lasted because Todd would have drained her of every penny she had. He could not resist a gamble and like all gamblers could not stop until he had lost."

But he did not live. "Todd Terminates," said *Variety* and he got the best press of his life. A great many people can remember exactly where they were when they heard the news.

I was alone in my apartment. I had a job on a newspaper and that particular Saturday morning I was not stuck on the weekend shift. A reporter who was called me from the office. What! Dead? No! Until Todd, I had stopped identifying with Elizabeth Taylor. Her movies were dreary, her husbands drearier. What use was beauty if that was all it could catch? But the Todd saga had fed into my own husband-and-baby-hunting fantasies. I had to talk to somebody and rang a girl friend who was on the same quest. The banalities we swapped were a tribute to how well Mike Todd's publicity machine had done its work. "Why did it have to happen to the only one she really loved!" "Think of the baby!"

The funeral in Chicago was a botched affair. Royalty and Mike Todd handled those things better. The widow, with dangling earrings about four inches long, her face gone blank again, was dragged onto the TWA Boeing 707 (thoughtfully loaned by Howard Hughes) by her brother, her doctor, Rex Kenamer, and Eddie Fisher.

Back at the city room, we all watched the wire photos as they crawled up the facsimile machine. The wire editor, a paunchy man who could not remember chasing his last fire engine, would not let us stand too near. It was the new technology and while he did not understand it, he was in charge of it. As the strip of the paper unrolled showing Taylor flinging herself on the casket (caption: "Mike, Mike! You can't leave me here alone!"), the Goldbogen brothers fighting each other, and the crowd tearing the widow's veil, the wire editor declared hopefully, "That funeral ain't over yet!" He stuffed the sheets into the basket and hoped for something better for the second edition.

When I left work that day, and got behind the wheel of my secondhand Plymouth, my eyes blurred with tears at the malevolence of fate. There was a shuddering crash. With my mind at the graveside, I had backed the car straight into the boundary wall of the parking lot. There was my funeral offering: two smashed taillights and a crumpled fender.

I took the car to my uncle, back in my hometown. He got a mechanic friend to weld it back together. It was never the same again, but it was legal by the standards of the Commonwealth of Massachusetts. The bill came to eighteen dollars—hardly in the Mike Todd class. "How'd you do it?" asked my uncle, puzzled, looking at the mess. I did not dream of telling him the truth— that I had been crying over the death of a movie star's third husband.

10

"I Think I May Be a Jew"

Has any goddess, classical or celluloid, been so multipurpose? Taylor's image changed from Grieving Widow to Scarlet Woman the week I met the man I was to marry. It was also the same time that I first learned of the existence of Richard Burton. I was in Geneva, reporting on a conference on atomic energy because the newspaper I worked for thought that someday the local shipyards might make atomic ships. The night before my husband and I saw each other across a crowded room (clichés are clichés because they're true), I was taken out to dinner in Celigny, a village near Geneva, by a pleasant man called Walter Hacket, a correspondent for my paper. Walter was too good to be what he sold himself as, a travel writer, but he liked his independence and living in Europe, and he liked to drop names. "You know that Welsh actor, Richard Burton?" he asked as we sat, drinking Calvados in the café garden at a table that crunched into the gravel. Never heard of him, I said.

Walter was disappointed but he kept on. "He has a villa near here. His brother, Ivor Jenkins, takes care of it for him. They've even got a British pub dart board for him in the café." Walter added, "He's in there now." Who? I asked, Richard Burton? "No, his brother."

A few days later, as I sat on the dry lawn at the Palais des Nations, I tried to sort out what was happening to me. He was Welsh, the man I fancied, and I had knowingly only seen one Welshman before. When I was in college, I had gone some distance on a freezing evening to hear Dylan Thomas and had found when I got there a stout red-faced little man who called his audience "Culture-Vultures." As my thoughts tumbled like clothes in a dryer, I noticed in the International *Herald Tribune* that Elizabeth Taylor was doing the New York night spots with Eddie Fisher, her late husband's best friend, her recent bridesmaid's husband. "How could she?" I wondered, which was blind of me as I was about to become the other woman myself.

Strange coincidence? Conjunction of stars? Not at all. Just the kind of tag memories movie stars, presidents, and hurricanes so usefully provide. Sometimes today when I look around our crowded table and think back to that week when my life changed direction, I find myself remembering the dry Swiss grass, the small item in the *Trib*, and Ivor Jenkins in the café, throwing darts.

Eddie Fisher? The *Coca-Cola Kid?* Of Taylor's long line of incongruous consorts, he was the most improbable. It was like Truman after Roosevelt.

Fisher was a crooner, a small animated Jewish boy from Philadelphia, born in 1928. With a boyish grin and a loud unmodulated baritone, he had made his way from Arthur Godfrey's Talent Scout Contest through the Borscht Belt hotel circuit in the Catskills to the top of the charts. His weekly television show—"Coke Time"—on NBC had a huge national audience. Teen-agers and their mothers loved him. They loved his wife too—pert blond Debbie Reynolds, the singing star of more musicals than anyone could count. When Debbie and Eddie married at Grossinger's Hotel, the capital of the Borscht Belt, in 1955, America thought they were just as cute and right for each other as the couple on top of the wedding cake.

Rumblings of scandal came out of the Catskills when Taylor was seen there with Fisher. There may be more public places than Grossinger's on a Labor Day weekend, but nobody who tried could think of one. Back in California with her two children, one of them a babe in arms newly named for Mike Todd, Debbie Reynolds laughed it all off. Confidently she waited for her husband to return from the East. She even went to the airport to meet his plane, but he wasn't on it.

If there was a single moment when Elizabeth Taylor fell from grace, it was on September 11, 1958, when Hedda Hopper got her on the telephone and asked what was going on. "Her reply," wrote Hedda, "was unprintable." What she did print was sufficient for Taylor's undoing.

The interview shows that old Hedda was more of a journalist than any of us had ever appreciated. In a sixteen-word lead, she established her authority. "I've known Elizabeth Taylor since she was nine years old—always liked her, always defended her." Then she steps back for a quick swipe at Elizabeth and Sara Taylor together: "She never wanted to be an actress. That was her mother's project."

Building with the gorgeous quotes that Taylor fed her: "You know I don't go about breaking up marriages. Besides you can't break up a happy marriage, Debbie's and Eddie's never has been . . ." Hedda proudly holds up her trophy. She has extracted from Taylor the words: "Mike's dead and I'm alive."

Then she packs in some gratuitous interesting information— Arthur Loew, Jr., the son of the chairman of the board of Metro, is in love with Taylor ("I can't help how he feels about me") and Taylor's three children are living at Loew's house. Then Hedda, the Hollywood seer, climbs to the battlements and abandons her former protégée to her fate: "Well, Liz, you'll probably hate me for the rest of your life for this, but I can't help it. I'm afraid you've lost all control over reason. Remember the nights you used to call me at two and three in the morning when you were having nightmares and had to talk to somebody and I let you talk your heart out? What you've just said to me bears not the slightest resemblance to that girl. Where, oh where, has she gone?"

Hedda got it all—one of the best stories she ever had—into eight hundred words, her usual space to fill.

Was it naïveté? It is hard to see how somebody who had been a Hollywood star for a dozen years could forget that Hedda Hopper had a typewriter. Taylor later claimed that she had been betrayed by her old friend. Did she believe that Hopper's long years of protecting her, never raising a shred of damaging gossip about her first two marriages, were based on genuine friendship going back to the Cazalet era? If she did, it meant that Elizabeth Taylor was still child-blind to some basic facts of Hollywood life. One was that the gossip harpies rarely attacked anybody in whom a major studio had a big investment. In earlier years, Taylor was MGM's. The studio would not have liked sordid gossip, even when her marriages went sour. But by 1958 her second seven-year contract with MGM was coming to an end. Taylor was on her way out. She was fair game.

The other plain truth was that Hedda Hopper, long divorced, was a prude. She had not, according to her biographer, George Eels, had a sexual experience for twenty-five years. She had as little understanding of physical love as she had of socialism. As such, she was the last person to whom Taylor should have delivered her unprintable remark. Hopper later printed it in her autobiography. It was: "What do you expect me to do? Sleep alone?"

The bowdlerized version—"Mike's dead and I'm alive"—was very reminiscent of the big dramatic line that Taylor had just delivered in *Cat on a Hot Tin Roof*. To her impotent husband, who is pining for his dead best friend, she spits: "Skipper's dead and I'm alive!" Yet as Taylor's words, not Tennessee Williams's, they were enough to create the image of a woman with an insatiable sexual craving and an indifference to public opinion. What the world couldn't know, as Hedda Hopper could have explained, was that Taylor, from Mummie to Todd, had had somebody with her virtually every second of her life. She never learned to live with loneliness, and how could she? There was always somebody waiting, in her old words, "to bring the same sense of love to me."

In fact, the loss of Todd was too overwhelming to be absorbed. Some thought that she might kill herself, she had been so dependent on him. Taylor was drawn to Fisher by the fact that he too had suffered the same shock: Todd had acted like a father to him.

For the first time, Elizabeth Taylor began to make the editorial pages. She even earned a cartoon in *The New Yorker*: a drunk, coming home late, explains to his wife: "I got to worrying about Debbie and Eddie." *Life* analyzed in depth how the Reynolds-Fisher marriage had been born in the MGM publicity department. In London the popular press went wild. "How *Can* She Behave like This?" demanded a four-column headline in the *Daily Herald*. "Fatal Liz," declared the *Daily Sketch*, lining up photographs of Taylor-men back to Glenn Davis.

Never had Taylor's lack of protection been so apparent. Her sanctuary for a while was the Beverly Hills Hotel. If she telephoned her friends and they weren't in, she didn't dare to leave her private number in case the press somehow got it. In fact, until Debbie Reynolds finally accepted the inevitable and filed for divorce in December 1958, Taylor and Fisher were so ostracized, they dared not go out in public even for a drive; people would shout insults at them when the car stopped at traffic lights.

In these days of free-screwing antistars, the whole scandal looks absurd. Stars themselves have a more realistic grasp of their relation to the world. But the Debbie-Eddie-Liz story broke precisely at the turn of the tide between the postwar coziness and the divorce revolution. The peak year for births,

1957, had passed. The divorce rate, at its lowest point since the war, was about to take off. And Debbie, with her two small children, Eddie, and Liz were like medieval mummers come to town to portray Wronged Wife, Helpless Male, and Femme Fatale for all the American families who were just beginning to go through just the same thing. And they spoke the perfect dialogue:

Debbie, wearing diaper pins in sweater (at, Hollywood said, her press agent's suggestion):

> It seems unbelievable to say that you can live happily with a man and not know that he doesn't love you, but as God is my witness, that is the truth.

Eddie:

> I know that I am not the great love of Elizabeth's life, but she is of mine.

Liz:

> I didn't take anything away from Debbie because she never really had it.

In retrospect, the popular anger that rose up against Taylor looks less hypocritical than it did at the time. The Widow Todd appeared to be breaking one of society's timeless and strongest unwritten rules: that the dead must be mourned and that it takes about a year. Because of Mike Todd's flair for publicity and because of his movie, which was still making the rounds, the world still loved Mike Todd and had itself not put his memory to rest.

Todd's death may have left Taylor as famous as the queen of England but a lot less rich. She was far from the wealthy widow that everybody supposed. Everything Todd had was tied up in his movie. Neither he nor Taylor owned a house. During the last year of his life, as the world knew, he had lived high. Some reports said he spent $1.5 million in 1957-58 alone and a friend of Richard Burton's, describing Taylor's financial woes fifteen years later, declared that a lot of them arose because "Mike Todd didn't read the fine print on his insurance."

Her actual legacy from Todd was a 50 percent share in the Michael Todd Company. The company's only asset was *Around the World in 80 Days* and it turned out to be even less of a golden hoard than it appeared when he died, with much of its production cost still to be paid and its backers reimbursed. They included United Artists, the distributors, who had put in $2 million, the Columbia Broadcasting System, which had bought an 8 percent share for $1 million, and Paramount Pictures, the source of another $750,000.

The expenses of promoting the film were, according to *The New York Times*, unusual. They ate deep into its income. After a year's showing, *Around the World in 80 Days* had, said the *Times*, grossed $33 million worldwide, but paid only about $3.75 million of its $7 million cost. Nonetheless, the entertainment industry confidently expected the picture to keep on grossing, eventually to surpass *Gone with the Wind* and possibly to reach $85 million to $100 million.

But it did less than half that amount of business when all was said and done. Today *Variety* lists its total domestic rentals as $23 million. Like the Todds, the movie was a fifties' wonder. It aged fast. Its re-release in 1968 brought in less than a million dollars, not the $6 million to $10 million anticipated. And when in 1971 Mike Todd, Jr., finally decided to sell it to television— something his father swore would never happen—he had to settle for $2 million from CBS, when four years earlier he had turned down the Ford Motor Company's offer of $3.5 million. What dated the movie was the jet age and color television. A sixties' public was in no mood to gasp in wonder over shots of a bullring in Spain. By then too the charm of the unflappable Englishman—David Niven's Phileas Fogg—had worn off. When the film was finally squeezed out of the television tube the Todd-AO wide-screen effects disappeared and the film drew very low ratings, both in the United States and Britain. It would take years to unravel Todd's finances; his back taxes were not settled until 1971. In any case, Elizabeth Taylor was only to receive income from her half of Todd's estate once the tax due from the film's earnings flowed into it. The other half was left to her stepson, with fewer strings attached.

Taylor clearly had to put aside all thoughts of retiring. She had three children, two aging parents, a personal staff, and a lavish style of living to maintain. Fisher, whom she intended to marry, had alimony to pay and, television being a more prurient medium than the movies, NBC had swiftly canceled his television show.

But Todd had also left her, for the first time in her career, among the top ten stars at the box office, and not near the bottom. The tumultuous year of 1958 landed her second only to Glenn Ford.

MGM got lucky again. *Cat on a Hot Tin Roof* was ready for release just as the Debbie-Eddie story broke, and the studio was glad it had made it in color. *Cat* became the top moneymaker of the year and the tenth biggest hit in MGM's history. It was a landmark for Taylor, too. She got the best notices of her career. *Time*, which had almost never liked her, said she played Maggie the Cat with "surprising sureness." Her performance secured her a nomination for the Academy Award for the second year in a row.

Even in 1958 homosexuality could not be mentioned by name on the screen, so exactly what is wrong with Paul Newman in *Cat on a Hot Tin Roof* is left to the audience to guess. He is an ex-athlete who drinks, sulks, and moans about his dead best friend, while his unbelievably seductive young wife tries every trick she can think of to get him back to bed long enough to get her pregnant so they can inherit Big Daddy's twenty-eight thousand acres.

Yet as Maggie lurks in the bedroom doorway, silky in her slip and satin pumps, the audience might well conclude that what is

wrong with the man is the woman. There is something menac-
ing in her demand to wring a baby out of the unwilling male. In
1958, before the Pill, before legal abortion, sexual intercourse
was still a cosmic act, something that could bring down Troy.
And whatever terror sex held for men, whatever danger the
female represented—*vagina dentata* in the psychoanalysts'
coy phrase—brunettes had more of it (as Hitchcock seems to
know), and Elizabeth Taylor embodied it.

Only ten years before, Ingrid Bergman had suffered because
scandal spoiled her image as Mrs. Nordic Clean. *Cat on a Hot
Tin Roof*, plus the Fisher uproar, only underlined the sexual
message that Todd's death blared out: Here was a fatal beauty,
and Taylor's career soared.

Now she was ready to cash in. There was no question of
signing a third contract with MGM. By then, with stars' fees
rising and the big studios becoming mere landlords for independent production units, working under contract to a studio
for a yearly salary began to seem like exploitation out of the
pages of Karl Marx. All around were the lessons of history.
Clark Gable made nothing except his salary for his part in *Gone
with the Wind*, yet the studio did not hesitate to cut him loose
in the fifties when it was through with him. Grace Kelly was
another who was conspicuously underpaid. She turned out one
financial bonanza after another for MGM for her regular salary,
and still Prince Rainier had to buy her out of her contract to get
her to Monaco. In contrast were the new kinds of deals shrewd
stars were making. For *War and Peace* in 1957 Audrey Hepburn was receiving $350,000.

As she prepared to operate as a free lance, Taylor got herself
Audrey Hepburn's agent. Kurt Frings was celebrated for the
big money he got for his clients—Lucille Ball and Brigitte
Bardot were also on his list. He has been called one of the men
who killed Hollywood. "How can they say that?" Frings asks in
a deceptively cute Austrian accent. "Hollywood is still here."
But not as it was. It has never recovered from the days when the
balance of power shifted to the stars.

Yet even Frings could not free Taylor from MGM with one bound. She still owed MGM one more picture under the contract from which she had hoped Todd would buy her release. However, she did not have to make it immediately. She was free to negotiate for other films, and Frings swiftly got her an offer that overnight put her in the news as the highest paid actress in the world. Half a million dollars, to make *Two for the Seesaw*, which had been a hit play on Broadway.

Freedom has its penalties and many an independent star has floundered in too much power of choice. Without the dictatorial studio, the star suddenly finds him- or herself with a veto power over the major jobs connected with a picture—with no experience to go on. Advice pours in from all sides; so do flattery and warnings, all delivered in a showbiz fortissimo. For somebody like Taylor, hypersensitive, resentful, needing money, the effect was to make her shrill, edgy, and imperious as never before. Her old habit of polarizing her feelings worsened. When she was told that Martin Ritt who had made *The Long Hot Summer* was going to direct *Two for the Seesaw*, she said, "I won't have him."

Why not? "I don't like him."

Sam Marx, who was present at the dickering that went on in Rome, heard her declare, "I'll give you a list of the directors I will work with." She listed only four: Joseph Mankiewicz, John Huston, Richard Brooks, and William Wyler. Then Marx spoke up. "I don't think you should make the picture," he said. "I can't see you as a little Jewish girl from New York who can't get a date and falls in love with a traveling salesman who goes back to his wife."

"She didn't like that," Marx says. "She said—and her remark showed a certain want of understanding, I think—'But I've just made a picture in which my husband wouldn't sleep with me.'"

"And I said, 'But he was a *homosexual*, Elizabeth. That was the point of the picture.'"

For various reasons, the contract was never signed and it was

Shirley MacLaine who made *Two for the Seesaw* in 1963. But Taylor swiftly got another contract for the same half-million price, to try her luck with Tennessee Williams and Montgomery Clift yet again and to make *Suddenly Last Summer* in London and Spain.

A test-yourself questionnaire in a Sunday magazine asked: "How stressful is your life?" A list of traumatic emotional experiences follows. One of these, the article maintained, was all that anybody could handle in a year. Two were enough to produce a nervous breakdown. By its measure, by 1959 Elizabeth Taylor should have been dead. Within the twelve months starting in August 1957 she had gone through childbirth, two major operations, loss of spouse by death, serious illness of child (Liza Todd nearly died of pneumonia), involvement in a divorce. And the next few months took her through a couple more—remarriage, change of employer and—something not on the list—change of religion.

Taylor converted to Judaism in March 1959. "Decision Not Hasty or Opportunistic," said the *Los Angeles Times*, "as Actress Had Long Considered Move." She had always been religious. Her shift to Judaism brought her closer to Todd. It also revealed how deeply persecuted Elizabeth Taylor has always felt. Even as a child, she said later, she used to daydream that she was Jewish, and was it surprising? MGM was like a Jewish second home, complete with L. B. Mayer's mother's chicken soup in the commissary. She also identified with the sufferings of the Jews during the war. She said, "I feel as if I have been a Jew all my life." Her words anticipated (and, who knows, may even have influenced) Sylvia Plath. Just before she put her head in her own gas oven in 1963, Plath wrote, in a bitter poem called "Daddy," "I think I may well be a Jew."

Converting when she did, scarred from a bad press and loss of friends, gave Taylor a fresh new identity. She even had a new name: Elisheba Rachel. The same month she bought $100,000 worth of bonds for Israel, which caused Elizabeth Taylor films promptly to be banned in Egypt, Jordan, and other Arab countries.

She did not get the Academy Award for *Cat on a Hot Tin Roof*. Perhaps it was the scandal. It had cost her some lesser honors: the University of California rescinded an invitation to lecture after receiving letters from angry housewives all over the United States, and the Theater Owners of America took back the title they had given her as actress of the year for *Cat*. Yet she was up against stiff competition for the Oscar. It included Deborah Kerr for *Separate Tables* and Susan Hayward (who won) for *I'll Cry Tomorrow*, and it would be hard to argue that Taylor was better than they were.

As her wedding to Fisher drew near, Taylor presided over nightclub tables in Las Vegas where he was singing, more like a Jewish mother than a Jewish wife. She brought her family, her friends, even her two little boys, to applaud Fisher's act at the Tropicana. If her movies lent themselves to double meanings, they were nothing compared to the songs Fisher chose to sing. Nothing seemed too near the bone for him, beaming in his neat blue suit. He even had a hardened Las Vegas audience looking at its shoetops when he came out with "Another bride, another groom, another sunny honeymoon . . ."

Taylor and Fisher were married in the gambling capital on May 12, 1959. It was her fourth wedding, second Jewish ceremony, and she said it again: "I want to devote my full time to being a wife and mother." She was quitting films forever—after she honored her outstanding commitments.

Hard as she tried, however, Taylor was never able to dispel the popular notion that she "stole" Fisher. She and Fisher, who as a couple seemed to move in a cloud of lawsuits, sued Associated Newspapers in London for libel—and won—for carrying what purported to be a personal interview: "Liz Taylor: 'I didn't steal Eddie.' "

That did not stop Mrs. Jacqueline Kennedy from using Taylor as a handy reference point. In 1965 when she tried to describe why public opinion was on her side in her lawsuit against the author William Manchester, Mrs. Kennedy said blithely, "Anybody who is against me will look like a rat unless I run off with Eddie Fisher."

Mrs. Kennedy found out herself a few years later how quickly the mystique of widows fades.

Suddenly Last Summer won Taylor her third nomination for the Academy Award. The film is a pretentious Tennessee Williams fantasy about a homosexual who is eaten by cannibals, but not before he had been devoured by his mother.

Katharine Hepburn played the mother, a mad southern aristocrat who rides in an elevator resembling a birdcage and keeps Venus flytraps as a hobby. The dead son, Sebastian, never appears. Montgomery Clift plays (but does not look like) a brain surgeon, with the awkward name of Dr. Cukrowicz—awkward because the principals have to shout it at each other. Sebastian's mother, it seems, wants the young man to perform a lobotomy on her dead son's cousin Catherine—a pretty girl who has been locked away in an asylum because of the obscenities she keeps babbling in her southern accent about the way Sebastian met his death.

At the time, the story seemed wildly daring and the censors, even slightly less fierce than in the past, threatened the film. Now it is clear the script was enough to ruin it and that the costumes alone could have done it. Columbia Pictures poured out warnings about how dreadful Elizabeth Taylor was bravely going to permit herself to look as a lunatic. We were in for disheveled hair, drab uniforms, and down-at-heel shoes. But when she saunters into the asylum's visitors' room, alas, it is not true. She is wearing beautifully smooth hair and a plain gray dress that she would do well to take back to civilian life. And if Taylor had courage, Columbia did not. After just one scene, Dr. Cukrowicz decides that Catherine-Liz's mental health would be improved if she went back to wearing the Paris frocks to which she was accustomed. (He is on her side—against

Katharine Hepburn—and is refusing to perform "The O-pe-ra-tion.") Then there is the problem of the bathing suit. The whole plot of the picture turns on it. Decadent Sebastian bought it for Cousin Catherine, it seems, so that she could wear it on the beaches of Europe and serve as a decoy, attracting the young men he would then take for himself. As a wicked trick, he bought the kind of suit (Tennessee Williams must have believed this technically possible) that turns transparent when wet.

Bathing suit scenes are not standard issue in Elizabeth Taylor pictures and at this time she was very heavy. In the Spanish resort town where the beach shots were filmed, the natives were very unkind. They were used to lean beauties in bikinis, and they said, in effect, what one of Taylor's directors said to me: "Elizabeth's face is her fortune. Her body belongs to somebody else." The shameful bathing suit, when it finally appears on the screen, turns out to be a white one-piece garment that would not cause offense on a waterfront counselor at Girl Scout camp. (The Spaniards were also pretty scathing when they found out that the easy work the movie was providing for local boys as extras had them portraying eaters of human flesh.)

In the movie's final scene, Taylor redeems all the silliness. Mankiewicz, one of Hollywood's most experienced directors, said he knew of no other actress who could have done it. In a long monologue (Mankiewicz called it an aria), Catherine-Liz forces herself to bring out the memory that has driven her mad. As she tells her story, her ice-cream face is used as a canvas over which images of unbearable horror are superimposed. A band of youths banging tin drums pursues a slim white-suited figure (who bears an unfortunate resemblance to Montgomery Clift) up and up a steep Mediterranean hillside until she shrieks the climatic line, "They ate him!" and collapses.

Jack Hildyard, who won an Academy Award for *Bridge on the River Kwai*, was in charge of photography. He later photographed Taylor again in *The VIPs*. Taylor's face has no bad angles, he says. Her features are absolutely symmetrical. In *Suddenly Last Summer* his camera inched over every pore of her face, eyelids, nostrils, and ears in what was by that time daring—black and white.

After doing the scene, Taylor sobbed for hours. She was beginning to realize that she had made the worst mistake of her life. Later she described the time as one in which "my despair became so black that I just couldn't face waking up anymore, couldn't face another divorce."

In the movie business, success is fiercely imitated. As the sixties drew near, the big studios were in one of their cyclical panics. The novelty of the wide screen had worn off and all were looking at each other to see what to try next. MGM, after being all wrong for so long, suddenly seemed to have all the right answers. Big epics, for one thing: *Ben-Hur* had earned MGM $80 million on a mere $15 million investment. And Elizabeth Taylor, for another, as *Cat on a Hot Tin Roof* proved. When she went on to turn *Suddenly Last Summer*, which got quite scathing reviews, into a tremendous money-maker for Columbia (about $12 million gross worldwide), the belief entered the head of Spyros Skouras over at Twentieth Century-Fox that Elizabeth Taylor in a remake of Fox's old blockbuster, *Cleopatra*, would save his studio, which was in dire straits.

Hollywood legend has it that Eddie Fisher took the telephone call when it came to the Dorchester in London. He relayed the request to his wife, and he relayed back her answer: She would do *Cleopatra* for a million dollars. Legend also has it that she asked for it as a joke, but if so, it was the kind of joke that Freud wrote a book about.

But like the wicked witch in a fairy tale, MGM reappeared. It reminded Taylor of her old contract. She still owed them one picture. The witch took the form of her old colleague, Pandro Berman, and he wanted her for *Butterfield 8*, John O'Hara's short story about a New York call girl.

"I made up my mind she was going to do it," he says. "I determined that she wasn't going to make *Cleopatra* until hell froze over unless she made *Butterfield* first. I forced her into it. I took a position and fortunately I was backed by the company."

Berman makes no attempt to conceal the qualities that made Taylor hate MGM or that made him a good moviemaker. He speaks in short sentences, qualifying nothing. He is sadistic, garrulous, egocentric, also candid and self-mocking. "You didn't see my last picture? That's lucky." He ranges and rages over the whole Elizabeth Taylor phenomenon. "I went through all the phases with her from the little girl wanting to get tall to the girl waiting for marriage. I went through hell with her. Sure, she had a lot of crummy parts, but they all did. I came to despise her. She let herself get as fat as a pig. I've been a woman chaser all my life and I never found her sexually attractive. Katharine Hepburn either. Those two."

Neither Berman nor John O'Hara ever accepted Taylor's explanation that she did not want to do *Butterfield 8* because the girl—Gloria Wandrous—was nothing better than a prostitute. "The trouble had nothing to do with the fact that Gloria was a call girl," says Berman. "It was that she had to do it for MGM, for one hundred twenty-five thousand dollars, and she wanted the million for *Cleopatra*."

Taylor gave in. She had to, otherwise MGM could have kept her off the screen for a couple of years, but she imposed a condition of her own—that Eddie Fisher be given a part.

Butterfield 8 had to be shot in New York, because of an Actors' Guild dispute on the West Coast. Berman recalls:

"Elizabeth never gave me a happy moment. She didn't like the clothes. She said she'd loaf. She wanted Eddie Fisher's part rewritten—he was worth two cents to the picture. I thought they were stalling. They called me up to their hotel room in New York. 'This is the new script for Eddie,' she said. They felt that Eddie wasn't getting a break in the old script, so she'd had some new lines written. The gall of her. I didn't want the bum in the picture anyhow. I walked over and dropped it—like this—into the wastebasket. I must tell you I pulled some pretty fast moves on the picture." As talks proceeded, Berman went out to dinner with Taylor and Kurt Frings. Berman, chuckling with hindsight at his foresight, remembers saying, " 'Play Gloria and you'll get the Academy Award.' They laughed and laughed." *Butterfield 8* was another fantastic financial success. It earned MGM about $15 million worldwide. It also got Taylor the Academy Award at last and made her, in 1961, the top box office attraction among stars of either sex.

The next spring, when Taylor collected her first Oscar, she still disparaged the picture. She was just recovering from near-fatal pneumonia. That, she said, not *Butterfield 8*, got her her award. Shirley MacLaine, another nominee, agreed. "I lost to a tracheotomy," she said.

But was it true? In *Butterfield 8* Taylor plays one of her rare contemporary women and gets her across with fierce accuracy. She looks as if she is on home ground: the sex war, according to John O'Hara, fought at its nastiest and most commercial, with mink coats, cigarette lighters, and expensive handbags. Anybody who has seen it will have to work hard to erase the memory of Taylor grinding her stiletto heel into Laurence Harvey's instep. (He takes it, of course, without flinching.) What's more, as Gloria, in hobbled skirt and bouffant hair, Taylor epitomizes how women wanted to look in 1960, and how men wanted them to look. To welcome *Butterfield 8*, the *Chicago Daily News*, unbothered by the call-girl veneer of the plot, sponsored a Liz Taylor Look-alike Contest. (And the winner, Rochelle Shane, when interviewed a few years later, came up with a quote worthy of the original: "I just want to be a homemaker someday.") Eddie Fisher, wherever he went, was besieged by people coming up to tell him that they had a cousin or a daughter who looked just like his wife.

As the fifties became the sixties, Taylor joined Monroe at the summit. They were the brunette and blonde of sexual fantasy. Each represented the ultimate in what a woman of her coloring could draw upon to tempt a man. Both, in their best films in those years, were thrown against impotents to see what they could do. Taylor in *Cat on a Hot Tin Roof* and Monroe, seminude in her shimmery gown in *Some Like It Hot*. Monroe was still a comic figure then and in that picture she is the butt of the joke as she rolls all over Tony Curtis, who is only faking as he says, "Can't you try harder?"

There was nothing funny about Taylor's sex appeal. She was the anti-Marilyn. Norman Mailer could have had Taylor in mind when he wrote about Monroe:

> She was not the dark contract of those passionate brunette depths that speak of blood, vows taken for life and the furies of vengeance if you are untrue to the depths of passion, no, Marilyn suggested sex might be difficult and dangerous with others but ice cream with her. "Take me," said her smile. "I'm easy."

"Take me," said the Elizabeth smile—"if you dare. I'm expensive. I'll cost you plenty, possibly your career, perhaps your life. If you survive, I may throw you away, but it will have been worth it."

There was something else that Taylor and Monroe had in common. Between them, they were about to bring Twentieth Century-Fox to the verge of liquidation.

11

Cleopatra

Who better to become the first star to charge a million dollars for a picture? Or to lead the most expensive movie ever made?

For sheer financial nightmares, only two other pictures in the history of Hollywood have approached *Cleopatra* and they hardly came close. The first was the 1925 *Ben-Hur*. The second was *Mutiny on the Bounty*, an indifferent MGM epic that ran out of control in the South Seas in 1962 soaking up $19 million and sending Marlon Brando's career into a decline from which he did not recover until *The Godfather* in 1972.

The story of the Egyptian queen who died for love, supported by a cast of thousands, has intrigued the men who make movies ever since the beginning of cinematography. Georges Méliès made a *Cleopatra* as one of his first projects with trick-motion cameras in Paris in 1899. An early Hollywood version, made by the original Fox Film Company in 1917 with Theda Bara, was a tremendous hit, and so was Cecil B. De-

Mille's remake with a sinuous Claudette Colbert in 1934. True Vivien Leigh's *Caesar and Cleopatra*, with Gabriel Pascal directing, in 1945 was a flop that managed to be the most expensive picture in British film history, but Spyros Skouras did not think that would happen to him.

Skouras was a Greek immigrant who was president of Twentieth Century-Fox in the fifties. He had risen from immigrant waiter to movie tycoon without dropping his thick accent or his worry beads. For a time, because he had gambled and won with CinemaScope, he was the hero of the American industry. But Skouras did not have a great gift for picture-making itself. When Darryl Zanuck, the aging boy genius who had put together Twentieth Century-Fox in 1934, left in 1956 to become an independent producer in Paris, Skouras found himself presiding over dud after dud and fewer and fewer of those.

From the very beginning, the new *Cleopatra* was clearly designed to save the studio. Fox had had only three hits in six years (and not artistic ones, either—*Peyton Place* in 1957 was its biggest earner) and no major Academy Awards for a decade. In New York dissident executives, shareholders, and various Wall Street bankers were maneuvering to get Skouras out; the studio was losing millions of dollars every year and the possibility that Twentieth Century-Fox, one of Hollywood's most famous names, might disappear was a real one.

Originally, Skouras was cool to the idea of Elizabeth Taylor as Cleopatra. She had not worked for Fox since *Jane Eyre* in 1943. He thought (and did not hesitate to remind people later) that she would be too much trouble. But Walter Wanger won him over. Wanger was producer of *Cleopatra* and, married to Joan Bennett, Taylor's old mother of the bride, he obviously liked the type. In his mind he had imagined Taylor as Cleopatra ever since *A Place in the Sun*. She became "my Cleopatra," "the quintessence of youthful femininity, of womanliness and strength, so beautiful and wise she also ruled the world." Once converted, Skouras was not half-hearted. It became a kind of *folie à deux* for both men: no Liz, no Cleo. In vain did others at

Fox try to get them to offer the part to actresses already on the studio's payroll—Joanne Woodward, Joan Collins, or Suzy Parker.

In October 1959 came the first big news about the new production: the size of Taylor's fee. Skouras did not balk at her demand for a million, just because Fox was nearly bankrupt. It was sound Hollywood logic: the higher the price, the better the goods. But it was a record-breaking sum. Kurt Frings, whose work it was, is still proud of it.

"I didn't use a gun," he says. "It was a big landmark. It was quite a long time before another star made a million a picture. Not until Steve McQueen, I think. The thing was that until that time none of her pictures had lost any money. Without a sure drawing card, Fox could not have considered the investment. It was a matter of whether they wanted to do the project or not." He adds, "It is up to the agent to know what a studio wants badly and to hold out for it. When we had to start again in Rome, we charged them a second million."

Taylor's "million" was, of course, a kind of symbolic reference to what she was actually to be paid, and even so, needs to be seen in perspective. Back in the early days of Hollywood, when a dollar was worth a lot more and income taxes were a lot lower, Mary Pickford earned a quarter of a million dollars for a single picture (*The Little Princess*, in 1916). In the twenties, Greta Garbo, beginning her American career in silent films, got as much as a third of a million per picture out of L. B. Mayer. Even more spectacular was Charles Boyer's fee for *Conquest* in 1937: $450,000. And the great leap forward, mentioned earlier, was taken by James Stewart in getting a percentage of the gross. By the time that *Cleopatra* was ready to roll, some male stars were already able to put more than a million per picture in the bank. John Wayne and William Holden each reportedly got $750,000 plus 20 percent of the gross for *The Horse Soldiers*.

In the movie business, that leaden phrase, "percentage of the gross," makes the blood run faster. What it means is that the actor or actress gets a share of the distributor's rental income before the bills are paid for making and selling the picture. To be a "gross player" is a mark of high status. Today perhaps only ten stars (almost all men) can claim it. Producers avoid such a deal if they can, but agree to it easily for a player like Robert Redford or Charles Bronson, who they believe will compensate his cost by pull at the box office.

If nobody goes to see the picture, however, a percentage of the gross is not worth very much. To have a gigantic flat fee is best of all. That way, the star takes no risk. That is how Elizabeth Taylor's million made movie history and brought home to the industry how precarious film investment had become once the studios no longer owned either the stars or the movie theaters.

In fact, Taylor not only got her salary but also owned 35 percent of the picture through a Swiss corporation called MCL Films. (The initials stood for her children, Michael, Christopher, and Liza.) Eddie Fisher and Kurt Frings also owned shares of MCL.

In her contract, Taylor had another stipulation that was to cost Fox dearly—that *Cleopatra* be made abroad. The movie could easily have been shot in California, but as an independent Taylor preferred to work outside the United States for tax reasons. Overseas filming suited Skouras fine. Not that he was intending to throw money around. Far from it. In spite of what he was paying his star, Skouras had in mind an economical blockbuster, to cost no more than $6 million in all. It was for reasons of economy that he decided to film at Pinewood Studios in England, where part of the production cost would be met by Eady money, the British government's subsidy to foreign films made with a preponderance of British staff. Skouras himself had helped work out the Eady plan with Harold Wilson, after the war, when Wilson was president of the Board of Trade.

On top of everything, Fox piled the kind of icing that all Hollywood players respect and that Elizabeth Taylor, in particular, adores: $3,000 a week for living expenses, two penthouses at the Dorchester in London, and round-trip first-class fares for her children, husband, and agent. Her favorite hair-dresser from MGM, Sidney Guilaroff, would be imported especially to do her hair; she would have the same Silver Cloud Rolls-Royce as during *Suddenly Last Summer* and the same driver. And Fox wouldn't use its CinemaScope. *Cleopatra* would be filmed in Todd-AO from which she would get royalties.

It was late in August at the end of an unusually sunless English summer when the Fisher entourage installed itself in Taylor's home-away-from-home on London's Park Lane. Taylor held court from bed. The royal comparison occurred to Walter Wanger, as it did and does to everybody who brushes with the Taylor presence. The queen, if not receiving in bed, was being fitted for costumes, or taking long-distance phone calls, while children, pets, sycophants, friends, people looking for deals surrounded her. Right from the beginning Taylor refused to see the press. Her Garboization had begun. "You want to interview her?" Cleopatra's press man asked the *Daily Mail*'s reporter incredulously. "She won't give you an interview. I'll tell you that."

There was no shortage of news though. Panic was in the air. Nothing was ready, certainly not the script. The frenzy was out of the early days of Hollywood. Two scriptwriters (first of an eventual fifteen) had been assigned to work on the screenplay, each unknown to the other. Nobody knew who was supposed to be controlling the cost, Hollywood, New York, or London. Out at Pinewood, a drafty combination of country house and warehouse near London Airport, workmen were trying to cover eight acres with pyramids and desert. Wanger confided despairingly to his diary, "Pinewood doesn't look like Egypt!" Nobody anticipated the obvious labor problems. There were two strikes on the first day of shooting, and what's more, the hairdressers' union absolutely refused to have Sidney Guilaroff on the set, while Taylor insisted that she would have no other hairdresser doing her hair. Props which in Hollywood would have been in the storerooms simply didn't exist and had to be ordered from scratch. To Fox's amazement they were not ready on time.

The one thing that was not behind schedule was the spending. Palm trees, brought in from California, were fitted out with fresh fronds daily, flown in from Egypt. All in all, it was a while before the papers began to notice that the star had hardly been seen.

Why? "Too fat," declared the *Daily Mail* and found itself on the losing end of a libel suit. Taylor was clearly unwell. She was immured in her hotel. Bad cold? Abscessed tooth? Meningism? Boil on the buttocks? All of these were possible, to judge from the reports emanating from numerous doctors and the London Clinic, an expensive private hospital. A psychiatrist friend of mine privately brought the opinion of his lunchtable at the psychoanalytical Tavistock Clinic: "Do you know what they're saying at the Tavvy? That Elizabeth Taylor is sick out of repressed guilt because she didn't mourn Mike Todd!"

At the time, I was working on Fleet Street, at Reuter's, and my editor had his own theory about Taylor. I was instructed to call up the Dorchester and put it to her. "Do I *have* to?" I wailed. It was my last assignment before leaving to get married and I was used to more serious subjects, like science and the royal family. I had to. With leaden fingers, I dialed and got through. A young Bronx male voice relayed my question to the interior. "Reuter's wants to know if you're pregnant!" Loud cackles rolled into the receiver before I got the freshly composed reply: "Mrs. Fisher would be very happy if she were pregnant, but she is not."

Whatever the cause, Taylor was not out at Pinewood making *Cleopatra*. By the end of October, Lloyd's of London, which had insured her for $3 million, was demanding that she be replaced. Lloyd's offered their own list of alternatives: Marilyn Monroe, Shirley MacLaine, or Kim Novak. Skouras refused. He also refused to get out of England, to shift to Rome, Egypt, or Turkey.

At the turn of the year, Rouben Mamoulian, who had been directing *Cleopatra*, resigned. Wanger replaced him with pipe-smoking, psychoanalytically oriented Joseph Mankiewicz, who was considered to "understand" Taylor as he had got *Suddenly Last Summer* out of her, and therefore to be worth the $3 million needed to buy him out of his other commitments. Mankiewicz, who was also going to be principal writer, needed time to think out his own concept of Cleopatra's relationship to Caesar and Mark Antony, so production did not resume right away. While waiting, Eddie Fisher got appendicitis and Taylor got Asian flu. Fisher recovered. Taylor did not.

On March 6, 1961, she was put on a stretcher and rushed from the Dorchester to the London Clinic. She had a rare form of staphylococcus pneumonia and was given an hour to live. One false press report gave out the news that she had died. It reached Skouras in Hollywood and it reached Marilyn Monroe. Hysterically, Marilyn telephoned John Springer, the New York publicist who looked after her, and Taylor, as well as many other great ladies of the screen. "Elizabeth is dead!" she sobbed.

But Taylor was not dead—at least not for long. (She claims to have stopped breathing four times.) Doctors saved her life by performing a tracheotomy, an incision in the windpipe. Sara and Francis Taylor were at her bedside, and Eddie Fisher was weeping. In the lobby, along with the press, hovered assorted Fox executives, worrying about what would happen to the picture if she died and what they would do about the scar on her throat if she lived.

Ten days later, Taylor was wheeled out of the clinic and flown straight back to the Californian sunshine. Skouras finally was convinced. England was no good. He scrapped the ten minutes of film—none of it with Taylor in it—that six months of anguish had yielded. Others in the cast were paid off: Peter Finch got $150,000 for his unfinished Caesar. Lloyd's contributed $2 million toward the losses of the English production—not the $7 million that Fox had wanted. As the company slid downhill, its earnings of $3 million in 1959 turned into losses of $6 million for 1960; Skouras announced that *Cleopatra* would begin again in Rome in September. The hairdressers' dispute was never settled.

The act of virtually dying gave the Elizabeth Taylor myth the brush with the afterlife that is essential for a goddess. Sylvia Plath, deified after her suicide in 1963, had nearly killed herself once before, and referred to herself in a poem as Lady Lazarus. But Taylor better deserves the title. Unlike Plath, Monroe, Lombard, and Garland, she has been there and back.

Although no poet, Taylor is a goddess who spins her own myth. She is given to reliving her encounter with death. Shortly after she returned to California, she appeared as a "symbol of the miracle of modern medicine" at a benefit dinner for the Cedars of Lebanon and Mount Sinai hospitals in California. With Senator Robert Kennedy beside her, she delivered a speech that suggested the fine hand of Joseph Mankiewicz, and also her old Christian Science teaching:

> Dying, as I remember it, is many things—but most of all, it is wanting to live. Throughout many critical hours in the operating theater, it was as if every nerve, every muscle, as if my whole physical being were being strained to the last ounce of my strength, to the last gasp of my breath.
>
> Gradually and inevitably that last ounce was drawn, and there was no more breath. I remember I had focused desperately on the hospital light hanging directly above me. It had become something I needed almost fanatically to continue to see, the vision of life itself. Slowly it faded and dimmed, like a well-done theatrical effect to blackness. I have never known, nor do I think there can be a greater loneliness. . . .

Later, in her memoirs, she told the story again, in unashamedly godlike terms. It was "like I was, I don't know, twenty-nine years old, but had just come out of my own womb." And in 1973, she confided to director Waris Hussein: "I died, Waris. Shall I tell you what it was like? Being down in a long dark tunnel and there was a small light at the end. I had to keep looking at that light. If I stopped, I died." For a more recent version, see *Vogue*, January 1977.

With Taylor recovering and still on salary, Twentieth Century-Fox had to find money to finish *Cleopatra*. Too much had been sunk into the picture to scrap it. In desperation, Fox plunged into a property deal that bordered on the suicidal. It sold its birthright—its backlot.

In the twenties, when the new movie companies edged into the dustlands west of Los Angeles where there was plenty of cheap empty space, they first built their lots—the sound stages, offices, and assorted buildings—and then they threw a fence around the rest—the backlot—empty acres where they filmed outdoor scenes of every variety. It was Twentieth Century-Fox's good fortune to have its backlot right on the edge of Beverly Hills. To anyone with half an eye to the future, this was one of the most desirable pieces of open ground in the United States outside of Central Park, and with stars fleeing abroad and air travel fast and cheap, who needed space to simulate foreign locations at home?

But Fox had to face the present. It sold 260 acres of its property to the famous developer William Zeckendorf, who roped in the Aluminum Company of America for $43 million. If it had not been in such a hurry, it might have developed the site itself, or let a developer do it on a lease. But Fox's cash was flowing into *Cleopatra* at the rate of half a million dollars a week, so it chose to make an outright sale. Just to keep its own studios, it had to lease back 80 acres from Alcoa. "It was *such* a bad deal," says John Gregory Dunne, whose witty book *The Studio* describes Fox's convulsions in the sixties. "That—more than *Cleopatra* itself—led to the downfall of Skouras."

In 1975 the Fox company bought back a corner of its birthright, paying Alcoa $21 million for 75 acres. But today Alcoa's development, Century City, stands overlooking Beverly Hills, a nest of trim skyscrapers, a monument to Fox's *Cleopatra* panic in 1961 and to Elizabeth Taylor's power to change even the skyline of her hometown.

September 1961. New site: Rome. New Caesar: Rex Harrison. New Antony: Richard Burton. New comforts for star: five-room dressing room at Cinecittà, plus fourteen-room Villa Papa. New unrealism: Skouras announces budget cut to $10 million when more than that already spent.

In Rome, *Cleopatra* was as chaotic as in London, but at least they were actually making the movie, at the painful rate of two minutes' worth a day. Mankiewicz was directing all day and composing the next day's lines at night, in longhand. The weather was, if anything, worse than in England. The fake Forum flooded. The owner of the hired elephants sued Twentieth Century-Fox for slander because someone said the elephants were wild. On the set, discipline was so slack that eager Romans were coming out to the studio in the morning, signing on as extras, going back to town for a day's work, then returning to climb into togas in the evening to collect their pay. The costs rose and rose; no one dared add them up. Peter Levathes, a Fox executive, arrived from corporate headquarters in New York to declare: "We are the laughing stock of the industry; this is the greatest disaster in show business!" At any point, it was possible that New York would blow the whistle on Hollywood, halt the production, and perhaps close the studio. What stayed New York's hand was the wan hope that a movie would emerge that might someday generate some income.

As 1962 came up on the calendar, Fox added up its losses for the previous year and found that they had more than tripled: $22 million in the red for 1961.

Elizabeth Taylor, at the same time, taking stock of her career, found herself number one at the box office. And in love with Richard Burton.

It was Mankiewicz who broke the news to Wanger on January 26, 1962. "I have been sitting on a volcano all alone for too long and I want to give you some facts you ought to know," he said. "Liz and Burton are not just playing Antony and Cleopatra!"

Imagine the terror at Fox. For the company, what the popular press had been saying was true—that Elizabeth Taylor as Cleopatra had more power than the real Cleopatra ever had. Fox's only hope of regaining its invested millions now rested on what was becoming the most public adultery in history. The world's press was camped on the doorstep while a corps of Fox PR men tried to answer the question that is as old as their profession: is *any* publicity good publicity?

The spectacle of one of the world's most famous women and one of Hollywood's most famous film companies out of control at the same time gave the heavies of the press an excuse to write about *Cleopatra*. Life and times had by then deposited me at the London *Economist*. *Cleopatra* was the first thing that landed on my desk. Would Fox survive? Would Hollywood unions' wage demand drive the whole American film industry abroad? In Rome a number of distinguished journalists dropped by Cinecittà. They all said they came to interview Mankiewicz. Walter Lippmann concluded that the Liz-Burton story was a good thing "because it took newspaper readers' minds off the daily world crisis." The Associated Press said that newspapers the world over were interested only in the Burton-Taylor romance. Art Buchwald, in the *Herald Tribune*, proposed a worldwide referendum on what Elizabeth Taylor should do.

In the spring of 1962 Cinecittà was as sealed and claustrophobic as Versailles. Burton and Taylor, like eighteenth-century royalty who were never alone, even on the commode, confided in their courtiers. In a memorandum to his boss back in New York, Fox's assistant publicity manager in Rome, Jack Brodsky, wrote:

Burton says to me, "Jack, love, I've had affairs before. How did I know the woman was so fucking famous? She knocks Khrushchev off the front page." So I say, "Rich, it's none of my business, but you can't very well deny everything in print and then go out on the Via Veneto until three in the morning." So he says, "I just got fed up with everyone telling us to be discreet. I said to Liz, 'Fuck it, let's go out to fucking Alfredo's and have some fucking fettucini!' "*

In March, with the picture only just past the halfway mark, Eddie Fisher had fled back to New York where he entered a hospital, described by the New York *Daily News* as "Private midtown psychiatric."

The affair was complicated by the fact that Fisher and Taylor had just begun proceedings to adopt a baby girl. How, in the middle of the chaos of *Cleopatra* and nearly dying, could she have thought of taking on another child?

To anyone who has seen Taylor with her children, the answer is easy. Her passion for mothering is fierce, constant, unstoppable; she is a matriarch out of the anthropology textbooks. As much as she dotes on her husbands, they are peripheral.

She has worried a lot about the impact of her marital career on her children. Her boys had loved Mike Todd, she has said, and thought of his death as a betrayal. "They liked Eddie Fisher, but when he left, they didn't even ask where he'd gone." But . . . "through everything, I've always been there—the one constant thing." All during *Cleopatra*, as on most of her films, she had her children with her. She rushed home at the end of work to be with them.

The adoption of Maria, a small handicapped German girl, Taylor's friends say was the most eloquent expression of a generosity and kindness unrecognized by the public. With Maria, she picked the most disabled child she could find. "Her legs were twisted so badly that one was practically facing

*Jack Brodsky and Nathan Weiss, *The Cleopatra Papers* (New York: Simon & Schuster, 1962).

around the other way," said one friend. When Taylor knew the child was hers, she sat up for three nights in the hospital nursing it. Walter Wanger, almost as practiced at Hollywood psychoanalysis as Mankiewicz, interpreted: "Liz sees herself as a mother-goddess figure. Part of her function, in her mind, is to bear a child by the man she loves." Because she had been told not to get pregnant again, Wanger theorized, the adoption of Maria was terribly important to her, to set the seal on her marriage to Fisher.

As events turned out, the child served the same purpose for the Burton marriage.

Probably the adoption of Maria from Catholic Bavaria was what moved the Vatican to speak. While Elizabeth Taylor was not mentioned by name, in an open letter from an anonymous reader, *L'Osservatore della Domenica*, piling on the metaphors of death, delivered the culmination of all the bad press she had received since Glenn Davis. It was her enthronement as Eve, the superstar's equivalent of the local girl's being denounced from the altar.

Dear Madame: When some time ago, you said that your marriage (your fourth) would last for your whole life, there were some who shook their heads in a rather skeptical way. We, always willing to believe the best, kept our heads steadily on our shoulders and did not say a word. Then, when you reached the point of adopting a baby girl, as if to make more stable this marriage which had no natural children, for a moment we really believed that things had changed. But children—whether they are natural or adopted—count little for illustrious ladies like you when there is nothing for them to hold together. It appears that you had the bad taste to state: "My marriage is dead and extra-dead." And what of the "whole life" you had declared it would last three years ago? Does your whole life mean only three years? And if your marriage is dead, then we must say, according to the Roman usage, it was killed dead. The trouble is, my dear lady, you are killing too many.

Poor Fisher came out of it worse even than the papers reported. The adoption of Maria, into which he presumably entered with some feeling, eventually went through without him, in Taylor's name alone.

But he also found himself deprived of Liza Todd. The summer before the Burton scandal, Fisher, Taylor, and Mike Todd's little daughter, aged four, went into the Santa Monica Courthouse in California to arrange an adoption. When they came out reporters asked the child, "What's your name now?" "Liza Todd Fisher," she replied and the wire services carried the news that Fisher had adopted Todd's daughter.

Today, however, Taylor's lawyer, Aaron Frosch, states categorically: "Eddie Fisher was never the adoptive father of Liza Todd."

What happened is not clear because information on adoption files is confidential under California law. But Los Angeles Superior Court records show that in March 1965 Fisher filed a complaint for partial custody of Liza Todd Fisher. He alleged that he had adopted her on September 6, 1961. The matter was later taken off the calendar and no further action was brought, which suggests that a legal means was found for setting the alleged adoption aside.

Le scandale, as Burton dubbed it, was in many ways the last gasp of the old morality. Cohabitations and adultery were still big sins in 1962, when the U.S. Census in 1960 had found only seventeen thousand couples bold enough to identify themselves as "People of the opposite sex sharing living quarters." How much coverage would the Taylor-Burton romance have drawn if anyone at the time had printed a story that the President of the United States was having affairs with the mistress of a Mafia chief, the wife of an American ambassador, and a Radcliffe undergraduate, to name but a few? But nobody did, although John Kennedy's adventures were common knowledge to the reporters who followed him around.

By June 1962, with *Cleopatra* still incomplete and the company's annual meeting approaching, the Fox top brass sent two heads rolling. One was Walter Wanger's. He was fired as producer. The other was Marilyn Monroe's.

Monroe's last days were lived in the shadow of *Cleopatra*. In the spring of 1962, she had returned to California to make the last of four films for which she was committed to Fox, her old studio. At thirty-six, she was a wreck. Her marriage to Miller was over, her latest picture, *The Misfits*, had a very lukewarm reception, and she was terrified about losing her physical appeal. And she was galled to find that Fox, which had once considered her queen, was paying her only $100,000 for *Something's Got to Give* while they were paying Elizabeth Taylor $1 million.

Marilyn turned her picture into a mini-*Cleopatra*. Shooting began in April. She had a virus. By May they had decided to shoot around her and on the rare days when she did appear on the set, she kept popping a thermometer into her mouth to see if she should go home. But frail health or not, there was one scene she wanted to do—a swimming-pool scene. Supposed to look nude, she threw off the camouflage bathing suit (a sign, they said later, of her impending final collapse). She did more than the scene required. She posed and frolicked for the delighted photographers, who were getting the first nude pictures of Marilyn Monroe in fourteen years. "I'll be happy," she said, "to see all those covers with me on them and no Liz."

When she flew to New York to sing "Happy Birthday, Mr. President," for John Kennedy at Madison Square Garden, she looked radiant. But the next week, back in California, she didn't come to work. To Fox, it looked like open defiance and they fired her. The studio wrote off *Something's Got to Give*, taking a $2 million loss, and someone murmured, "No studio can afford her and *Cleopatra*." The studio had made its choice.

By August 1962, it was all over, including Monroe's life.

Would Fox have been more patient with her if *Cleopatra* had finished as scheduled on May 15? It is a question that could be asked in the endless speculations about the death of Monroe.

As she is safely dead, there is no shortage of people ready to say what Marilyn's innermost thoughts were during those last bitter months. But what it felt like to be Taylor at the center of that corporate and personal cataclysm, she has not deigned to tell, except in the most superficial terms. We do know that at the height of the *Cleopatra* crisis, she summoned her parents to be with her in Rome. And we know that the senior Taylors had really loved Eddie Fisher—he was more of a son-in-law than anything they'd had previously. Wanger revealed that Francis Taylor gave his daughter a scolding that upset her so much she cried all night and could not work the next day. (Yet it was also clear that Sara and Francis Taylor adapted readily to Burton. They accompanied him to Bulgari's, in a procession, according to Jack Brodsky, "of parents, hairdresser, faggots, and other members of the court" to purchase a jewel Taylor had previously suggested she wanted; it was Francis Taylor who selected an emerald.)

It was an international news story when Taylor was carried off to a Rome hospital in the middle of the night. The studio's diagnosis—"food poisoning from eating baked beans"—had to be withdrawn. The owner of the restaurant where all the cast were known to eat objected to this implied criticism of his cuisine. Skouras later said that Taylor tried to commit suicide four times because she felt that Burton was losing interest in her.

Was the stress intolerable? Or does Taylor have an emotional hide like leather? The certain thing is that Elizabeth Taylor is a survivor, and not a victim like Monroe, because she is full of energy and unreflective. Fights she may have, and the occasional black eye. But she does not sit around lacerating herself and analyzing her motives. She has never been to a psychiatrist, she says. She also has been sustained by the solid family ties that Monroe and Garland wanted so much and couldn't even fake. Whatever she felt, Taylor kept going and finished her picture.

Cleopatra claimed other victims, less tragic. Skouras resigned as president—only to be made chairman of the board. Darryl Zanuck was brought back from Paris to be president and to save the studio. Mankiewicz fell under the ax. He was denied permission to cut and edit the movie.

And the movie? So dull as not to be believed. Taylor was all wrong for the part. It opened at the Rivoli Theater in New York in June 1963. I covered it for *The Economist*. I had had a baby four weeks before, and *Cleopatra* was the first time I had left her with a nurse and, worse guilt, a bottle. With aching front, I taxied to the Rivoli and met my deadline with visceral copy, which began:

> Mr. Walter Wanger, the film producer, must be forgiven for declaring that in 1962 there was more world interest in *Cleopatra* and its stars than in any other news event. Now that the elephantine film has finally emerged from its painful gestation, it is clear that this distorted perspective affected its parts as well as its whole. Cleavage takes precedence over character, pageant over plot, matter over mind. *Cleopatra* is the costliest film ever made at somewhere between $40 million and $50 million. It is also the longest. What Shakespeare and Shaw put asunder, Twentieth Century-Fox has joined together. The laborious four-hour unwinding of the encounters of both Caesar and Mark Antony with the bosom-proud Egyptian queen gives value for money on tickets costing as much as $5.50. Thanks to an interval it is possible to fall asleep twice.

Cleopatra inspired other critics to pyrotechnics of ridicule. The prize should probably go to John Coleman of the *New Statesman* for: "Miss Taylor is monotony in a slit skirt, a pre-Christian Elizabeth Arden with sequined eyelids and occasions constantly too large for her." *The Herald Tribune* (Judith Crist) said, "The mountain of notoriety has produced a mouse." However, the trade press liked it, and so did Bosley Crowther of the *Times*. Some unkindly say that Crowther, historian of Hollywood, praised *Cleopatra* because he was afraid that its failure might kill the American movie industry. "Nonsense," he says, in retrospect. "I was very impressed by it as a motion-picture epic. I had studied early epics. I felt that Mankiewicz pulled out of this story a remarkable piece of work. He was encouraged to spend a whole lot of money. Unfortunately, the consequences of the Taylor-Burton romance, and the expense, made the intellectuals so ready to be supercritical. It came out with two strikes against it."

Crowther's claim is borne out by the success of *Cleopatra* abroad where its static opulent pageantry went down well. In Japan, it is twenty-seventh on the list of the fifty top-grossing films of all time—the only Elizabeth Taylor movie on the list. In India it was still drawing crowds in 1975.

The lawsuits arising from *Cleopatra* dragged on for years. Taylor and Eddie Fisher, bound together in the MCL corporation far longer than in marriage, accused Fox of bungling the distribution, thereby lowering gross receipts. Fox, in turn, sued Taylor and Burton, claiming that by their conduct they damaged the value of the film. Skouras said that Taylor personally had added $5 million to the cost of the film.

Taylor eventually settled with Fox for about $2 million, making her earnings from *Cleopatra*, including her salary, about $4 million. Fisher's share of MCL was not settled until 1967 when he remarried and had a new child.

(The scandal, so good for Taylor's finances, was ruinous for Fisher's. Although he managed to get bookings, mainly in nightclubs during the sixties, he never recaptured anything like his old fame, and in 1970 he filed a petition for bankruptcy in Puerto Rico, listing debts of $916,000 and assets of $40,000. But what withered Fisher's career, of course, was not Liz, but Elvis. Crooning went out of style.)

Now that the books are closed, it is clear that *Cleopatra* was not the biggest money-losing film of all time. But neither was it the great financial success that some now like to claim. By 1976, the theatrical gross revenues for *Cleopatra* totaled $40.3 million worldwide, of which $22.1 million represented U.S.-Canada in revenues. The cost of making it was at very minimum $31 million, excluding payment for prints, advertising, and distribution.

But Fox survived. By 1963, under Zanuck, the studio was back in the black (thanks to one of Zanuck's own films, *The Longest Day*, with Richard Burton). And by 1965 the company achieved its dream of making the biggest grossing film of all time. It did it with the help of the Madonna, not Eve: Julie Andrews in *The Sound of Music* finally pushed *Gone with the Wind* from first place.

The star system was not destroyed by *Cleopatra*, nor was Taylor. After *Cleopatra* she feared she might never work again. Instead, she went on to collect a million dollars a picture through most of the sixties, capping her earning performance with a million-and-a-quarter-dollar fee from—you guessed it—Twentieth Century-Fox.

12

The Burtons Ascendant

When Richard Burton went to Hollywood in 1953, turning his back on Stratford-on-Avon and one of the most dazzling first seasons as a Shakespearean actor that anyone could remember, he had relentlessly and cheerfully pursued contracts in six figures. On the West Coast, he and his Welsh wife, Sybil, never succumbed to the common delusion that the fairy gold would last forever. They rented a small house with no pool. They went to others' parties but did not entertain. Frugality paid off: by 1958 Burton was earning enough to be a tax exile in Switzerland, part owner of a Swiss bank, and full owner of an income-producing house in London. He had bought new homes for his many brothers and sisters. But as a movie star, he was considered washed up. In spite of dark smoldering good looks that had been compared to Montgomery Clift's, he was never as good on the screen as on the stage—either because his voice and his presence were too strong or because, some say, he

looked down on the craft of screen acting. At the time when
Cleopatra was being recast in 1961 he was enjoying a
tremendous success on Broadway as King Arthur in *Camelot*.
Yet he was depressed and drinking a lot. He identified success
with money and knew that movies were where the big money
lay. And in Elizabeth Taylor, with her black eyepaint and
Nefertiti hat, he saw the secret of a million dollars a picture.

"It is not true," says his Welsh friend, the broadcaster John
Morgan, "that after going to bed with her the first time Richard
said, 'I am worth four million dollars more than I was yester-
day.' It is not true that he *said* it, that is, but it *was* true in fact."

Being Welsh, however, Burton did say quite a lot to quite a
few. To David Lewin, the veteran film reporter in whom he
often confides, he told how he had rifled through Taylor's desk
and found her contract: "It's true. She *is* getting a million
dollars for the picture. That's more than I'm getting!" (He was
getting $250,000.) Even to Sheilah Graham, no confidante, he
boasted that the romance had boosted his price per picture to
half a million.

One man who did not need to be told was Burton's agent,
Hugh French. French, now dead, was a Hollywood English-
man, the suave David Niven type, who could chat comfortably
in a black silk dressing gown with his bare legs sticking out. As
Burton's professional representative from his earliest Hollywood days until the seventies, Hugh French did not take
offense at the suggestion that he anticipated the affair. "Yes, I
did," he replied. "I had thought something like that might
happen. Richard is *so* attractive, *so* intelligent, never boring. I
had trouble selling him to Fox, though Wanger always wanted
him. I arranged for Fox to buy him out of the second year of
Camelot. Then came the scandal. What a saga! Every detail in
the papers! They were together, they were separate. . . . Each
time I thought to myself, well, that'll put up his salary a bit."

It did more than put up his salary. Burton finished what Mike
Todd began. Allied to the fifties' queen of the movies, he
turned her, with himself as partner, into one of the biggest

money-making factories in the history of the movies. By the late sixties, the Burtons were probably the top-earning husband-and-wife team in any business in the world apart from the British and Dutch monarchies.

After *Cleopatra* was completed the scandal did not waft away. It intensified as they traveled together while the labyrinth of their emotions, companies, and custody rights was sorted out. They made a picture together in London, living in separate suites at the Dorchester, with Burton slipping out occasionally, followed only by reporters, to visit Sybil and his little girls in Hampstead. Taylor accompanied Burton to Puerto Vallarta, Mexico, where he made *Night of the Iguana* with Ava Gardner and Sue (*Lolita*) Lyon, bringing with her her parents, her children, her brother, her brother's children, and forty bikinis. The press hounded them even though it was hard to do, hiring rowboats to get out to the then unknown Mexican port and telephoning stories out by means of the single phone at a local café. In Canada, less secluded, they were booed as Burton arrived to play *Hamlet*. In Boston they were nearly crushed to death by a mob trying to get a look at them entering the Copley Plaza. It all made news—a fact that enraged many people even though they read every word. The *Los Angeles Times* got so many letters complaining about the coverage given the pair that it defended itself and scolded Taylor in the same breath: "Miss Taylor is the world's premier motion-picture attraction. Public appearance is her trade. Thanks to recent publicity she may discover her obligation to be seemly."

So far had Taylor moved into the news and off the entertainment pages that she even made the Drew Pearson column. On July 12, 1963, Pearson quoted a leak from the secret hearings of the House of Representatives' immigration subcommittee:

> "I want to know," inquired Rep. Arch Moore (R-W.Va.), "is Richard Burton guilty of adultery?"
> "I have no knowledge," said Schwarz helplessly.

Schwarz was Abba Schwarz, then in charge of consular affairs at the State Department. The hearings were called by Representative Michael Feighan (D-Ohio) who was trying to revoke Burton's American visa.

It all seems a long way from David Bowie. Yet at the time, as another episode in the long-running comic strip, The Life and Loves of Elizabeth Taylor: The Girl with the Woman's Body and the Child's Emotions, it was not boring.

Taylor was not in the habit of trying to appear seemly. (Her friends say this is an example of her extraordinary honesty.) And Burton was essential to her. If she had made the worst mistake of her life in marrying Eddie Fisher, at last she had found a man who could help her grow. Nothing is more irresistible to women, as Arthur Miller found with Marilyn Monroe. Yet Burton was not at all eager to divorce his wife, Sybil, and in any case was an unlikely candidate for eternal fidelity. He had replaced Dylan Thomas as the world's Welshman, and for the same qualities.

"What's the difference between the Welsh and the Irish?" I once asked Donald Baverstock, the small Welshman once known as the BBC's whiz kid. Like a shot he replied: "Sex." The Irish, he amplified, take their religion seriously. They really do not like women and far prefer drink. In contrast, the Welsh are blessedly hypocritical about their religion and are fiercely randy. The pleasure they find in drink is in addition to and not a substitute for bed.

Richard Burton genuinely likes women. He enjoys talking to them, remembers if he has met them before, and has a nice way of expressing himself. "Richard calls me Ocean," said Taylor.

His exploits in Hollywood were fabulous. Fredric March has said, "I don't think he has missed more than half a dozen." Burton himself contributed to the lore with, "Sure, movie executives in those days were spending all their time making love to starlets but so were most of us actors." His wife, Sybil, a prematurely gray, friendly girl, enjoyed a reputation for being understanding because Burton always was true in his fashion.

For a long time, she did not believe he wanted a divorce. (Even during the encounter with Taylor in *Cleopatra*, Burton had in his company a chorus girl from the cast of *Camelot* until Walter Wanger asked her to leave.)

As the struggle between Taylor and Burton raged on, *Time* neatly defined the stakes. The game must yield up a loser, it said. "If he should ever marry her, he will be the Oxford boy who became the fifth husband of the Wife of Bath. If she loses him, she loses her reputation as a fatal beauty, an all-consuming man-eater, the Cleopatra of the twentieth century."

Burton surrendered at a Unitarian ceremony in Montreal in March 1964.

A week earlier Francis and Sara Taylor had recognized the changing order and remade their will. "To Richard Burton, our beloved soon-to-be-son-in-law," they bequeathed "the Masson painting snow scene which hangs over the fireplace" and Francis Taylor's Viking cuff links.

The Burtons were born. There was no talk about retiring into house and garden this time. They were a team of high-priced actors looking for deals. It was a quick matter to blend entourages: Her Dick Hanley stayed on as press secretary; his dresser, Bob Wilson, did double duty as bodyguard and best man. Pink-faced John Springer did their publicity. (So entwined were the Taylor-Burton careers that when they divorced for the first time the joke around New York was, "Who will get custody of John Springer?") Hugh French took over as Taylor's agent and his British representative, John Heyman, became their British agent and adviser on tax shelters. Marjorie Lee of the Dorchester Hotel served as a kind of friendly English aunt, arranging air tickets for children and relatives, making sure that the Burtons got suites at the Dorchester when they wanted. (Once the hotel was so full that when they telephoned, Miss Lee had to book them at the Savoy, to Taylor's distress. "But the Dorchester is home to me!" she wailed. Luckily, by the time the Burtons reached London, space at the Dorchester had opened up.) There were many many others: hairdressers, makeup men, personal photographers, and assorted residential staff needed to run their houses—two in Switzerland, one in Mexico, one in London.

Superficially Taylor seemed the gainer. Burton represented what her face looked as if it had—education, culture, sophistication. No wonder she always seemed to be clutching him. Her diction improved, and so did her powers of expression. (On *Cleopatra* these were noted to range from "crazy" [good] to "balls" [bad].) With Burton, Taylor moved out of the show business cloister into a wider world. She went to Welsh rugby matches. If Senator Mansfield was in town, then Senator Mansfield was invited for drinks. She met the theatrical greats and admired Burton for being able to recite virtually all of Shakespeare. And she basked in his sympathy for the dangers she had passed. "Poor Elizabeth," he would tell friends, "she was educated at MGM."

Welshness slid over her adopted Jewishness very comfortably. Perhaps naturally. Freud's biographer, the Welsh psychoanalyst Dr. Ernest Jones, called the Welsh the Jews of Britain. If so, Burton was her third Jewish husband.

But Burton himself was much enhanced by the marriage and not only financially. He was much more a movie star in the classic pattern—that is, a motherless child, a cuckoo in the nest, nothing like his brothers and sisters. He was born Richard Jenkins in Pontrhydyfen, a small town in South Wales, and later moved to the nearby coastal town of Port Talbot, where he lived with his eldest sister and went to school. A teacher, Philip Burton, recognized his brilliance and adopted him, giving him his name. Burton had always wanted to be big, and he loved playing the poor miner's son who comes home with the queen of the movies. (It was a game he could also play against her. Once he pointed to John Morgan's wife, Mary, an old classmate of his at Port Talbot, and said, "You wouldn't understand a woman like Mary, Elizabeth. She's only had one husband in her whole life.")

At first Burton's old friends despised Taylor. Emlyn Williams, the actor and writer who had encouraged his early career, and who had gone to Rome to try to get him to go back to Sybil, called Taylor a third-rate chorus girl. But after a time Williams changed his mind. So did John Morgan. When the film came out he wrote a wicked anonymous profile of Burton in the *New Statesman*, entitled "Mr. Cleopatra." In it he said:

> Welsh romanticism has a startling arrogance. Ideally, it likes its heroes to die young; the dream is of the golden boy of natural genius who effortlessly conquers the English world. The romance lies in the ascent. Early death is attractive because it rules out the chance of solid middle age. The Welsh have all the talents, except for being 45. What to do with all that talent is the perennial problem.
>
> Dylan Thomas, thus, is the perfect hero. This arrogance—an arrogance that masquerades as modesty—infects the performer because this is how he sees himself. Perversely pleasure lies in the waste of talent.

Rather than contributing to Burton's pursuit of self-destruction, Morgan says with hindsight, Taylor rescued him, temporarily at least. Because of her, "Richard recovered a lot and had five good years." Morgan himself was won over.

"Sober, she can be a boring woman," Morgan says. "The tedium of her conversation is noticeable. She talks about her children mainly. But when she's got a few drinks in her, she becomes very lively and flirtatious. Sexually attractive? I'll say. I liked her. But women can't stand her."

Other friends liked the way she could deflate him. Burton can be pompous, especially in his cups, when he is given to long recitations of poetry. Once, left out of a conversation about The Theater, Taylor confessed: "I don't know anything about the theater. But," defiantly flinging her arm over her head, "I don't need to! I'm a star!" At a bar in Puerto Vallarta one night, she was embarrassed when Burton kept inviting her to recite some poetry. "I don't know any," she kept protesting. "Oh, come on, love, you must know *some*," he insisted between sonorous outpourings. Finally, she obliged. It was a poem her father taught her, she said, and she recited it in her little voice:

> "What'll you have," the waiter said,
> As he stood there picking his nose.
> "Hard boiled eggs, you son of a bitch!
> You can't put your fingers in those!"

To women the world over, however, Taylor remained a figure of terror and fascination. When I got married I found that my Welsh mother-in-law, who lives in a village not far from Pontrhydyfen, reacted to Elizabeth Taylor in the same way as my own mother three thousand miles away. And with the same double standard. On the one hand, here was female Satan. "That Liz Taylor. I'd like to take her by the scruff of the neck and shake her! I hear she was in a pub over Port Talbot the other night and nobody took any notice. *She* didn't like that one bit!" On the other hand, Taylor was the ideal beauty. "Look at her!" said my mother-in-law, watching her little granddaughter play on the floor. "Isn't she a pretty little thing! Just like Liz Taylor! We've never had anything like that in our family!"

The effect of Taylor on Burton's career was instantaneous. His *Hamlet* on Broadway made more money than any Shakespearean production in history. With *Night of the Iguana*, he began a string of movie roles that were to produce the best performances of his career. Taylor brought him to the cover of *Life* twice within a year. Yet he paid the price early and, apparently, willingly. He had to join the myth, following Taylor in blending public with private life. After their wedding in Montreal, while he was playing *Hamlet* there, he stepped forth after the final curtain and tossed the audience a line from the play: "There will be no more marriages." Once they were married, they gave themselves over to the part of rabble king and queen. Or rather queen and prince: they knew which monarchy they were aping. In New York during the run of

Hamlet she developed a ritual of coming to fetch him home
from work, which turned into a Times Square Changing of the
Guard. Every night at eleven-thirty, a Rolls-Royce would drive
up to the Lunt-Fontanne Theater and, as police struggled to
hold back crowds twelve deep, there would emerge, in full
regalia, Elizabeth Taylor. With a gloved wave of the hand she
would go into the theater and emerge with her consort in tow.
Try as she would to build him up, however, the reality of her
rank obtruded. Even in little day-to-day matters, she often
could not help overwhelming him. S. J. Perelman recalls a day
in London in the early sixties:

"We were coming back from lunch at a pub on St. Martin's
Lane when we passed the Reform Club. I mentioned that the
club was the setting for *Around the World in 80 Days*. 'I must
go in!' Elizabeth said, and the Rolls slid to a halt. Richard and I
tried to pull her back. Women weren't allowed in the Reform
Club in the afternoon and that day Elizabeth was wearing, as I
recall, a towering busby hat in gray caracul, a chubby coat, and
she had stretch pants tucked into jackboots. We couldn't stop
her. She headed up the steps and got to the door just as the
club's secretary was coming out. "Miss Taylor!" he cried and
instead of keeping her out, he took her in and gave her a tour of
the whole club, from cellar to library. You can imagine those
old men dozing in their chairs suddenly seeing Elizabeth Taylor
in the club in the middle of the afternoon!

"Well, when we got back into the Rolls, Elizabeth said, 'You
ought to join that club, Richard,' and he told her, 'You can't just
join a club. You have to be invited.' And she said to him . . .'"
Perelman has to stop to laugh—"She went right on as if he
hadn't spoken, and as if he was out of work instead of making
that picture with Peter O'Toole, she said, 'You ought to join that
club. It would give you something to do in the afternoon.' "

As the money rolled, the Burtons allowed themselves to
flaunt it in a way that no genuine monarchy would dare. Why?
The answer for Taylor lies locked somewhere in the blend of
her family and her MGM upbringing; she developed an inse-

curity and lack of trust that only jewels and visible proof of wealth could stanch. For Burton, the answer in part lies in the place he came from.

Pontrhydyfen is the kind of gray wet Welsh valley town that produces socialists, miners, and exiles. On a December morning as we make our way there in the family car, the stone houses give off mist like cold steam. It is one of those days that divide the Welsh into two classes, those who ride in cars and those who wait in bus shelters. As we set out, my father-in-law instructs us not to miss the local landmark, Pontrhydyfen's viaduct. He does not tell us, however, that we have to drive right over it—a precarious 150-year-old line of arches that hangs over a dry riverbed seventy-five feet below and looks as if it were built during the Roman occupation instead of the industrial revolution. Safe across, we navigate down a slippery street of small row houses with smoking chimney pots. A woman's head darts out of a doorway. "Do you think that's the place?" my husband asks. "Does she look like Richard Burton?" I ask. "Incredibly," says my daughter from the back seat.

Mrs. Hilda Owen is Richard Burton in a blue housedress, broad of face and chest, spindly in the legs. Her house lies in the middle of a terrace and looks like a million others: three tiny rooms lead into each other and coal fires burn in hygienic tile fireplaces. (There are fires in two rooms at the same time only because company is expected.) On the mantelpiece are a pair of china dogs and bronzed glass mugs. A few photographs of a well-known actor are around the room, but they might have been cut out of a Sunday newspaper.

Seating herself in a businesslike way, Hilda Owen sets about giving a superb demonstration of what I think is the greatest Welsh gift of all: the total lack of a sense of awe. Her brother Richard has never got out of touch with his many brothers and sisters, Verdun in Port Talbot, Tom in Cwmavon, Cissie in Hampstead—the list is long—and why should he? They always knew he was going to be famous. "Even when he was two, he was extraordinary. Richard could really recite, little verses from the Bible and hymns—all Welsh and no English." His mother died when he was two. Today it is as if his whole clan are his parents. He flies them out to Budapest or Geneva or his yacht and they go along as matter-of-factly as if they were going into Port Talbot or Swansea. "And it doesn't cost us a penny."

"At that last party they gave in London, I told Rich the only two I wanted to meet were Dame Margot Fonteyn and who was it played Churchill's mother? Oh yes, Lee Remick. Just those two. I'd met all the rest.

"What do we talk to them about? Well, they seem mainly to be coming to us, like. We had no problem. You know the Welsh. We're good at singing. We're good at parties and we don't feel shy. Anyway, we're happy because we're together as a family."

Does she mind that her brother sacrificed the chance of becoming the greatest Shakespearean actor of his generation? "Well, when he left the stage . . . let's be honest. He looks after us all. The money was no good. He is so generous. Every September we all get our annual check, and another one at Christmas. Elizabeth is very generous too, mind. She's very kind. They're both too generous for their own good. And the letters they get, the begging letters! Richard, he can't say no. But, of course, now everything has to go through lawyers."

At the time of the great scandal, the village kept its mouth shut. "They're very nice around here. They wouldn't say anything. My sister Cissie took it worst. [Mrs. Cissie James, who brought Richard Burton up, is the eldest sister.] She's on the staid side. She doesn't believe in divorce and she always liked Sybil. Anyway, whenever there's a rift, the phone goes. I always say, 'If Rich is happy, I'm happy. He couldn't be a better brother.' Anyway, that's how they all are nowadays, isn't it? But my husband and I did have an awful shock when Ringo and Maureen split up. We sat with them at the Duma in Budapest."

The Owens were just recovering from a Taylor-Burton visit. If possible, Mrs. Owen prefers to see her famous brother away from Wales. "It's not really good when they come here in the village. He never tells us when he's coming. The first thing we notice is the day and night press start to hang about, and then the BBC. And the next thing we know, out of the blue, there they are on the doorstep. Richard and Elizabeth. It was like a fair here when they arrived. There was busloads coming to see them. We were eating when they came, so they joined us. Even the chauffeur. I wouldn't leave him sitting out there in the Daimler. Even the press came in. That's how we are in the village, we couldn't keep them out.

"Rich was playing hymns on the piano. And Elizabeth said, 'Next time I come down, I'll just send the ring. That's what they come to see, not me.' "

When Burton comes home, Mrs. Owen speaks only in Welsh and cooks him Welsh soul food: laver bread,* faggots and peas, and gooseberry tart. On her last visit Elizabeth Taylor had stomach trouble, picked up in Leningrad during the filming of *The Blue Bird*, and her then sister-in-law observed, "It was unusual to see Elizabeth not eating, I mean, not eating a lot." Nonetheless, when she did get hungry between meals, they all slipped down to Cwmavon and got some fish and chips.

Burton likes to see the women in his family dressed in style. Whenever there's a grand event, he sends Mrs. Owen and her daughters money for clothes. Sometimes they go on a shopping spree to Cardiff or Swansea. Sometimes they wear Taylor's castoffs.

"Elizabeth used to send trunks of clothes," says Mrs. Owen. She runs upstairs to fetch an armful. The sight is incredible: those hideous movie queen gowns from the news photos spread out over a Welsh cretonne sofa. They are short and wide, almost square. There was a black-and-white silk from the days of the mini-skirt: its brief length made even shorter by a low square neck, and a thick velvet belt and the large print in the fabric. There were silver sequins on blue silk, and a fuchsia and

*Seaweed mixed with oatmeal and fried with bacon.

yellow filmy caftan from Robinson's of Beverly Hills. "She loves caftans," says Mrs. Owen, whose shape caftans also suit. "I wore that one to the Royal Film Performance of *Taming of the Shrew*." One dress, however, is genuinely eye-stopping, a heavy crotcheted white lace gown by Sybil Connally of Dublin. "Megan wore that to the premiere of *Under Milk Wood*," Mrs. Owen ventures uncertainly. Her husband calls in from his chair in front of the kitchen fire: "That one cost a thousand pounds!"

In general, the Owen girls like the long dresses, but the short ones are too short, even with the hems let down. When the trunks arrive, the women of Pontrhydyfen turn out for what Mrs. Owen calls "a pick-through." After everybody has helped herself, the rest goes to charity.

As we part, Mrs. Owen gives me her recipe for pastry—use lard, not butter—and her husband, Dai, puts down his paper and sums up their situation. "I'm a carpenter, a working man. I've been a working man all my life. But it doesn't hurt to have people like that in the family."

I get back into the car and wonder: does Burton's apparent greed come from a desire to help his family?

The big money years started right after *Cleopatra*. Together they made *The VIPs*, directed by Anthony Asquith, based on a frothy collection of stories written by Terence Rattigan and set in fog-bound London Airport. The producer, Anatole de Grunwald, took a chance and worked with Taylor uninsured. There was no trouble, no illness, no lateness. For *The VIPs* she got a million dollars and Burton half a million, against 20 percent of the gross. When the gross rose to a hefty $14 million worldwide, the Burtons' share came to $2.8 million. Burton got the same fee for *Becket* and *Night of the Iguana* and found that his *Hamlet* had grossed $6 million, of which he took 15 percent.

Why, you might ask, after the *Cleopatra* debacle, was Elizabeth Taylor still able to charge a million dollars a picture? One answer lies in the movie industry habit of admiring big numbers. "You fail upwards here," a nameless young agent explains in Dunne's *The Studio*. "A guy makes a ten-million-dollar bomb, the big thing is not that he's made a bomb, but that he put together a ten-million-dollar picture."

The other answer is that for about five years after *Cleopatra* the public's curiosity about the sexual combination of Taylor and Burton remained insatiable.

All the Burton pictures cashed in on this voyeurism, but few so shamefacedly as *The Sandpiper*, a Technicolor soap opera set in Big Sur, California. This, their next number after *The VIPs*, brought Burton up to three-fourths of Taylor's million, and showed that no story was too silly to keep people away from a screen on which they imagined were scenes from the Burtons' home life. The critic Kenneth Tynan described the plot: "a plump unmarried atheist (Elizabeth Taylor) and a stocky married clergyman (Richard Burton) who go to bed on the coast of Upper California." Its gross was $7 million in North America alone.

By 1964 Burton had suddenly emerged as the world's number-one film box-office attraction and he began for the first time in a twelve-year movie career to pick up Academy Award nominations: for *Becket*, *The Spy Who Came in from the Cold*, and *Who's Afraid of Virginia Woolf?* Even early on, nonetheless, there were rumors of drinking and late arrivals on the set. Vincente Minnelli directed *The Sandpiper*. I asked him if lateness were not common with superstars. He squirmed. "Not to the extent that we had it in this situation. Time . . . it's very serious when you're making a movie."

How did he, as director, explain it to the crew? Minnelli shrugged. "There was just the two of them. Without them there was no picture."

As the money rolled in, Taylor began to accumulate real wealth at last.

In 1966 she dropped her American citizenship and took British nationality exclusively. At reports that she wanted to become British to escape tax, she laughed mirthlessly. "Funny, really," she said. "Taxes are higher in Britain."

But—she did not add—only if you lived in Britain. At that time British subjects who lived abroad had a far better tax deal than Americans living away from their own country. While Americans enjoyed an exemption of only $20,000 on their income earned abroad—peanuts to a movie star—British subjects did not have to pay any British tax on their foreign earnings if they ordinarily resided abroad and did not spend more than 183 days a year in Britain.

Burton never pretended that he was anything but a tax exile. A homesick one. In Dublin in 1965 he said, "I want to go back to England and pay taxes like everybody else." (It is not really fair to quote Richard Burton, because he is so eloquent and garrulous that he can be found to have said almost anything—pro-Churchill, anti-Churchill, and so on.) So far he has resisted the temptation presented by Britain's confiscatory tax on the upper brackets and remained a legal resident of Switzerland. What Taylor was doing in changing citizenships was to make her tax status resemble her husband's.

"It would be uncharitable," says John Heyman, "to say that she became British for tax purposes. It was a terribly emotional thing with her. I cannot tell you how much in love she was at that time."

But the U.S. Internal Revenue Service is uncharitable, and was to Taylor. In 1972 according to a news report, the IRS had asked for $350,000 in back taxes, and advised that "one of the principal purposes of your expatriation was the avoidance of U.S. income tax." Her lawyer denied that she either owed or had tried to dodge tax.

In 1966 the Burtons reached their financial and artistic climax. They did it in two films, one in color, one in black and white, in which the public, as never before, believed the real Burtons were on show.

Playboy enjoyed *Taming of the Shrew*. "A news event— another colorful episode in the lives of Elizabeth Taylor and Richard Burton, whose supposed follies happen to fit into a comedy from the first folio. . . . The royal rowdies of filmdom may not have quite everything, but there is glitter in everything they've got."

Shrew was the first of the Burtons' own productions. They invested their own money, waived salaries, hadn't expected to make much, and were rewarded with a modest fortune. The initial worldwide gross was $7 million, which eventually swelled to $12.6 million. The production was flamboyantly self-indulgent and neatly tailored to the international market: minutes pass without any words at all. With the enthusiastic assistance of Franco Zeffirelli, the opera director, Burton threw out two fifths of Shakespeare's text and concentrated on a feast for the eyes. Taylor, terrified of Shakespeare and of competing with Burton on his home territory, was an exquisite shrew—a fiery, patrician beauty, wearing the kind of Renaissance costume that suits her. She spoke her lines not badly, considering the handicap of her voice. And the plot deftly allows Burton, as Petruchio-Mike Todd, to tame his Shrew—who first appears as a single beautiful, terrible eye—by physical force that no female could match.

Before *Shrew*, the Burtons made *Who's Afraid of Virginia Woolf?* When the news was out that Elizabeth Taylor was to play Martha, all those who had been stirred and shattered by Edward Albee's play were appalled. Hollywood was at it again—a slick commercial bit of miscasting as bad as putting Audrey Hepburn into Julie Andrews's part for the film of *My Fair Lady*. It actually seemed worse than *My Fair Lady*, for Albee's play about a childless embittered academic couple was savage, raw reality. Elizabeth Taylor was celluloid. Never had she, apart from her brief implausible scenes as a mental patient in *Suddenly Last Summer*, played a female who was not a beauty. What's more, *Virginia Woolf*'s Martha is not only a blowzy fifty-two-year-old, but an academic bitch, the well-read daughter of the president of the university who never lets her husband forget that he's never made it out of the history department.

Stories differ of how Taylor came to want the part. Some say Burton challenged her with the script, saying, "I don't think you're old enough to be Martha. And you don't have the passion and the power. Anyway, you'd better play it to stop anyone else from doing it and causing a sensation." Hugh French says he suggested it to her. Whoever did, once the idea took root, she was hungry for the part, desperate to do it—but not so desperate that she waived her usual million fee plus "overages"—that is, she was entitled to excess payments of $175,000 a week if the film ran over its shooting schedule. (But generously she did not claim the $1.5 million in overages to which she was entitled when the film took a very long time to make.)

Virginia Woolf was made in Hollywood by Warner Brothers. The Burtons were glad when their friend, Mike Nichols, was chosen as director. Nichols looked a bigger risk than Elizabeth Taylor. A satirist who turned Broadway director, he had never made a movie before. He didn't even know where the cameras should be placed. "So I said to myself, 'Schmuck, you don't know anything and you have to pretend that you do!' " To prepare, Nichols read books, asked questions, and went to the movies. And the movie he learned most from was George Stevens's *A Place in the Sun*: "having something sexual happen when it's so dark that you really have to make up what you *think* you're seeing physically."

What Nichols did realize, however, was exactly what lay hidden in Elizabeth Taylor:

My first reaction was: Yes, I can see it. I know what they mean. I absolutely can see something in Elizabeth that can play Martha. The age never concerned me. . . . The brilliant, overeducated, ball-cutting woman who also has womanly feelings and alternates between them is a very specific type. No movie star that I've ever known or heard of could be expected to capture that specific character element. It's that very specific poet's wife, or professor's wife, whose hair escapes from the knot at the back of her head, whose dress doesn't quite fit, who's read everything and laughs at Simone de Beauvoir, who says what in effect Martha said in the play: "Abstruse in the sense of recondite. Don't you tell me words." That's very far outside most actresses' experience.

The fact is that Elizabeth does know about what you could call the center of the piece, which is the intimate and possibly painful connection between people. I think that's what she did, that's what she brought.*

Burton's casting as George came later. He was uneasy about playing such a repressed, henpecked male—and one with an American accent. As it turned out he was as brilliant as she was, and was nominated again for the Academy Award. He did not win it. Of all the gifts Burton ever gave Taylor, his George in *Virginia Woolf* may have been the greatest and the most self-sacrificing. With his superb quiet underplaying of the academic sadist in plastic-rimmed glasses and Dagwood cardigan, he handed her the picture.

Taylor is only as good as her directors and Mike Nichols turned out to be a genius. At first when she swaggers into her filthy kitchen, you feel that it is not going to work. In spite of the twenty pounds she happily put on, in spite of the frowzy wig and the faculty-wife duffel coat, she is too pretty. But then she spits out the famous opening line—"What a dump!"—and you know that it is going to be all right. You can almost see Mike Nichols walking through the scene first—chomping on a drumstick, throwing the uneaten half back into the refrigerator.

It is not a subtle performance. Taylor enjoys bellowing "God damn you!" too much. But it is a powerful and controlled study of menopausal terror: the hard lewd female, panicky about an empty uterus and an empty future. Taylor nods knowingly to herself as she admires her young guest's biceps; she writhes obscenely with him through a twist at a roadhouse. By the final scene at dawn when the guests have gone and George, having

*Nichols's views on the picture appear in *The Film Director as Superstar* by Joseph Gelmis (New York: Doubleday, 1970).

demolished their imaginary son, taunts her lightly with her own joke: "Who's afraid of Virginia Woolf?" and she whimpers, "I am, George, I am," the crumpled woman on the screen does not even resemble Elizabeth Taylor.

Virginia Woolf earned Taylor virtually every acting prize going: her second Academy Award, the New York Critics Circle prize (shared with Lynn Redgrave), the National Board of Review Award, the British Film Critic Award, and the Foreign Press Association Award. It also must have been satisfying for her to carve another niche in Hollywood history. *Virginia Woolf* broke the Production Code that had kept movieland dialogue sky-blue pink since 1930. Most of the credit has to go to Jack Warner of Warner Brothers and to Edward Albee, who refused to bowdlerize the script for the movies. But it was Taylor who said the words. Her heartfelt screw you's and sons of bitches were so essential that the Production Board accepted Warner Brothers' offer to restrict admission to the film to the over-eighteen-year-olds. The board finally gave *Virginia Woolf* a seal of approval because it reflected "the tragic realism of life." Having itself faced reality, the board abandoned the code altogether. In its place came the film classification system and R-rating, with what consequences for censorship we all know.

Who's Afraid of Virginia Woolf? is as central to the Elizabeth Taylor myth as Mike Todd is. People liked Taylor for playing it. Dismissing all her other pictures but *National Velvet*, they still rave about it. For her public image, it was the death of the fatal beauty. Not surprisingly, women began to like her better. While they don't warm to ravishing beauties, they sympathize with women who have trouble with their weight. In her press coverage, Taylor made another major jump: off the editorial pages and onto the women's pages. The Chicago *Sun-Times* lady readers were treated to a friendly cartoon of Taylor, bulging out of toreador pants, in among the recipes for sour cream coffee cake. There was a poem too:

Elizabeth Taylor, we give you our hearts,
Our hot fudge sundaes and cherry tarts.
For "Virginia Woolf" you've earned our prizes
By bringing glamour to half-sizes.

Yet something ugly was also revealed. It is a measure of Taylor's willingness to become a Method actress that she let it show. Martha, like Maggie in *Cat on a Hot Tin Roof*, is a homosexual's nightmare of a woman. She is all mouth, a campus Martha Mitchell. She drinks, she devours, she swears—even her baby comes out of her mouth. Even though Albee's plot has George triumph thinly in the end, Martha is the woman all men fear. "You can stand it!" she snarls at George. "You married me for it!"

Who's Afraid of Virginia Woolf? marked Elizabeth Taylor's debut as Medusa, the monster-woman with snaky hair and raging eyes that can transform mortals to stone.

13

The Burtons Descendant

After such a winning streak, the Burtons might be forgiven for believing they had the Midas touch. *Variety* thought so. "Burtons can't take holiday," it declared over five columns in December 1967. "An extended vacation causing them to skip an acting assignment means one film less and a rock-bottom minimum loss of $12 million in industry revenues." Between 1962 and 1966, *Variety* said, quoting John Heyman, pictures starring one or both Burtons earned distributor grosses in the neighborhood of $167 million.

In Cannes, where she was filming, Taylor refused to see the press when she won her Oscar for *Virginia Woolf*. She was too bitter, she said, because Burton and Mike Nichols had not won as well. But at their celebration party, the Burtons were not depressed or weeping. "Not at all," says John Morgan, who was there. "They were thinking how much money they were going to make when the picture was re-released." And they were right. *Who's Afraid of Virginia Woolf?* eventually grossed $28 million, out of which the Burtons took home about $5 million— more than she earned from *Cleopatra*.

As the bigger earner in the dual-career family, Elizabeth Taylor had never looked better value for money. "She is one of the few stars—many say the *only* star—who is regarded as a true gilt-edged investment," declared *Saturday Review* in 1967. "Her presence in a picture is a sure guarantee that audiences will turn out in sufficient quantity to offset even the staggering costs of a *Cleopatra*."

Suddenly her audiences mysteriously began to stay at home. In 1968 she had two flops in a row—*Reflections in a Golden Eye*, without Burton, and *The Comedians*, with him, which began for both of them a downhill slide at the box office which, as much as any other single reason, delivered their marriage to the divorce court in 1974.

On paper, *Reflections in a Golden Eye* looked like the old successful formula as before. How could it miss? A southern horror tale of adultery and impotence at an army camp, John Huston directing from a script drawn from Carson McCullers. Taylor's part was her usual overripe southern belle afflicted with a limp male; her costar, playing the latent homosexual army major, was to be Montgomery Clift, who was always good for her.

It's a fact of Hollywood history that there is an Oscar jinx that can blight the career of those who get the Academy Award— Marlon Brando after *On the Waterfront*, Julie Andrews after *Sound of Music*—but nobody expected it to land on Elizabeth Taylor. She had, after all, survived *Butterfield 8* rather well.

But Elizabeth Taylor does not need Hollywood jinxes when she has such a powerful one of her own. Shortly before shooting began on *Reflections*, Montgomery Clift was found dead in his apartment in Manhattan. He was forty-six; the coroner's verdict: coronary occlusion. It was a terrible blow for Taylor, professional as well as personal. The only reason she'd agreed to do the picture was that she hoped it would get Monty back on his feet. Since he had made *Freud* in 1963, his career had shriveled and he had been pursuing self-destruction with renewed determination. But there was no getting out of the deal; her million-dollar contract had been signed. "It was a case of a generous lady helping somebody out and getting lumbered," says John Heyman, who negotiated the contract.

At first, Taylor resisted going on. She said she would do the picture only if Marlon Brando played the male lead. To everybody's surprise, Brando said yes. He even consented to take second billing for the first time since *Streetcar Named Desire* with Vivien Leigh. "The attraction to me of a neurotic role like Major Pendleton?" said Brando. "Seven hundred fifty thousand dollars plus ten percent of the gross receipts if we break even."

They didn't. The supposedly unbeatable combination of Taylor and Brando did not generate anything like the electricity of Taylor and Newman in *Cat on a Hot Tin Roof*, and Taylor found herself, somewhat astonished, associated with a flop.

It was sad, for she was at her raging best. *Reflections* began a long line of Elizabeth Taylor pictures in which she acts her heart out, and even gets good personal reviews, only to be stigmatized by the failure of the picture as a whole. There was plenty that was wrong with *Reflections*. John Huston was below par. The script was terrible. The kind of grotesque dialogue that got by in *Suddenly Last Summer* drew laughs in *Reflections*. (Perhaps nobody could sneer, "She cut off her nipples with garden shears! You call that *normal*?" and not get a laugh.) Brando wasn't much help. Expressionless as the homosexual guardsman, he slurred more than usual and stood in front of the mirror, morosely putting cold cream on his face. Yet Taylor does have a scene that makes the whole farce worth sitting through. She is the major's wife, a dumb southern broad, planning a party. Proudly she stacks up her invitations, *cordially* spelled with one *l*. Then her eyes light up. The food! She counts on her fingers what she is going to serve: spareribs and ham and barbecued chicken! Is it good acting or the real

Elizabeth Taylor coming through? Either way, it's a memorable moment.

But the *Reflections* flop set off a wave of anxiety in the film industry. Were the big stars worth their price if two of the biggest names in the business, putting $1.75 million on the bill before a foot of film was shot, could not sell tickets?

By the late sixties, failure could hurt a star's bankability. By then movies had become package deals, financed by an assortment of investors who looked at each proposed project very coldly. They wanted to win big each time. The film studios, when they handled financing themselves, had the same philosophy, and so did the unsentimental conglomerates that were buying them up. (Gulf and Western Corporation had bought Paramount; Warner Brothers-Seven Arts, which made *Reflections*, was taken over by Kinney National Service, Inc.)

The Burtons' next film, *The Comedians*, had two distinctions: (1) it was the first time that Burton was paid more than Taylor—$750,000 to her $500,000 (but as she was on the screen for only about twenty minutes, her rate per hour was still higher) and (2) it was their first picture that lost money.

Again, it was a picture that looked good on paper. *The Comedians* was based on a Graham Greene script and set in "Papa Doc" Duvalier's Haiti, with sinister black police, the Ton-Tons Macoutes, swaggering around with billy clubs and dark glasses, ready to dispatch anybody, white or black, who so much as whispers against the regime. Burton was cast as the world-weary burnt-out case who in the final moments, like Rick in *Casablanca*, throws his lot in with the fight against tyranny. Taylor was Burton's mistress, the German wife of an ambassador, played by always-good Peter Ustinov. And Alec Guinness was a shifty likable British drifter caught and crushed in the debacle.

The reviews weren't bad. Taylor's German accent was good in places and the political message of the film was strong enough to have Duvalier lodge an official protest with the United States government. But the financial results were terrible. In its first year of release in North America, *The Come-dians* grossed only $1.8 million, nearly half of which went in salary to the Burtons. What had gone wrong? Overproduction, mainly. The Burtons had made too many movies. *The Come-dians* was their seventh together in five years. Suddenly the public had had enough. "It's time the Burtons realized they are not the Lunts," said the *New Statesman*, "and kept their private partnership out of the realms of art." Another critic dismissed the film as "another glimpse into the private life of the Burtons—a favor I personally could do without." There are long necking scenes in which Burton's mouth crawls over Taylor's arched throat (arched, says one of her directors, to hide her double chins). It was Bosley Crowther in *The New York Times* who spotted the sexual ingredient that was souring the partnership. "Elizabeth Taylor simply plays her [the ambas-sador's wife] so cruelly and confidently that she appears more ferocious than usual, especially in the kissing scenes."

In fact, there were two sexual elements in the Burtons' decline. On screen, they were incompatible. Taylor was simply too strong for Burton. She obliterated him. It was Sunset Strip against Stratford-on-Avon. More and more, his performances with her left him looking weak and washed out, and those who didn't like him said he was bored. Yet there was something else working against them.

Sexually, they had become anachronisms. Movie audiences were dominated by the under-thirties, and by 1968 the image of Woman projected by Taylor had gone out of style. There she was in *The Comedians* in *haute couture* and teased hair, reek-ing doom, just as Vanessa Redgrave was removing her plain checked shirt and baring a bony chest to the camera in *Blow-Up*. And in *The Comedians* Burton actually had to refer to sexual intercourse as "the two-backed beast" ("Every time I see the boy in bed, I think of the two-backed beast that led to his making") while in *Blow-Up* Sarah Miles in the nude and part-ner copulated very matter-of-factly for the camera.

The sexual revolution had come. Sex was a giveaway, not a

dare. Nudity was honesty, while cleavage—the separation but not the breasts—was meretricious. When the script of *Reflections in a Golden Eye* called for a nude scene, Taylor refused to play it. The flesh that appears on the screen—rear view of a nude ascending a staircase—belongs to an Italian stand-in.

Nobody who worked with them underestimates the Burtons' personal contribution to their own decline. In the late sixties, they were superpowers and their power worked against them, chiefly by giving them the right to approve every detail of a picture: the script, the director, the producer, the costumes, lighting, still photographs and, most important, location.

Elizabeth Taylor could insist on being decked out by her personal troupe of body servants in every picture. As a result, she fell more than ever into playing against herself—the real-life Liz against some screen character with a forgettable name like Laura or Leonora. Liz won every time. You can see what sabotaged the picture when the credits roll up at the end: "Hairstyles for Miss Taylor . . . Alexandre de Paris," "Miss Taylor's Gowns . . . Tiziani of Rome." In *Reflections*, she appears at her Georgia army wife's party in a getup that would make her look overdressed at Princess Grace's Red Cross gala at Monte Carlo.

Dominated as they were by the need to minimize their income tax, the Burtons chose the locations for their films less by what was best for the picture than by what was best for their tax returns. *Reflections in a Golden Eye* was shot in Rome. Someone doing a postmortem on the flop said acidly, "You do not make pictures about the Deep South in Rome." Not unless your star demands it, that is. Taylor's need to work abroad also cut her off from her Hollywood roots, and put her out of step with the younger American stars. Gradually, as American tax became more lenient on the upper brackets, the new generation of movie stars stayed at home and many became politically involved.

As the Burtons became wealthier, they became more monar-

chical, and ostentatious. Their entourage thickened. People
wanting to see them on the set had to wear badges and pass
security guards. Sometimes when they got to London or L.A.
their friends could not even reach them on the telephone,
while they would sit in their hotel rooms wondering why various people hadn't called. The entourage flattered them while
overprotecting them. You can see a photograph of the Court of
the Burtons. Taylor, maternal and full-busted, holding a glass,
beams proudly at Burton, who is surrounded by people, laughing wildly. Most of them are on his payroll. The Burtons
became as confined as Nixon was in the White House. They
couldn't shop; goods were brought in. If they went out, they
didn't carry money. Somebody else paid. They ate a lot of room
service meals. Often they would vary their diet by ordering
carry-out food from another continent. (When in Rome, Taylor
tends to crave chili con carne from Chasen's in Los Angeles.
When in Leningrad, she asks for pork sausages from the Dorchester or Fortnum and Mason's in London.) A new element
began to enter stories about them: fear of the Burtons. Someone who worked on *Reflections* in Rome described the mixed
feelings that they aroused:

"I liked Elizabeth enormously. But I'm used to movie stars.
That helped. Some are frightened of them. The Burtons didn't
like people who cringed. If you were timid and afraid of them,
they would snap at you. She sent Ray Stark [producer of the
film] off to buy her a bracelet she wanted. 'Did you hear what I
just asked him for?' she said, laughing. She *is* an incredibly
spoiled lady, but she's always been indulged since she was
about ten and so she gets away with what she can. He's not easy
either. Their entourage was not very pleasant, the sort of male
secretaries they have. But there are less of them than there
were with Marilyn Monroe. The difference between Marilyn
and Elizabeth is that Elizabeth is not an idiot. Elizabeth can
comb her hair and make her children's breakfast, and the
Burtons were infinitely more generous and pay well. They did a
lot of good things that people don't know about. But she's quite

neurotic about jewelry. Jewels are her security blanket. Every time she's depressed, she calls the jewelers."

Taylor has said, "The jewelry I have has been given to me. I don't buy jewelry for myself." That is one of the half truths that mark her public statements. She may not buy them, but she tells other people what to buy for her. There is a movie custom of giving presents when a film is completed and Taylor's ability to communicate what end-of-film gift she would like is legendary. As soon as *Taming of the Shrew* got under way, she laughingly instructed Franco Zeffirelli about "a little shop in the Via Condotti . . ." Bulgari's, in other words. Zeffirelli demurred, but eventually came back with a gold bracelet that had belonged to Napoleon's sister. Most others complied, but not Jack Warner of Warner Brothers. According to Sheilah Graham, when told that Taylor wanted an $80,000 ruby brooch for *Virginia Woolf*, Warner said, "I'm paying her a million dollars plus ten percent of the gross. Let her buy her own jewelry." Another who resisted was Taylor's companion during 1974-75, Henry Wynberg, the car dealer from Los Angeles. When they were in London during a break from filming *The Blue Bird* in Russia, while waiting for the elevator at the Dorchester, Taylor spotted a jeweled bluebird that had somehow found its way into the display case. "Oh, Henry, buy it for me!" she was heard to say. It cost £1,100 (then about $2,500). "Ask George Cukor," Wynberg said. "Let him buy it for you." Cukor was directing *The Blue Bird*. A few days later Twentieth Century-Fox, the American producers of the movie, rang to confirm the purchase.

If the Burtons had realized they were slipping, they might not have made *Doctor Faustus*. Bad reviews are bad reviews. But because of the time lag between the making of a film and its release, the Burtons carried on like potentates for at least three more movies before the truth hit the screen. *Faustus* was finished before *The Comedians* was out. True, Burton did it as an act of charity. But he did not intend it to lose money, nor did

Columbia Pictures, which handled distribution. And he was not prepared for his film to be ridiculed as evidence of his overweening vanity.

Everybody thinks of Richard Burton as an Oxford man. Yet he is an Oxford man the way Gatsby was an Oxford man. Burton attended the university for six months in 1944 as an air force cadet enrolled in the wartime short course. He was there long enough to do some acting and for Nevill Coghill, professor of English at Merton College, to decide that Richard Burton was one of the two geniuses he had taught in his life. (The other: W. H. Auden). Under Coghill, Burton did his first Shakespeare—Angelo in *Measure for Measure*. The greater an actor he became, the more his loyalty to Oxford increased. The trouble is that, as a born actor, he overdoes it. Burton continues to portray himself as an academic *manqué*—Faust, in other words, the scholar who sold his soul to the devil. (He never makes it clear whether the devil is the movies or Elizabeth Taylor.)

A director who is a nonadmirer of Burton says, "Richard thinks his tragedy is that he's Doctor Faustus. His tragedy is that he knows he's not." In a reflective moment, Burton himself acknowledged that academia might not have suited him. "If I had become a don in the first place," he told David Lewin, "there would have been trouble. I am very sexually attractive and I certainly would have gone to bed with the wives of all the other professors, so in the end I would have been expelled."

The dream of being a don's wife appealed to Taylor. She and Burton occasionally talked of buying a house in Oxfordshire. He could teach at Oxford while she bred horses. She even offered to teach a seminar herself, in Tennessee Williams.

In 1965, the Burtons personally appeared with the Oxford University Dramatic Society (OUDS), in a performance of *Doctor Faustus*. They took a terrible panning from the critics. As Faustus, Burton was underrehearsed and the London *Times* called his performance "almost as embarrassing as those of the undergraduate actors." Taylor had a walk-on role as Helen of

Troy. Undaunted, Burton decided to make a movie of the play, with the undergraduates as supporting cast, and to send it out for international distribution.

For this project, Burton put on the triple crown: producer, director, and actor. Together he and Coghill improved on Christopher Marlowe's text, by inserting a juicy speech from *Tamburlaine* and a film clip from Olivier's *Henry V*. They also expanded Taylor's part, giving her repeated entrances, each time coated with a different shade of body paint. They flew the OUDS cast to Rome for the filming and themselves worked for actors' minimum salaries. The whole thing cost Burton an estimated million dollars out of his own pocket and even Alexandre de Paris was caught up in the spirit of the thing. ("Miss Taylor's wigs donated by . . .")

Was it, as playwright Wolf Mankowitz maintained in a letter to *The Guardian*, "the largest individual act of philanthropy made toward the amateur or professional theater in this country?" Or was it an ego trip that only a superstar could afford?

Time had no doubt. "Lots of grads bring their wives back to the old school and ham it up for movies—but this is ridiculous. Richard Burton is charging admission." For Taylor, *Time* capped twenty years of insult: "When she welcomes Burton to an eternity of damnation, her eyeballs and teeth are dripping pink in what seems to be a hellish combination of conjunctivitis and trench mouth." The public agreed. *Doctor Faustus* grossed only $610,000, of which only $110,000 came from the United States and Canada.

In London, the press was just as scathing. *The Times* described Burton and Taylor traveling together down to hell "on a moving staircase—a journey enlivened by writhing, intertwined torsos at whom Mr. Burton furtively glances as if they were corset advertisements on the London Underground." If he sounded flippant, the critic said, "it is only because its combination of self-indulgence and visual vulgarity provokes such a response."

And only because the critic had not seen *Boom!* Everything

about the Burtons' next film, from its title to its costumes, was so much a commentary on them and their lifestyle that you can only interpret it as a sign of their determination to destroy themselves through caricature.

Taylor consented to play, believe it or not, an aging hypochondriacal, diamond-studded American millionairess exiled in Europe, who has had five husbands. And one lover. Burton plays the Angel of Death whose vocation in life is to help just such women shuffle off, or to borrow the language of Tennessee Williams whose script it was, "to pass into eternal night." Taylor's screen name is Flora Goforth and the part was originally played on Broadway, where the play bore its original title, *The Milk Train Doesn't Stop Here Anymore*, by an actress whom she was beginning vocally to resemble: Tallulah Bankhead.

In Joseph Losey, Taylor had perhaps the most cerebral director of her career. Losey, an American exile in Britain since the Hollywood witch-hunt, is called an *auteur* by those who like their cinema heavy, and pretentious by those who do not. An *auteur* is a director who controls every element of a film as a novelist controls his book. When they began *Boom!* Losey might have posed himself the question: Does not the screen presence of a mind-blowing superstar like Elizabeth Taylor automatically sabotage the *auteur*'s approach?

Still, Losey and Taylor might have made a good combination. In his films, people eat. Losey is fascinated by food and the ceremony of the table, especially English tables. The tensest moments in *The Go Between* and *Accident*, two of his best films, come as people munch through kippers and toast or cold ham and salad. Unhappily, everything in *Boom!* is bizarre, so while there is a lot of talk about food, nobody gets to eat any. In one scene, Taylor, the decadent hostess, entertains Noël Coward to dinner at a sumptuous moonlit table set outdoors on the terrace of her clifftop villa overlooking the Mediterranean. (Coward's screen name is the Witch of Capri, no help to him or the picture.) As he seats himself expectantly, a servant uncovers a dish containing a fish so revolting (a coelacanth?) that he has to leave the table. And poor Burton. Costumed grotesquely in a Kabuki robe with a sword thrusting from below the belt, he has to deliver the passionate utterance: "I'm starving and all you've offered me in two days is black coffee!"

There is nothing for the audience either. Taylor is so fat that the white loose gowns by Tiziani look like nightdresses from the Outsize Shop. Her spiky jeweled wig by Alexandre merely confirms her as Medusa. And Tennessee Williams gave Taylor the plummiest double entendres of her long screen life: "My bedroom is full of treasures, including myself." "If you have a world-famous figure, why not show it off?" (Another nude scene refused here.) The double meanings reach a climax when Taylor-Goforth has closed her eyes for the last time and Burton-Death removes an enormous square diamond (jewels by Bulgari of Rome) from her finger. He holds it aloft and dramatically drops it (but it's only a movie) into the pounding sea far below.

The resulting crash was so loud that the Burtons decided not to make any more movies together for a while. They had an estimated million each out of *Boom!* John Heyman's World Film Services and Universal Films who made the film bore the financial disappointment. Before it was released an excited Universal executive had exclaimed: "We've got *Virginia Woolf* in color!" Afterward, it was easy to see that the Burtons were a mistake. She was too beauteous, said Tennessee Williams, and too young, while Burton was too old. Jay Kanter of Universal admitted that "when the Burtons were involved, a lot of my judgment was colored by the magnitude of the star she was considered to be."

By now the critics were aiming straight for the Burtons as Burtons. The Chicago *Sun-Times* was politer than many: it called *Boom!* a film for voyeurs. "Elizabeth Taylor and Richard Burton remain the nearest thing we have in the movies to a reigning royal family no matter how uneven their acting abilities. We know so much about them—or think we do—that there is a gruesome satisfaction at the sight of them bogged down in Tennessee Williams's belabored script, especially since its broad lines seem to resemble the Burton and Taylor private lives." *Life* did not attempt restraint.

> When people reach a certain status in showbiz—have plenty of "clout" as they like to say—a kind of arrogance seems to set in. They get to thinking, perhaps unconsciously, that they can dare us to reject anything they feel like shoveling out. The Burtons are peculiarly afflicted with this malaise. . . . Suitably stimulated, as they were apparently by *Virginia Woolf*, the Burtons can still be effective. But there is a tired, slack quality in most of their work that is, by now, a form of insult. They don't so much act as deign to appear before us and there is neither discipline nor dignity in what they do. She is fat and will do nothing about her most glaring defect, an unpleasant voice which she cannot adequately control. He, conversely, acts with nothing but his voice, rolling out his lines with much elegance but with no feeling at all. . . . Perhaps the Burtons are doing the very best they can, laden as they are by their celebrity. . . . But if they are not cynics, overestimating their charisma and underestimating our intelligence, then they are guilty of a lack of aesthetic and self-awareness that is just as disheartening.

As all that came out, Universal and World Film Services found themselves with another completed Taylor-Losey movie awaiting release.

One good thing about *Secret Ceremony* is the way Losey lets Taylor eat. She plays a fat middle-aged tart who is adopted as a mother substitute by a psychotic orphaned heiress, Mia Farrow. With the camera watching every mouthful, Taylor consumes an English breakfast of sausage, bacon, and eggs. When she's finished, she emits a belch like a pistol shot.

The orphan takes her new mother home to the kind of baroque London house (8 Addison Road) that Losey loves; he says they remind him of the mansions of his Mississippi childhood. This one has a splendid upstairs-downstairs kitchen with an enormous scrubbed-top table, carefully cluttered with stale toast and cheese. Losey skillfully weaves an eery mood of psychosis and possible lesbianism as the older woman joins the younger in her fantasy—and at one point, her circular bath. (But they are only nude from the armpits upward.) Once again Taylor, by her mere presence, shatters the mood. When I saw *Secret Ceremony*, the audience laughed when she took off her coat.

"Ooh, isn't she fat!" said the girl next to me as an enormous fat-lady expanse of black satin was revealed. Unfortunate for the plot too is that the orphaned girl's late mother had left behind closets full of caftans by Marc Bohan of the House of Dior. Soon, lo and behold, Taylor is eating in expensive restaurants, exotically gowned, with her hair in the distinctive coils, cascades, and enameled butterflies of Alexandre de Paris. Farrow, on the other hand, never suggests her off-screen self from the first moment she appears, with dark hair and mad eyes, crying "Mummie" in a spooky little voice.

Posters for the film showed the two ladies in their tub—a brave attempt to suggest a trendy bisexuality, but audiences did not respond. By the time the film was out, Taylor had slid in box-office rank from third in 1966 to sixth in 1967 to tenth in 1968. She then slid off, never again—so far—to reappear.

If too much power of choice was part of the Burtons' problem, so too much to choose from was another. Everybody wanted them in a movie. Wherever they went, they were besieged by offers and by advisers, experts, and friends telling them what they ought to do. Hugh French, who guided much of the choosing during those seven-figure contracts, described the decision-making process that led to Taylor's next film, *The Only Game in Town*.

"I was staying at the Beverly Hills Hotel with Richard and Elizabeth and I went with them to a party given by Frank Sinatra. Frank was at that time married to Mia Farrow. The next morning Frank was on the phone. 'What's the name of that dog you bought for Elizabeth last Christmas? I want to give Mia one.' I tried and tried but I couldn't think of the name of it. But something started working in my head. Frank and Elizabeth. Elizabeth and Frank. Jesus! What a combination! I called Dickie Zanuck, who was running Fox at the time and said, 'I've got a hell of an idea. Frank and Elizabeth! What have you bought lately that they could do together?' I went over and we went through the scripts and I picked out *Only Game in Town*. I read it to Elizabeth. 'Stop it, you're making me cry,' she said."

That meant she liked it. She liked it also when George Stevens, old and forgiven after *Giant*, was brought in as director. She also liked her fee; her highest ever: a million and a quarter dollars. Why did she think Fox was willing to pay so much? "They must be out of their tiny Chinese minds," she replied amiably.

Better still, Hugh French garnered from Fox equal pay for Burton. He was to make *Staircase* with Rex Harrison, a play about two aging English homosexuals, for $1.25 million. The fact that the Burton magic was fading was not at all apparent. He had just made *Where Eagles Dare* for MGM, the biggest money-maker of 1969. Besides, Fox was still stuck in the belief that very big, very expensive pictures were the way to make money.

Ungrudgingly, therefore, Fox agreed to the Burtons' contracts, including a rumored stipulation that they not work more than forty-five minutes apart by any form of transport. That bit of sentiment, plus the Burtons' preference for the French tax climate, determined that both pictures be made in Paris. In other words, to get the Burtons, Fox had to build a fake Las Vegas and a fake London at two studios in the French capital.

If one thing is predictable about moviemaking it is that the best-laid plans will go awry. In the summer of 1969, Taylor had a nagging abdominal pain. Another major operation. After it was over, Dick Hanley announced a "partial hysterectomy"— just the womb not the ovaries. But the start of *Only Game in Town* was delayed and Frank Sinatra pulled out. In his place went Warren Beatty. Warren and Elizabeth, Elizabeth and Warren. Jesus! What a combination. He looked young enough to be her brother and far too fresh and sassy to be depressed by a few gambling losses.

Only Game in Town turned out to be a dull and embarrassing picture, implausible as a love story and as a social commentary on the human wrecks of Las Vegas. George Stevens did not have much American landscape to inspire him (although some exterior shots were done in Nevada). Taylor tried hard. She teeters convincingly like a divorcée behind a supermarket shopping cart but is dressed disastrously in ponchos and stretch pants. *Playboy* found her hopeless, looking like a well-heeled suburban matron having a fling at community theatricals. And Liz is still there. In one scene, Fran Walker, the heroine, has to react to the sight of a diamond ring in a jeweler's box. "Don't tell me how many carats? Ten?" She feigns awe and the plot goes out the window as you snicker and think, "Liz Taylor, if anybody, should know."

Only Game lost nearly $8 million. *Staircase* lost $5.8 million. Shades of 1962-63. Twentieth Century-Fox had twenty-four losers in 1970 and the shareholders attacked the Zanuck management. Elizabeth Taylor was frowned upon by far worse than the Vatican; *Variety* observed that she had had a "three-flop year." "There was wonderment," it said, among Fox shareholders about the cost of the Burtons' pictures. "But husband and wife enjoyed togetherness."

Was the star system dead, killed by the Burtons? It looked possible. Every studio's dream was to make an *Easy Rider*, a low-budget picture that made a fortune. The big names and the big money did return, however, but only for others. For two years after *Only Game*, Elizabeth Taylor did not appear in a motion picture. Since then she has tended to work for expenses, plus a percentage of the profits, which, often as not, have failed to appear. With *Anne of a Thousand Days* in which he played Henry VIII, Burton had one more resounding success, and another Academy Award nomination. But then he too hit the skids, with *Hammersmith Is Out* (with Taylor), *The Assassination of Trotsky*, and *The Loves of Bluebeard*.

Richard Burton, said *Time*, "once an actor now performs mainly as a buffoon." The Burton boom was over.

But they were rich. Together they made about $88 million. By the time of their divorce their joint holdings were estimated at $23 million. Their stake in Welsh commercial television (about which more later), probably the least of their investments, was worth about $500,000 in 1974. They invested in a Paris fashion boutique and in property in Mexico, Ireland, and the Virgin Islands, as well as in London and in Switzerland. They had an undisclosed amount in Swiss banks and a valuable collection of fine art (Taylor bought a Monet for $130,000 in 1968) as well as the appurtenances of stardom—a yacht, a plane, and the much-publicized jewels. Oddly, after *Taming of the Shrew*, little of their investment seems to have been plowed into motion pictures. ("What I don't like about the Burtons," said somebody from the industry, "is that they take the money and run.") In 1967 *The New York Times* reported that the Burtons had set up a company called Taybur Productions, to produce international films starring the Burtons. But it never made any films. Perhaps their decline discouraged them, or perhaps Taybur was never intended to be more than a holding company for their other financial interests.

Of the two, Burton enjoyed high finance more. Interviewers who came to talk about the usual movie star matters—what he ate for breakfast and what he gave his wife—found him obsessed with his money. He liked to boast, for example, about how much his Virgin Island land had appreciated.

Taylor was far less interested in money for its own sake. She is not the type of rich woman who calls up her brokers every morning. Her basic preoccupations are love and her family. But she adored having, at last, the power to buy what she wanted and to do what she wanted. Hugh French said, "I would explain the deals in her contracts to her and she was always more excited about what expenses she was going to get than the actual salary."

Diamonds were the investment for which the Burtons were and probably will remain best known. The big jewels hit the news almost exactly in step with their box-office decline, and may have contributed to it. First Burton bought his wife the Krupp diamond, a 33.19-carat square-cut diamond for $305,000. Next he bought not a diamond but a pearl: La Peregrina, which King Philip of Spain gave to Mary Tudor in 1554, which cost him $37,000. Then came the inch-thick Cartier Burton diamond priced at the sum associated with Taylor's name, one million dollars.

It was all too much for many people, including the editorial writers of *The New York Times*. (Question: How many women have been criticized by both the *Times* and the Vatican?) The *Times* gave the Burtons a whole editorial:

The peasants have been lining up outside Cartier's this week to gawk at a diamond as big as the Ritz that costs well over a million dollars. It is destined to hang around the neck of Mrs. Richard Burton. As somebody said, it would have been nice to wear in the tumbril on the way to the guillotine.

Actually, the inch-long, inch-thick Cartier diamond is a smart buy because it goes with everything. It won't clash with the smaller Krupp diamond already given by Mr. Burton as a modest gift to his wife. It won't seem out of place on the yacht parked in the Bahamas or the Mediterranean where the Beautiful People spend much time, not to mention money, impressing each other.

In this Age of Vulgarity marked by such minor matters as war and poverty, it gets harder every day to scale the heights of true vulgarity. But given some loose millions, it can be done—and worse, admired.

Taylor's friends are uneasy on the subject of the diamonds. Clearly they've worried about them too. "Why shouldn't Richard and Elizabeth do what they want with their money?" they retort. "They've earned it!" Then they add: "Anyway, the diamonds are an investment."

Even the *Times* could not quarrel with that. In the sixties, as prices rose and currencies wobbled, the rich everywhere sought to protect their fortunes by investing in durables whose price was also rising rapidly. The Cartier diamond alone has increased in value to $2.5 million since Burton bought it.

But to the Burtons, the diamonds represented much more than a hedge against inflation. Burton often spoke of the pleasure he got from being the miner's son buying the world's biggest diamonds. But for Taylor I think they meant even more.

The Krupp, a great brute of a stone that she used for everyday wear, ensured that just as through her entire life, all eyes instantly and instinctively turned to her when she entered a room, although people now looked at her hand as soon as they recognized her face. What's more, the Krupp looked like a talisman, a relic of evil to ward off evil. Taylor knew where it came from—the hand of the wife of the German munitions maker. "I think it is nice that a little Jewish girl has it now," she has said. Above all, the ring was a badge of office, the symbol of the biggest goddamned movie star in the whole world. Cardinals let people kiss their ring. Taylor let people try hers on.

In 1968 after she received the ring, she and Burton, along with Noël Coward, the Queen Mother, and Princess Margaret went down to Kent to attend the wedding of Sheran Cazalet to Simon Hornby. It was the society wedding of the year. To get to the church the guests had to walk up a long path across a green up to the church door, as the villagers crowded around to gawk at the greats. As Taylor and Burton headed up the path, Lady d'Avigdor-Goldsmid, another guest, recalls, "Elizabeth removed her glove and held her hand with that enormous rock against her throat. They all knew she had it because they'd all read about it in the papers. The crowd cheered. They just loved it. *Of course*, it was vulgar. *You* wouldn't have done it. *I* wouldn't have done it. She is *vulgar*, tremendously. But she's a *star*, and it was just right."

Taylor herself accepts the charge. She will sit in an armchair, wagging her Krupp. "I know I'm vulgar," she says, "but would you have me any other way?" "And, of course, we wouldn't," say her friends.

As their financial interests grew, their entourage was swelled by processions of lawyers and accountants pressing for decisions, holding up papers to be signed. Yet the Burtons did not act like tycoons or even politicians. Burton especially retains a reputation for not answering letters.

"You have no idea of the amount of mail they get," a friend said during the late Burton era. "Sacks and sacks of it. It comes to any hotel where they're staying and half the time they don't even open it—with checks inside and everything. Sure, they make lots of money. He's good at it, better than her, but the waste is fantastic. They have all these houses and they invest in crazy things on the stock market. They keep suites at hotels in cities they don't even visit during a year. And the way they pick their staff . . . !"

Burton himself said at the time that their living expenses were a million dollars a year and "don't forget, we've got a staff of thirty to support."

For people who made their money through publicity, the Burtons were curiously inept in their relations with the press. Nevill Coghill said they had "the worst newspaper-image (deliberately and wickedly fostered) of any famous actors in the world." Burton instructed Taylor, who needed no reminding, to be extremely suspicious of journalists. Then he would himself talk for hours whenever he found one congenial, always conscious that the interviewer would rather be talking to her than to him. Sometimes their naïveté was astonishing. In 1971 they sold *Look* some photographs of themselves necking on a Pacific beach, with Taylor wearing a mink coat costing $120,000 over her bikini. *Look* did not put nice words under the picture. It called Taylor "the big getter . . . a fading movie queen who has much, and wants more." The Burtons were hurt and so was John Springer.

Taylor hates interviews. (While he lived, it was probably easier to get to see Mao Tse-tung.) She had too many when she was young. She says there is nothing left to say. The writers she has favored with good long chats have been ones she trusted: Liz Smith, Tommy Thompson, Rex Reed, and David Wigg. It is trust that has had to be built up over the years, in the knowledge that it could all be blown in an instant by the wrong questions or quote. If compelled by advisers, she will see others, usually with a resigned shrug. Reporters who meet her for the first time, having passed the John Springer barrier, do not know what reception they might get, maybe warm, maybe ice cold. Humility is advisable. Someone explained, "You do *not* interview Liz Taylor as if you were bigger than Liz Taylor."

The Burtons' press relations had their peak low in the late sixties by which time, as a couple, they had developed a monumental capacity for giving offense. The special yacht anchored in the Thames in London that they rented just for their dogs did not win them many friends, although there was a perfectly good explanation: the dogs couldn't join them at the Dorchester because of the British quarantine regulations. And then came that fortieth-birthday party in Budapest.

Elizabeth Taylor turning forty might have made the papers in its own right. But the Burtons decided to give a party, inviting some of the world's flashiest names to join them for four days in the Hungarian capital. Then, when the newsmen started to arrive, they were aghast. It was a *private* party.

Picture the scene. The Burtons ensconced in the Duma Hotel in Budapest, with Princess Grace, Ringo Starr, Raquel Welch, and Stephen Spender, to name but a few, at their side. Along come seventy journalists from the corners of the world, pockets full of expense-account money, each with an inescapable assignment to file at least one story a day. Any county sheriff knows how to manipulate such a situation. Not the Burtons. They told the press to stay in the lobby. Most certainly, Elizabeth Taylor was not going to appear, not even to be photographed—except by one Spanish magazine photographer she decided to let into the party.

Burton, the workingman's friend, did let himself be seen at a press conference. He came with a nugget of news: He was giving his wife a new diamond, one that the Mogul Emperor Shah Jehan had given his wife in 1621 before she died, when he gave her the Taj Mahal. He also delivered a good quote: "I set out to try to buy the Taj Mahal, but it was a little difficult to transport to Switzerland." And he had something for the photographers: He draped the jewel over his forehead. That was all.

They got the press they deserved. Someone found out that Alan Williams, son of Emlyn Williams, had confronted Taylor. "Have any Hungarians been invited?" he demanded. "What does the Hungarian revolution mean to you?" and she burst into tears before Nevill Coghill intervened. Alan Williams's description of Taylor in her festive dress also got out: "a beautiful doughnut covered in diamonds and paint." Others wrote about lavish extravagance.

The spectacle inspired the Hungarian writer Georges Mikes to assert that the Burtons richly deserved the Stalin prize for socialism. "The Burton party must have gained more adherents to the creed in a week than the Communist party in a quarter of a century," he wrote to the London *Times*.

It all looked very different from the inside. To Francis Warner, the Budapest weekend was a great act of generosity. The Burtons knew how to enjoy their money. "They were not hoarding it all for themselves. They gathered their friends around them. Who wouldn't if he could?" Another guest remembers it as "a quiet family party. Not many famous, lots of Jenkinses, teachers, and ex-army buddies of Burton's. No ostentation, but very thoughtfully organized. They had it in Budapest because Burton was filming there at the time and they were living at the hotel. Apart from the relatives, everybody bought their own tickets. Elizabeth was quiet. She didn't dance much. She wore a kind of billowing smock and looked fat, with a sweet joyful face. Burton circulated more, talking to people. Their personal staff was overprotective, gave them bad

advice. There was no need to keep the press out. It just got their
backs up."

Belatedly the Burtons realized how the party looked to the
Western world: a capitalist spit in the eye of threadbare communism. (The Hungarians, in fact, loved it; it was just how they
liked to see things done.) As criticism for their extravagance
rose, Burton said he would match the cost of the party with a
gift to UNICEF and the cost of the diamond with a contribution
to another charity. Later a check for $45,000 went to UNICEF.
The other gift, if made, did not get the same publicity.

Anybody who knew the Burtons speaks of their almost reck-
less generosity. An actor abandoned his child and the Burtons,
unbeknown to the child, paid for its education. Another
youngster had ballet lessons thanks to an anonymous sponsor.
Another got an eye operation. Burton gave a hefty quarter of a
million dollars toward the Oxford Samuel Beckett Theater run
by Francis Warner. Together the Burtons paid for the building
of a small rehearsal theater for the Oxford dramatic society;
they saved *Isis*, the Oxford magazine, with a £1,000 donation.
They showered their staff with Rolls-Royces, and Hermès
handbags and pensions and have each looked after very large
families for a very long time. Taylor has made a lot of appearances for Israel, as well as buying bonds. *Life* said in 1972 that
they gave a million dollars a year to charity, most of it
anonymously.

Yet some of their publicized acts of charity are difficult to
track down. If the Burtons had a passion for anonymous giving,
it is curious how unsecret they could be in advance of the gift.
In 1966, when Montgomery Clift died, Elizabeth Taylor was
reported as announcing that she was going to set up a special
research foundation into coronary disease in Clift's name. She
was going to endow it with one million dollars and have it run,
so the papers said, under the auspices of the American Heart
Association. (To say that Clift died of heart disease might seem

like saying that James Dean was the victim of poor road conditions, but never mind.)

The American Heart Association is still waiting to hear from her. When it inquired whether there was any substance to the report of her million-dollar gift, the AHA received this reply:

> The form of such memorial and the organization through which it will be administered has not as yet been determined. Mrs. Burton's concern is not with any tribute to her or any acknowledgment on her part but rather the application of a sum of money to research in the area of cardiovascular disorders. The contributions that she will make may well be anonymous.

A recent biography of Taylor, listing "charities and acts of kindness" reported the Clift Foundation as a fact (which it may be, somewhere). It went on to say that "Britain's National Society for Mentally Handicapped Children is dear to her heart. All the profits on her Harlech TV stock go to this society." The society was surprised to hear that. In 1960 a bingo club working on behalf of the society presented it with a check for £100,000. "In view of the size of this check, it was felt that a distinguished member of the showbiz world should be invited to present the check to us at a publicity party. This Miss Taylor kindly agreed to do . . . and that was the full extent of her involvement with us. We have no knowledge at all of 'profits from Harlech TV stock.' This must clearly be for another charity."

In 1964 Richard Burton announced that he would set up a Richard Burton Hemophilia Fund to aid research. Burton who suffers from a mild form of the disease ("I have been a bleeder all my life") announced at a press conference that "I want to do—and my wife wants to do—all we can to help." She was to be chairman of the fund. They did help. The National Hemophilia Foundation is very grateful to them. But research funds have been launched with larger financial propulsion by those whose names they bear. The Burtons gave from $5,000 to $10,000 apiece and made available to the foundation the receipts from the charity benefit premieres of *Who's Afraid of Virginia Woolf?* in Los Angeles and also in New York with half of the latter proceeds shared with Burton's adopted father's American Musical and Dramatic Academy.

In 1970, during the outcry over the extravagance of the million-dollar Cartier diamond, there was another news item. Elizabeth Taylor, it said, announced through a spokesman that she would either choose a charity or form a special foundation to which she would donate the cost of that diamond.

Then there was the gift to Botswana. When they remarried in the remote African country in 1975, Burton announced that he had given Taylor a new million-dollar diamond, a pink one. But she declined it. "Liz to Trade in Ring for Botswana Hospital," said the headlines. "After long discussion," she said, "we both decided that we would like to build a hospital-clinic in Kasane, Botswana, on the border of the Chobe Game Reserve. They need one badly and I certainly don't need another ring."

The gift was complicated by the fact that the new marriage split up almost immediately. And also that hospitals cost more than one million dollars. I tried to find out about the hospital. I rang up Burton's accountant in London. (Did I detect a groan?) "Did the papers say that?" he said. "I haven't heard about it." I tried the Botswana High Commission. They had read the story in the papers but knew no more about it. "Try Botswana's Commission of Health." No answer. From Aaron Frosch, there was the reply, "I am informed that Ms. Taylor is active in raising funds for a hospital(s) in Botswana." Later the press reported that Taylor had appeared before the Senate Foreign Relations Committee seeking funds for the project, and that she had hired a professional fund-raiser to help.

After making further inquiries, I received the following letter from the Ministry of Health in Gabarone:

9th June 1977

Dear Madame,

With reference to your letter to the Botswana High Commissioner in London, we are able to provide you with the following information.

The assistance for health in Botswana which Ms. Taylor's representatives initially discussed with this Ministry in October, 1975, has not yet been forthcoming. We were informed in April of this year that Ms. Taylor had changed her mind and could not consider funding a hospital at Kasane. We had asked for assistance to expand the present health centre at Kasane at a cost of roughly P310.000 [$374,000]. This has also been turned down.

Ms. Taylor has instead offered the Government about $50,000 to build two health clinics. The Government has accepted this offer but we are not aware when (or if) the funds will actually be forthcoming.

We hope that this has sufficiently clarified the situation for you so that an accurate account of Ms. Taylor's assistance can be rendered.

Yours sincerely,
M. Kam
for/PERMANENT SECRETARY

When in 1976 Burton went on to marry Susan Hunt, the story went out that Taylor generously had given her ex-husband her share of their yacht, *Kalizma*. It didn't mention that the Burtons had been trying to sell it for years, and couldn't even when the price was cut in half. In these days, diesel-fueled yachts are not very tempting. One possible purchaser said he would be interested in the *Kalizma* only if it were wood-burning; another only if Elizabeth Taylor were on board.

Obviously Taylor and Burton, like all wealthy people, are prey to false reports, hangers-on, and people who use their names without asking them. There was a mix-up in South Wales when the mistaken impression was given by one of Burton's brothers that Burton would pay half the cost of a holiday center for the disabled at Porthcawl. And all who know them know that

Elizabeth Taylor and Richard Burton are impulsive, warm, sympathetic individuals, who have given away a great amount of their money. They admired each other for their generosity. (Burton: "I think she's supported the entire Biafran war effort on her own.")

But as the true facts of their philanthropy cannot be known unless the now ex-Burtons choose to be less secret, one is left with the open question: did their gifts to charity amount to anything like what superstars who stay in the United States or Britain pay in less emotionally gratifying income tax?

Gifts to the Burtons were another matter. They tantalized people, like courtiers, to give them things to make them laugh, and what else could you give to the couple who had everything? It was a constant worry to their relatives and friends. Brook Williams hit upon the perfect present when Burton was trying to cut out drinking: a water divining kit. Norma Heyman scored once with sunglasses with windshield wipers. The big birthday was hard for all the guests: Norma Heyman gave her a framed copy of the announcement of her birth in the London *Times*, Francis Warner a first edition of Sir Walter Raleigh's *History of the World* and a sonnet written especially for her. Burton's relatives give him books ("Rich loves reading"). Victor Spinetti, the Welsh actor, gave Taylor a can of diamond polish. Hugh French once impulsively gave her a small simple ring. "You can give her anything, something in a box from Marks and Spencer," he said. "She goes mad. It's a lovely thing about her." Even journalists try. Liz Smith, who was admitted to the Burtons' suite after the premiere of *Doctor Faustus* in New York, went in bearing some Avis Rent-a-car buttons with "We Try Harder" written in Welsh ("Yndrechwn yn galetach") and two packages of Wick Fowler's 2-Alarm Chili Mix. Even I have given her something. I sent her a copy of a book I wrote and got a reply from a minion: "Mrs. Burton conveys her thanks for the book that you sent her and wishes you much luck with it. She would love to have a copy of the book you are busy preparing on her career when it is complete."

Two quasi-philanthropic gestures in the direction of Wales gave a glimpse of the Burtons operating as a business team. When Richard Burton agreed to appear in the film of Dylan Thomas's radio play *Under Milk Wood*, director Andrew Sinclair, the historian and novelist, was delighted. The famous opening lines: "To begin at the beginning" would go out in the richest Welsh speaking voice since Thomas's own. A friend of Burton says he cautioned Sinclair: "Watch out."

Under Milk Wood was supposed to be more than an art movie that would make money. It was to be a trend-setting partnership between private finance and government money. The British National Film Finance Corporation was to put up two thirds of the money and a London merchant bank, Hill Samuel, Ltd., offered to put up most of the rest—on the condition that the Burton deal went through. When it did, with not only Elizabeth Taylor but also their friend Peter O'Toole agreeing to appear, all three to draw only $24,000 each, Hill Samuel came in willingly. The Burtons' presence seemed to ensure that both sides would get their money back.

The film was made, with the British government's contribution of $480,000, and was shown as the opening entry in the 1971 Venice Film Festival. Andrew Sinclair was rapturous. "We came in under budget and on schedule for six hundred and eighty-four thousand dollars, with the three stars and all the actors working like worshipers for the dead Dylan," he said.

Yet the deal that had been struck saw to it that if anybody made money out of the dead Dylan it would be the Burtons and O'Toole ahead of the British taxpayers or the bank that carried the risk. The stars had agreed to work for small fees—on the condition that through their agents, Hugh French and Jules Buck, who were named executive producers, they held the rights to a major share of the profits, and to handle sales to television and overseas movie theaters as well. At that time a lucrative American television showing seemed virtually certain, and the stars' share of profits would more than compensate for their labors.

There were two other conditions. Elizabeth Taylor had to play Rosie Probert, the village prostitute, even though she did not look or sound Welsh, and the shooting schedule had to be adapted to fit what little time the Burtons could provide, five and a half days for him, two days for her.

When the first of her two days came, Taylor did not appear until just before lunch. She was accompanied by her personal photographer, Gianni Bozzachi, who according to an observer, "kept flinging himself to the ground to photograph her from below so that her double chins wouldn't show." She was also wearing full Cleopatra eye makeup. When it was suggested that this was inappropriate, she replied, "I always do my own makeup." The cameramen were dismayed to find that she did not look as young as she once had. They solved it with two ancient Hollywood tricks: filming her face through gauze, with a strip of cardboard held between the light and her chin to cast a shadow beneath it.

Reviewing the film, the critic Stanley Kaufman smelled the truth: "Cosmetized and fineried, she looks less like a small-town Welsh whore than like part of the deal that included Burton." Generally, the picture got fine notices in Venice and in New York. ("I have seen it three times! I shall see it three times more!" wrote Judith Crist.) Then it disappeared.

Did the Burtons milk *Under Milk Wood*? They might have if they had sold it to television, but they couldn't. The word had got around: the public was sick of the Burtons. Instead, none of the backers saw much money back, and the film to date has incurred a substantial loss for its investors.

The drama of Harlech Television took longer to play out.

In 1967 John Morgan was putting together an investment group that was trying to get hold of the franchise for commercial (that is, supported by advertisers) television in Wales. At that time all of the commercial TV franchises in Britain were coming up for renewal. The original franchises given the separate regional companies that together form Britain's advertising sponsored channel (the rival to the BBC) were aptly described by Roy Thomson, the newspaper magnate who held one, as "a license to print money." But there was a lot of discontent in Britain with the then tawdry content of commercial television. And the regulatory body, the Independent Television Authority, before handing out renewals, was openly looking for new contenders, new groups that might do more to tap the cultural roots of the various regions where the television stations operated.

Morgan took himself to Nice. Would Burton join his team? Burton was more than willing. How much did they need? Two million? Three million? And he was bubbling with ideas.

That was just the impetus the consortium needed. "Indeed," says Morgan, "no one would support my conception until Richard had expressed his generous interest." Subsequently, the only living man as strongly associated with Wales as is Richard Burton was enlisted: Lord Harlech, the former Sir David Ormsby-Gore, British ambassador to Washington during the Kennedy Administration. And soon the Harlech-Burton company, called Harlech Television, had won the Welsh franchise away from the existing holders.

Because the rules forbade any dominant investor, Burton's financial contribution to Harlech TV was limited to about £100,000 ($240,000), making him, along with the bandleader Geraldo, the largest individual shareholder. But there were no limits on his artistic contribution. All sat back and waited to see what it would be.

The Burtons did appear for the opening of Harlech TV. Sort of. There was a boozy train ride from London to Bristol in the west of England, where one of the Harlech studios was located. On the trip, Burton draped some of the guests with some of his wife's jewels, which were traveling with them in a small case.

Unfortunately for Harlech, its opening, like the Cazalet wedding, coincided with Taylor's acquisition of the Krupp diamond. In Bristol, the Burtons took refuge in two luxury trailers. Jack Pugsley, in charge of publicity, remembers the day with a shudder. "The whole of the nation's press was there, and they didn't care two hoots about Harlech Television. All they wanted were pictures of that diamond. But we couldn't get the Burtons out. Their language was appalling. I thought they were a couple of stinkers. Finally we had to send Lord Harlech in to persuade them to come out."

Out they came. Pugsley's reaction: "She was absolutely gorgeous. She was perhaps the most beautiful woman I had ever seen. Her face was absolutely Madonna-like. So photogenic I was flabbergasted."

The couple did appear for the opening telecast. And one of the first sights transmitted by Welsh television under its new folk-oriented management was that of Elizabeth Taylor's Krupp diamond.

As the years went by, the other glittering Welshies on Harlech TV's list appeared on the screen—Geraint Evans, the opera singer; Stanley Baker, the actor; Wynford Vaughan-Thomas, the writer and broadcaster—but not Burton. He did not attend board meetings, either, although he was a director of the company; he deputized his accountant, James Wishart. And pressure mounted from the ITA in London, because the authority itself was under fire. It had handed out a lot of new franchises and much of British commercial TV was the same dreary mixture as before.

The Burtons were extremely busy with film assignments, but he kept promising. In 1970, Burton announced: "We are definitely committing ourselves to making at least one film each a year. We are all [Stanley Baker too] very excited about it. No other regional television company could afford to make these films if it meant paying us our normal salaries. But I would work for nothing."

In 1971, a plan for a television film was finally made. "We

own so much of Harlech Television that we thought we should really do some work for them," said Burton. Taylor and Burton would star in a pair of television plays, written especially for them by the brilliant writer John Hopkins. They would tell the story of a divorce, one from the woman's point of view, the other from the man's. The Harlech studios at Bristol were cleared for five weeks for the stars' descent, although filming was to begin in Rome.

Divorce His, Divorce Hers was such agony for all concerned that nobody today mentions it without wincing. It was to be the final nail in the coffin of the Acting Burtons. It also was one of the chain of events that ended with Burton's being pushed off the board of Harlech TV.

Burton got to Rome first. He began rehearsing with the director Waris Hussein. Hussein, a Cambridge graduate whose work included *The Six Wives of Henry VIII* for BBC television and *The Millstone* with Sandy Dennis, was not part of the original team but was a replacement for John Frankenheimer, who dropped out. Taylor arrived late, straight from making *Night Watch* in London with Laurence Harvey, a picture that had run overtime because Harvey was ill with terminal cancer. Taylor ran out of tax time as a result, and could not work in Britain.

The whole project had to stay abroad. It was moved to film studios in Munich. At Bristol, the crew were not sorry. "The staff—you can quote me—were not happy about working with him," says George McWatters, Harlech's vice-chairman. "The younger people despised him."

By then *Divorce His, Divorce Hers* had become decidedly less Welsh. Although Harlech TV was investing about $72,000, John Heyman had found a bigger partner: ABC television in the United States. ABC's $1 million investment meant that the plays, already written, had to be altered to suit American tastes and commercial breaks.

Munich was a nightmare. The Burtons and Hussein did not get along. He appeared overawed by the Burtons. Taylor resisted rehearsing. Burton lost his temper. "Fuck you!" he bellowed at Hussein one day, and the director retreated to his dressing room and would not come out.

The Burtons did not look as if they were trying to save money for their television company. However, they were under greater strain than anybody realized at the time. Their marriage was breaking up. Burton was drinking heavily, and young actresses were vying for his attentions. Taylor was watching yet another old friend die. Laurence Harvey's illness had made her exceedingly morbid—so much so that when she visited him at his Hampstead house, she lay down beside him on the bed, saying, "I wish we could go together." (With his eyes, Harvey implored his doctor to take her out and her visits were finally banned. Privately the doctor later observed, "She struck me as very, very shallow—interested in only her own feelings and not anyone else's.")

Never had the Burtons looked so cut off from the real world. The photographer Zoë Dominic, sent by ABC to do four days of work to publicize the film, found when she got to Munich that a nervous PR man asked her to wait a whole day before being introduced to the stars. "Everyone was so frightened of the Burtons," she said. When she started taking pictures, Taylor's personal photographer threw a tantrum. It took negotiations with New York before Dominic could resume. "I came away with a profound sense of misery about them as people. When you have opted out of ordinary living, what is there: food, jewels? But her face was lovely, absolutely lovely. Otherwise, she was a small plump Jewish woman. Well, maybe she is just a convert but she looks Jewish."

By then Taylor's confusion between screen world and reality looked total. Playing the part of an American business executive's wife in Rome, drifting around in Edith Head nighties, she insisted on wearing her La Peregrina pearl. "*I* know what people come to see," she said, when advised against it.

A memorable portrait of the disintegrating Burtons was done for *Time* by Carrie Nye, Dick Cavett's wife, who was also in the

Divorce cast. "It became apparent that Mr. Burton did not do an awful lot of work after lunch," she wrote, while Mrs. Burton "did not generally arrive until about a quarter to three in the afternoon." Most of those who lunched with them were in their employ, she observed.

What was eaten, if anything, is lost to memory. What was imbibed will be permanently inscribed on my liver. And the talk was about who mixed what drink with what in what European capital, South American port or Balkan satellite. All this good fun would be punctuated by phone calls from the anguished director to inquire when, if ever, work could be resumed. Mr. Burton could generally be relied upon to knock off work early—usually with a magnificent display of temper, foot stamping, and a few exit lines delivered in finest St. Crispin's Day style. My favorite was, "I am old and gray and incredibly gifted!"

If there is one thing for a movie actor worse than failing at the box office, it is failing on television. Few investors want to put money into a film unless a hefty television sale seems likely, and it was "that television thing," as one big producer later described it, that really put the knife into the Burtons.

Divorce His, Divorce Hers was an utter disaster. When it was shown on ABC on two successive nights in February 1973, the audience ratings were very poor. And the critical abuse whistled: boring, sickening, tedious, hopeless. The *Village Voice* said, "Perhaps the Burtons really talk this way. . . . 'Beat me black and blue, do anything as long as you stay with me.' " It noticed "the vulgar medallion" between "her projectile-like tits" and also her "gross finger-ring." *Variety* watched it with all the joy of being present at an autopsy.

Five months later when the Burtons formally announced their separation, memory of the films had so faded that nobody even commented on their double meaning. The fiasco reportedly sent Burton into a deep depression and Waris Hussein's growing reputation took a temporary dip.

The Burtons were divorced in Berne, Switzerland, in June

1974. They divided their property equally, with Taylor keeping her jewelry and getting custody of their adopted daughter.

Richard Burton remained a director of Harlech TV until 1975. When from undisclosed motives he delivered himself of a fierce outburst against Winston Churchill after playing him in *Walk with Destiny* some members of the board of Harlech Television took great offense. Although they were reminded that there would have been no Harlech TV without Burton, they wanted his resignation. Lord Harlech was more embarassed by Burton's failure to attend board meetings. He had written repeatedly suggesting that Burton might show up, even briefly, but to no avail. Finally concluding that Burton was a liability to the company, Harlech wrote and asked for his resignation, and Burton obliged.

However, Burton and his ex-wife were not left empty-handed. They still had their shares. With about 120,000 each, they were still the largest individual shareholders in Harlech TV. And their work for their company had not exactly been performed for nothing. The Burtons' fee for *Divorce His, Divorce Hers* was half a million dollars. And Taylor had her end-of-film present. In Munich Waris Hussein had been instructed as to precisely which necklace in what Munich jeweler's shop Elizabeth Taylor would like. "I bought it," he shrugged. "It went on the bill."

If the Burtons had been as reticent as real royalty, they might have survived at the box office. "I have never over the past fifteen years made any comment about my private life," said Lord Snowdon, separating from Princess Margaret, "and I have no intention of doing so."

Compare the Burtons. Him: "Elizabeth has beautiful breasts. I don't like to see them trussed up." Or, "My wife says that if I'm not home in forty-five minutes I can have any woman in the world but her." Her: "Terrible fights we have. Sometimes they're in public and we hear whispers of 'that marriage won't last long.' But we both know that once we're cuddled up in bed it will all be forgotten."

The Burtons' remarriage in Botswana in October 1975 was accompanied by torrents of words, almost all of which were proved false within weeks of their printing.

Their reunification was virtually a diplomatic event. After their reconciliation was announced by John Springer in August 1975 Taylor and Burton flew to Israel. Israeli crowds mobbed them, but one Israeli diplomat sourly ventured that the whole trip was a publicity stunt to take advantage of the fact that Henry Kissinger, the American Secretary of State, and the world's press were there at the same time. If so, Kissinger didn't mind. He likes famous people and he gave the Burtons a party (Burton not drinking). Next the couple went to South Africa with Peter Lawford and Ringo Starr to attend a black tennis tournament. More mobs, to look at her. "It was like the second coming of Christ," says Peter Lawford. "They don't see movie stars down there every day, you know." And then north to Botswana. A friend of mine who works there for the Peace Corps was grateful. After the Burtons' visit, people no longer asked, "Where?" when he said where he worked.

In Botswana they remarried and for any who missed the news reports, Taylor's own story, written in Caitlin Thomassy prose, soon appeared in the *Ladies' Home Journal*, in *Woman* in Britain, and in Scandinavian publications. Several women have said they blushed to read it under the hairdryer. What they did not appreciate was that it was the full flowering of the prose talent first seen in *Nibbles and Me*.

"To Live in Love" unwinds like a film. It opens with a shot of X rays. Taylor's had a pain in her chest. Big C? No, but the scare has made them, Liz and Dick, realize they belong together. So back they go to Botswana, Africa: "the gut earth, back to where it all began."

Remarrying is her idea. Burton says marriage is just a piece of paper. But she wants the piece of paper.

Finally he gives in; the day is set; he gets dead drunk. She chooses her bridal dress. White won't do, nor blue jeans. She settles (a low blow) on a dress given her by Burton's late brother, Ivor—a kind of Druid garment of green trimmed with beads and bird feathers. For her hair, leaves and more beads. He threatens to spoil the scene with his old slacks and shapeless sweater, but she makes him change. He reappears in white (white is all right for him) trousers and a red turtleneck. Then they go and say their vows before "a legal-looking gentleman." (An actor too, perhaps?) Their voices quaver so badly that "if we'd been auditioning we would have been turned down instantly." Stage directions are supplied: "We exchanged rings, fathomless looks." The scene now shifts outdoors: "But the ceremony wasn't really completed until we went back to our riverbank and repeated our vows again with a Bible and all God's beauty around us." Back at her writing desk, possibly with a candle dripping onto the page, Mrs. Burton writes to Mr. Burton:

Dear Husb.

How about that? You really are my husband again and I have news for thee, there will be bloody no more marriages—or divorces.

We are stuck like chicken feathers to tar—for lovely always. Do you realize that we *shall* grow old together and I know the best is yet to be!

Why write that? Tempting fate? No. She writes it because she knows she is a public myth and dutifully writes letters to her constituents, just like a politician, to tell them what is going on. But by the time they appeared in print, Burton had left her for Susan Hunt, whom he married shortly after, and she was considering candidates for her seventh husband, a post now filled by John Warner of Virginia, former Secretary of the Navy.

The remarriage would have made a good ending to a movie,

or a book. It was deeply satisfying: two halves back together. "So Liz is back with Dick, huh?" (New York cab drivers are always reliable.) In the *Boston Globe*, columnist Ellen Goodman rejoiced: "Sturm has remarried Drang and all is right with the world. . . . In an era of friendly divorces and meaningful relationships, they stand for a marriage that is an all-consuming affair, not a partnership. None of this respecting each other's freedom but instead, saying 'I can't live without you.' Wow."

Francis Warner, moved, wrote an epithalamium for Burton's fiftieth birthday. (Note what the first letters of each line spell.)

> *Richard Quinquagenarian*
> If distant ages look back on our years
> Curious to know the myths by which we live—
> How our imagination dried our tears
> As Empire's actions grew contemplative—
> Richard, they'll thank you that retreat from power
> Diademed into all the arts that flower.
>
> Acknowledged round Earth's little ocean ball
> Now seen against its lighting-chart of space
> Deified with your lady, loved by all,
> Euridice herself returns with grace.
> Love is life's drama, poetry its land:
> Interpret still until all understand
>
> Zeitgeist and zest crystallize in the part
> Applauding History calls you to share
> Because you two make life a work of art
> Endowing myth with joy, and joy with care.
> Take up the tale, embody our ideals—
> Happy the night that rings these wedding peals.

"With whom can you compare Elizabeth," asks Francis Warner, "but Euridice?"

But Orpheus and Euridice did not manage to stick together for keeps, and neither did Liz and Dick. They exited, talking.

"Listen to this." I read to my Welsh in-laws from the *South Wales Evening Post*, shortly after the remarriage:

> "It is written into our wills that, when we die, we are to be placed next to my parents in the Jerusalem Chapel graveyard," he [Burton] revealed during a rare visit to his old home at the weekend.
>
> "Show me exactly where I'm to be buried, darling," urged Elizabeth Taylor, slender and beautiful in green slacks and a beige sweater adorned with a magnificent diamond pendant.
>
> Turning to me [wrote reporter Betty Hughes], she confided, "Do you know, during the two years Richard and I were separated, I never changed the clause in my will to have my grave here."

My mother-in-law, eighty, sighed with disgust. "In't it soppy!" she said.

Three weeks later the Burtons parted and headed for their second divorce. Why had they remarried? Taylor likes to be married, that's obvious. Also, Burton told a friend she was short of cash. Talking with David Lewin a few months before, Burton had acknowledged that she had a liquidity problem. "I know she is a very wealthy lady but all her money is tied up in assets like jewelry and she doesn't like selling anything." In fact, the remarriage was a second try worth making, a coda to a good long marriage, by anybody's measurement, and one that looked as if, in spite of the Medicean trappings, it might last for life.

The more interesting question is what finally snapped the marriage. Burton has made heroic efforts in recent years to give up drinking and even at its heaviest, Taylor was adept in dealing with it. Yet those close to them felt that it cannot help but have harmed their home life. Burton himself dismissed the booze factor. She understood that, he said. It was their careers. He spoke of the shame of acting, for a man. "It isn't natural to put on make-up and wear costumes on the stage and say someone else's lines," he told David Lewin. "So you drink to overcome the shame. . . . perhaps most actors are latent homosexuals and we cover it with drink. I was a homosexual once but not for long. But I tried it. It didn't work so I gave it up."

Isn't it strange that in all the public fascination with the Burtons, the essential truth never sunk home—that they were *actors?* Not royalty. Not Mr. and Mrs. Everyperson. Put actors in a situation and they inhabit the part. Burton is an Oxford man at Oxford, a hemophiliac among the hemophiliacs, a boyo at a rugby match, a Communist in Russia. (It was in Moscow in 1973 that he uttered my favorite Richard Burton quote: "I am a Communist at heart . . . I'm a multimillionaire. I make one and a quarter million dollars a picture. I realize that it sounds strange to say that I am a Communist at heart, but there is no contradiction because my earnings do not entail the exploitation of others." Taylor is wholeheartedly the devoted wife of each man she marries. Together the Burtons immersed themselves totally in the roles of the most famous movie stars in the world.

When the day comes for the story conference on the "Burton and Taylor" movie and they want a happy ending, there are at least two possibilities to try. One would be to give Burton a life peerage and let Taylor play Lady Burton. The other would be to give Burton an Academy Award for *Who's Afraid of Virginia Woolf?*

14

Elizabeth the Third

Part of me is sorry I became a public utility.
Elizabeth Taylor

But they will probably make the movie about her alone. Even at the height of his fame, Richard Burton could pass unnoticed in a crowd if he was without his lady. Taylor, never. Her face, as Andy Warhol showed, is like "Jackie," "Marilyn," "Elvis," and the Campbell soup can, one of the images by which we live. For sheer fame, she is with Dr. Spock and Muhammad Ali in the universal class, known far beyond the English-speaking world. She may be more widely known than Elizabeth II (a good research project for UNESCO?). A schoolchild in Toledo, Ohio, according to a news report, believes that Queen Elizabeth Taylor is on the British throne. Lucille Ball curtsied when the Burtons appeared on "I Love Lucy" and called Taylor "Your Highness" and "Your Majesty." And she's a less remote queen. We feel we know her so well. Mention her name and stand back. Out come pouring opinions, memories, dreams, fantasies, extravagant opinions about her life. Few are indifferent. Academics rush to recite the names of her husbands like bright kids rattling off their multiplication tables.

Elizabeth Taylor has more in common with Elizabeth II than a high voice, an odd shape, and conspicuous handbags. They are growing older in the same way, taking on the sexless look of Oriental potentates, with their geological gems and turbans that hide every shred of hair. And like primitive tribal chieftains, both women carry the royal taboo. The tremendous curiosity that surrounds them is a very thin covering for an intense envy of their privileges and mystical power. People feel an uncontrollable urge to see and if possible to touch, and then to gloat about having seen signs of ordinary imperfect humanity.

The emanations radiating from Taylor have not diminished with her appeal at the box office. If anything, they've increased, for the longer she survives, the more memories people retain of her, the more they feel there is a connection between her and them. "You have only to walk down the street with this lady to feel the electricity," says the producer Elliott Kastner. "It's mind-boggling. But she's got her act together. She handles it with enormous dignity." Even in celebrity-hardened Washington, she excites. In the *Washington Post* newsroom, defense reporter George Wilson watched Taylor walk in with publisher Katherine Graham. "That's Liz Taylor!" he said. "I can't stand it." He walked up and introduced himself—"Miss Taylor, I'm George Wilson"—and walked back to his desk. In Leningrad, American Ambassador Walter Stoessel and his wife visited the set of *Blue Bird*. They stood at the side, shy and grateful, as the star graciously came over to give a benediction.

All royalty have to pay a heavy price for their privileges. The ancient Mikado of Japan, says James Frazer in *The Golden Bough*, was obliged to sit every morning with the imperial crown on his head, without stirring hands, feet, head, or eyes, in order to preserve peace and tranquillity in his empire. The endurance trials in self-control and spartan self-denial that the British royal family go through are well known. The penalty for Elizabeth Taylor is to have to be oblivious to staring eyes. "Doesn't that bother you, Elizabeth?" George Cukor asked when the flashbulbs popped every time she walked onto the set. "No, not a bit," she said, "I just wipe them off." Burton used to describe the invisible shield that came down when she faced a crowd. She has often attributed it to something she learned from her father. Christian Science stoicism, perhaps? Whatever it is, her escorts don't carry it. They notice the mob. It bothers them. Perhaps that's why Taylor always seems to end up inhabiting her myth alone.

"Once in New York, I took her to see *Hello, Dolly*," said Brook Williams. "While we sat waiting for the curtain to go up, I heard a terrible buzzing noise." Williams imitated the noise. "I looked round. And it was the whole dress circle leaning over to get a look at her! The theater manager presented himself, and when we went out to get a drink at Sardi's, there were four hundred people in the street watching, and four policemen. And she didn't seem to notice at all!"

If you were a friend of Elizabeth Taylor's, you would insist that under the goddess there is an absolutely ordinary woman —full of fun, liberal, generous, unselfconscious. You wouldn't worry about entertaining her. She would like nothing better than to come over for some scrambled eggs and gossip. If you lived in England, she would bring her own Jack Daniel's and if you were in trouble, she would help you out, perhaps lend you her house in Mexico. Your children and your dogs would run over to her, and you would wonder if you dared to tell her she is far more beautiful without makeup and that her clothes are all wrong. ("Sim-*pli*-city, Elizabeth!" Elliott Kastner stretches out his hands pleadingly to an imaginary companion. He shrugs and gives up. "Elizabeth has taste up her ass. If she were low key, she'd leave Grace Kelly in the dust.") And all the while you were describing how plain and simple your friend was, you would brim over images of magic and divinity that make her ordinariness seem absolutely extraordinary.

Norma Heyman recalls meeting Taylor for the first time. A small, pretty woman, a former actress, she recognizes in herself "that tiny bit of jealousy we all have" in confronting great beauty.

"I had long been enchanted with Elizabeth Taylor," she said, "but from afar. When I was married to John Heyman, I was used to meeting film stars, but Elizabeth Taylor was different. She was the most awesome creature. I dreaded meeting her. I didn't know what to wear. I was pregnant and felt too fat. I put it off twice. But Elizabeth and Richard were clients of John's, and Elizabeth kept asking him where his wife was. Finally I agreed to go—to the theater. Mike Nichols was with us. I put on something nondescript. I was a vision in black remoteness. (Now I dress to make her laugh.) She sat next to me and the play went out of the window as far as I was concerned. I was conscious that she was smaller than I had expected and that she was dressed like a normal mortal . . . and that she had the most perfect face in profile that I had ever seen. At the interval, we went for drinks, and my husband said to me, 'Would you please take Miss Taylor to the bathroom?' And I was angry. 'This silly creature,' I said to myself. 'She can't even go to the loo by herself!' But then I realized that every woman in the theater had decided to go to the ladies' room. The whole room filled up. She seemed oblivious. And when she came out, she smiled and said to me, 'Thank you so much. That was very kind of you.' And I was completely won over. The jealousy went completely. I felt very protective. Of course, now I say to her, 'When I met you, you couldn't even pee on your own!' "

Can an ordinary mortal *be* oblivious? Of course not. Taylor often speaks of her myth as if it were something she viewed at a distance. At a charity auction for Israel in Amsterdam, for instance, she apologized, "The reason I'm doing this kind of Elizabeth Taylor stunt is that we must help the bereaved." Yet she plays the goddess too often and too readily to pretend that it is not a basic part of her. She knows the primitive power of her eyes, that people are afraid of them. (Because of both their width and their clarity, the eyes give the impression of an inner person watching, like portraits on detective-story walls.) She knows how to turn on their power. Norma Heyman calls it "the frost in her eyes." Burton used to like to demonstrate it.

"Come on, Elizabeth, give us The Look," he would say. And she would oblige. Everybody knows The Look. It's in all her movies. Back goes the head. The nostrils pinch in. The eyes widen and the power of a thousand cold blue lightbulbs flares out. It's a terrifying sight, accentuated by all the little winking glittering diamond eyes on her fingers and ears.

Who's afraid of that Elizabeth Taylor? We all are. She's the Queen of the Night, ready to make Eddie Fishers of us all. And it's my hunch that as long as she continues to play it, she will find it difficult to make her "all I want to be is a good wife to Nicky-Michael-Mike-Eddie-Richard-Johns" come true.

In recent years, as her career declined, her public image has become more likable. She has never had such a good press since the late forties. Her decision to ride high the New York-Washington circuit, after Burton departed, exhilarated a lot of divorced women. "I'm having a good time," she said, and just like flashing her diamond at the wedding crowd, it was just right. *Newsweek* called it "Liz Taylor's Brave New World." She could have had a good reign as Ms. Taylor, but she couldn't sustain it. "Elizabeth *has* to be in love," says Sheran Hornby. And love is always waiting. She entered her seventh marriage (WASP husband, Episcopalian rite) just over four months after her second divorce from Burton.

Can she act? Elizabeth Taylor's fame, now radiating from her diamonds and her marriages, rests on a life's production of more than fifty motion pictures that have issued with astonishing regularity every year with few exceptions since 1942, through husbands, divorces, near-deaths, childbirths, and scandals. Compared to her, Grace and Marilyn were streaks in the night. Marilyn had ten big years, from 1952 to 1962, and Grace reigned for a mere five. Taylor is one of the Stakhanovite stars; like John Wayne, Barbara Stanwyck, and Joan Crawford, who started in the twenties, she'll hit the seventy-picture mark if she keeps on going.

In 1950, after *Conspirator*, the Harvard *Lampoon* awarded Taylor its Roscoe Award, "for so gallantly persisting in her career despite the total inability to act." Today, in spite of her two Academy Awards and three nominations, many people hold the same view. "I suppose you're writing about her acting ability," they say, and giggle.

Few in the film world disparage her skill. Taylor is regarded as a true professional. Late to the set she may sometimes be, but she is totally in command of her craft when she gets there. According to Paul Newman, "She's not afraid to take chances in front of people. Visually, stars become very protective of themselves and very self-indulgent, but she's got a lot of guts. She'd go ahead and explore and risk falling on her face." Joseph Mankiewicz has said that if she were not a beauty, she'd be hailed as a great actress. Emlyn Williams says, "I have always thought her fame obscured her talent, which is very great." Burton said flatly that she was the best movie actress in the business and Waris Hussein, who had such a dismal experience with their *Divorce* films, says, "No one could say she couldn't act."

When George Cukor, known as a woman's director, worked with Taylor for the first time it was late in both their careers. Students at the American Film Institute asked him what it was like. "She's capable of enormous concentration," he said. "Also, she's a very accomplished actress; she knows what she's doing. But also, she's to be influenced and you say, 'It was too slow,' or if it was not believable you have to have an absolutely honest rapport. That's all. Only a stupid woman is absolutely inflexible and I've never had trouble with a good actor and she's a really very gifted actress and she tries all the time."

One reason her ability is underappreciated is that she was so dead-awful as a postadolescent actress that her reputation has never recovered. Yet from *A Place in the Sun* on, critics have been discovering that she is good and giving out the news: "Miss Taylor is breathtakingly beautiful. But more important, the kid can act—" (1951). "Rising twenty-four, she is now something of an actress. She ought not to be wasted so shamelessly" (1955). "Perhaps best of all, because least to be expected, is the performance of Elizabeth Taylor" (1960). "Suddenly Elizabeth Taylor is everywhere hailed as an actress; why suddenly? She has been not simply a temperamental beauty but an actress, a disciplined and distinguished performer on the stretched nerve, for years" (1972).

Yet she is also underrated because she is not consistently good. She needs a strong director. What does seem unfair to her is that lately she has grown much better, yet few have noticed because her pictures have been so bad. Here is a sample of notices she has collected for her flops:

NEW YORK HERALD TRIBUNE, *Reflections in a Golden Eye*: A Healthy Liz Taylor Shines in an Unsound Golden Eye.

NEW YORK, *Ash Wednesday*: The rottenness of this almost perfectly awful garbage about a middle-aged matron who goes under the plastic surgery knife (in nauseating bloody clinical close-ups) is flawed by tiny touches of value, among them a reasonable—and wasted—performance by Liz Taylor as the black-n-blue oversutured surgeree.

THE SPECTATOR, *Hammersmith Is Out*: There is nothing to do except watch Elizabeth Taylor as a dumb redhead act everyone else out of the picture.

THE GUARDIAN, *X, Y and Zee*: Go see it for Miss Taylor, a great professional who gets better as all around her get worse.

THE NEW YORKER, *Only Game in Town*: Elizabeth Taylor has a sweetness and despite her rather shapeless look a touching quality of frailty . . . but the plot makes her look ridiculous.

As her career wallowed in the doldrums, Taylor made two films that failed so quickly that they were hardly seen at all. *The Driver's Seat* (1974), also titled *Identikit*, was made in Rome from a Muriel Spark novel about a mad woman who pursues death until she finally persuades someone to strangle her. It was not released either in the United States or in Britain. Thanks to the intervention of Princess Grace, *The Driver's Seat* was screened at Monte Carlo during the 1974 Cannes Film Festival and busloads of critics from Cannes were shipped over to take a look. The other was *The Blue Bird*, the first American-Soviet major coproduction of a feature film (one of Mike Todd's old dreams). *The Blue Bird* had a very limited showing in the United States, none at all in Britain. Yet Taylor worked hard and well in both. Rex Reed called *The Driver's Seat* her most imaginative performance in years. "Taylor allows the camera to search out her daring flight into insanity with penetrating self-assurance." As for *The Blue Bird*, in which she played four parts and which kept her and the rest of the cast in Leningrad for months over schedule, *Variety* found her performance as Light, "dominant and dazzling," and as Maternal Love, "elegantly simple and believable."

If she got better as she went along, was it because Richard Burton taught her? Burton himself was always gallant. He sang hymns of praise to her ability. *He* had learned from *her*. "She taught me to cut down. I was obviously a very stagy actor—still am, I'm afraid, but I have picked up a lot of tricks from Elizabeth, because when I first worked with Elizabeth, when she was actually playing in the flesh before the cameras, I thought: She can't do it, she's not doing anything." But when he saw what the film had captured, especially from her eyes, the effect was overwhelming.

In 1966 the *Cleveland Plain Dealer*, taking a second look at *Cat on a Hot Tin Roof* and *Butterfield 8*, decided "pre-Burton Liz Was Talented. Revivals Here Prove It." It said that it was "unfair to conclude that whatever acting she does now or in the future is because some histrionic talent has rubbed off him and stuck on her." David Thomson, in his *Biographical Dictionary of the Cinema*, went one step further. "Marriage to Burton may have unsettled her by showing her how simple her own dramatic taste was. She altered from a presence to an actress. Not a bad actress but one unable to regain the shallow brittle clarity of *Butterfield 8*."

Bosley Crowther's summary view, offered from retirement, is nicely balanced: "She can be very good—but in a narrow range."

Unfortunately, Burton did nothing for her worse defects, her voice and her weight. Probably because of these and her notoriety, when Taylor is bad as an actress, she is infuriating. Male critics especially pour on her the kind of ridicule usually reserved for beauty queens who try for screen careers. *Time*'s treatment of her has been mentioned. Rex Reed of the *New York Daily News* can hit below the belt. Of *Hammersmith Is Out* (1973), he wrote: "Wobbling her enormous derriere across the screen in a manner so offensive, it would bring litigation from any dignified, self-respecting performer, and saying lines like 'I'm the biggest mother of them all,' she inspires pity instead of laughs. A good time to retire." For a sheer annihilating attack, Wilfred Sheed's in *Esquire* in 1968 has hardly been equaled. In "The Burtons Must Go" he dismissed *Virginia Woolf* as "their tiny triumph." He called Taylor herself "a subaverage film actress." "They have tried to exploit her fiery, earthy womanliness again and again . . ." he said, "but every time it comes out air and water because she hasn't the idiosyncrasy of voice and manner that colorful women have in real life. She can shout and lunge about with the best of them but this isn't interesting, just noisy. . . ." Pandro Berman delivers much the same verdict, in fewer words. "She's a shitty actress, the worst in the business. I can't look at her."

But women critics, like the rest of their sex, are now nicer to Taylor. She may have become a monster but they're on her side. Molly Haskell in *The Village Voice*: "She began with a period of maximum beauty and minimum talent, survived a time when she was just a dazzling embarrassment and at last her essence seems to have caught up with her image, and she has relaxed into one ripe, raucous, caterwauling paper tigress of a woman." Pauline Kael of *The New Yorker*, going to see *X, Y and Zee* (1972), gave Taylor the review she's always needed, one that judges the Life peeping through the Art:

> She wears her hair like upholstery, to balance the upholstery of flesh. The weight she has put on in these last years has not made her gracefully voluptuous; she's too hardboiled to be Ruben-esque. The weight seems to have brought out this coarseness, and now she basks in vulgarity. She uses it as a form of assault in *X, Y & Zee* and I don't think she's ever before been as strong a star personality.

What a loud uncontrolled performer like Taylor offers her audience, says Kael, is the element of accident and risk, the possibility that something grotesque may be revealed.

> But there is also the excitement of seeing a woman who has vast reserves of personality and who wants to come forward, who wants to make contact. There's a documentary going on inside this movie. . . . It's of a woman declaring herself to be what she has become. Like everyone else I adored the child Elizabeth Taylor, but I have never liked her as much since as in this bizarre exhibition. She's Beverly Hills Chaucerian, and that's as high and low as you can get.

It is ironic that the critics now seem to have a higher opinion of Elizabeth Taylor as an actress than the public does. Yet there is a reason. The critics can forget the myth. The public cannot. The novelist Penelope Mortimer, reviewing *Secret Ceremony*, described very acutely just what it is that comes between Taylor and her audience.

> In spite of her skill I have an irresistible compulsion to think of her as the Queen Mother playing charades.

Whatever the part, she is always and inescapably Elizabeth Taylor. In this picture, she is often very good, particularly when she is being snarlingly common: I have never seen anyone eat more convincingly on the screen, and her body, teetering along on high heels, conveys a lifetime of self-indulgence and sin. She is also very bad when she has to express emotion, or any subtlety of feeling. But good or bad, that face rides above the performance like a postage stamp: impeccable, bland, perfect, and not, by me, to be taken seriously.

Can she act? I think only a man from Mars could tell. If acting is the ability to portray someone else, she is almost always a total and utter failure. By choice. By allowing herself to become a public utility, she forfeited the possibility of being popularly recognized as an actress.

But she probably will never retire. Taylor may be as emotionally dependent on making movies as she is on being married.

While she has rarely conceded that she likes working, it is clear that whatever dressing up and playacting meant to her, it is still as important to her as when she was a child. Because she still blurs her screen and private worlds, she uses those double meanings in her scripts to explain her life to herself. Just before marrying John Warner in 1976, for example, she told David Wigg, "There is one particular line in the film *Night Music* that sounds like a cry from my heart—and the line is to my daughter: 'How would you feel about having a home of our very own and my acting when I really felt like it?'" Richard Brooks hopes that she will continue her career: "It's the only part of her life that's functioned," he says, "but she needs to choose well." Elliott Kastner too sees her as a great professional, a true thoroughbred, only waiting for her "Maggio"—the part that will do for her what the part in *From Here to Eternity* did for Frank Sinatra. If she does keep on working and gets the right parts, she could become, like Ingrid Bergman, one of the rare actresses who ages in public.

At the same time, she has always been deeply ambivalent

about her career. She means it when she says (Hugh French's version): "I'd like to be a hausfrau and then I could eat as much as I want and drink as much as I want." Part of her really hates her career and the public Elizabeth Taylor. If she hadn't, she would have worked on her voice—any girl in summer stock has a richer instrument—and she would not eat five-course meals. Compulsive eating looks like a protest, against her mother, against MGM, against the world for forcing her to be a star.

"There's nowhere to go when you retire from movies, except oblivion," says the fading actress in Tennessee Williams's *Sweet Bird of Youth*. Maybe Taylor now can face oblivion— that is, private life.

Today the world waits to see whether the Elizabeth Taylor myth will do for John Warner's ambitions what it did for Mike Todd's and Richard Burton's. The actress is now immersed in a new life, in the shadow of the Blue Ridge Mountains of Virginia. As a political wife, she is visible and accessible as never before. Full-face, the legendary beauty is gone, buried in weight that seems out of control. The natural light is cruel to its lines, as is the MGM makeup. But the profile, tilted up, is still perfect, and the eyes are eternal. As Mrs. Warner, Taylor is cultivating ordinariness. She clambers up windy hillsides and presents ribbons at pony competitions. She smiles patiently through Republican committee suppers. She is a patroness of local arts. The hair is held in place more often by a headscarf than by Alexandre. She shops at Safeway, and she stands (wearing treacherous flowing sleeves) in front of the kitchen stove, frying chicken.

She is aware of the suspicion that she is playing another part. "No," she has said, "I'm very much myself—which people either like or don't like. But I'm still me, and John's wife."

True? Or is she still fundamentally a movie queen, a femme fatale who by her very presence diminishes the man at her side? Time and the ballot box will tell. It is clear that she still likes top billing: "Mr. and Mrs. John Warner and the American Cancer Society request your presence . . ." It is also undeniable that certain elements in her Mrs. Warner contain echoes of past roles. She has begun giving seminars to drama students, not at Oxford, but at Virginia educational institutions. To the challenge that she has become an instant Republican, she replies, "I'm Republican by osmosis." Re-exhibiting her morbid fascination with her own death, she volunteers that she and Warner have chosen their grave sites. "I think that's sweet," she laughs for Joy Billington of the Washington *Star.* "We're going to be buried next to each other."

Soon after settling on Warner's 25,000-acre farm near Middleburg, she announced that she had found her roots at last. Perhaps she has. Still Jewish, she is back among the WASPs where she started. She may rebecome American. Perhaps as Mrs. Warner, she has found the identity—the politically tuned-in, horsy Virginia millionairess, a short-waisted Jackie—that will take her through middle age. If not, ahead lies Sunset Boulevard, the aging star with an unsettled love life, plotting her comeback.

By now virtually everybody carries a private Liz in his or her head. If there is one common thought about her, it is the hope that she will be settled and happy. She's tired, and we're tired. And guilty. Is it our fault that she's married so often—a kind of Hawthorne effect in which by observing we altered what we were watching? If we hadn't looked at the paparazzi photos and bought strapless dresses and chatted with cab drivers about Liz and Dick, could the ordinary mortal called Elizabeth Taylor have had a more tranquil existence?

It has to be an open question. Taylor is a survivor, a thirty-year veteran of the toughest game in the world. "I always swore I wouldn't end up like Judy," she once said, and she hasn't. She has not put her head in a gas oven or taken too many pills. Neither has she retreated like Garbo and Grace or gone into the boardroom as Joan Crawford did. She always looks as if she's having a good time—a warm shallow woman who loves her children, her jewels, her dogs and who is not greatly disturbed that the great untutored intellect that Burton used to boast about devotes itself to remembering everything she owns down to the last yellow chiffon scarf. She doesn't feel guilty, nor do those who started her on her career. Certainly not Pandro Berman.

"Do I feel responsible? Hell, no. Why should I? What changed her was becoming a superstar. George Stevens—he was responsible. He's dead. Let him be responsible. He got her at the psychologically right moment with *A Place in the Sun* and *Giant*. But listen, I don't feel sorry for them, these big stars who've gotten married lots of times. I feel sorry for the girl who's worked all her life and never got a husband. That's who I feel sorry for."

If she should die young, she will go up to heaven with Saint Marilyn. Ex-loves will sell their memoirs and there will be retrospectives of her work at film societies and exhibitions of her photographs at art galleries. *Father of the Bride* will be ranked above *Virginia Woolf* as a seminal film, a corrosive commentary on American marriage.

There can be no more Elizabeth Taylors. Richard Schickel, the film historian, has called her the last star. Sex will never be so dangerous again, nor will marriage. Nobody is going to live by Lives of the Stars and there are no movie studios left capable of spraying on a celestial glow.

And what of the Liz we're left with? She is still in the papers all the time. There are two of her, really. One is Elizabeth the Terrible, the movie monarch, fat and caftanish, still performing the most public private life in the world. The other is Fifties' Woman, someone who lived off her looks, spent her youth looking for great love in marriage, and realized too late that she could be good at her job. My guess is that it is the second Liz that now fascinates. With her bouffant hair, black-rimmed eyes, and indomitable faith in marriage and her Man, she's more valuable than her diamonds: a cultural icon, a living relic of the days when the prettiest girl had to have a man at her side or she was nothing. She's where we have been, the way we were, the way I was.

Taylor's Box Office Ratings Among the Top Ten

1958—2
1959—off list
1960—4
1961—1
1962—6
1963—6
1964—off list (Taylor was eleventh; Richard Burton was first.)
1965—9
1966—3
1967—6
1968—10

SOURCE: Quigley Publications Poll, Motion Picture Herald's Annual Exhibition Poll

Films of
Elizabeth Taylor

1. *Man or Mouse* (Universal, 1942)
2. *There's One Born Every Minute* (Universal, 1942)
3. *Lassie Come Home* (MGM, 1943)
4. *Jane Eyre* (Fox, 1943)
5. *The White Cliffs of Dover* (MGM, 1944)
6. *National Velvet* (MGM, 1944)
7. *Courage of Lassie* (MGM, 1946)
8. *Cynthia* (MGM, 1947)
9. *Life with Father* (Warner Brothers, 1947)
10. *A Date with Judy* (MGM, 1948)
11. *Julia Misbehaves* (MGM, 1948)
12. *Little Women* (MGM, 1949)
13. *Conspirator* (MGM—Britain, 1949)
14. *The Big Hangover* (MGM, 1949)
15. *Father of the Bride* (MGM, 1950)
16. *Father's Little Dividend* (MGM, 1951)
17. *A Place in the Sun* (Paramount, 1951)
18. *Callaway Went Thataway* (MGM, 1951)
19. *Love Is Better Than Ever* (MGM, 1951) (Britain—*The Light Fantastic*)

20. *Ivanhoe* (MGM—Britain, 1952)
21. *The Girl Who Had Everything* (MGM, 1952)
22. *Rhapsody* (MGM, 1952)
23. *Elephant Walk* (MGM, 1954)
24. *Beau Brummell* (MGM—Britain, 1954)
25. *The Last Time I Saw Paris* (MGM, 1954)
26. *Giant* (Warner Brothers, 1956)
27. *Raintree County* (MGM, 1957)
28. *Cat on a Hot Tin Roof* (MGM, 1958)
29. *Suddenly Last Summer* (Columbia, 1959)
30. *Butterfield 8* (MGM, 1960)
31. *Scent of Mystery* (Michael Todd, Jr., 1960)
32. *Cleopatra* (Twentieth Century-Fox, 1963)
33. *The VIPs* (MGM—Britain, 1963)
34. *The Sandpiper* (MGM, 1965)
35. *Who's Afraid of Virginia Woolf?* (Warner Brothers, 1966)
36. *The Taming of the Shrew* (Columbia, 1967)
37. *Doctor Faustus* (Columbia, 1967)
38. *Reflections in a Golden Eye* (Warner Brothers-Seven Arts, 1967)
39. *The Comedians* (MGM, 1967)
40. *Boom!* (Universal-World Film Services, 1968)
41. *Secret Ceremony* (Universal-World Film Services, 1968)
42. *The Only Game in Town* (Twentieth Century-Fox, 1969)
43. *X, Y and Zee* (Columbia, 1971) (Britain—*Zee & Co.*)
44. *Under Milk Wood* (Timon Films, 1971)
45. *Hammersmith Is Out* (J. Cornelius Cream Films, 1972)
46. *Night Watch* (Avco—Embassy, 1973)
47. *Divorce His, Divorce Hers* (ABC-TV-Harlech TV, 1973)
48. *Ash Wednesday* (Paramount, 1973)
49. *The Driver's Seat* (also titled *Identikit*) (Franco Rosselini, 1974)
50. *The Blue Bird* (Twentieth Century-Fox-Soviet Films, 1976)
51. *Victory at Entebbe* (Columbia—Warner, 1976)
52. *A Little Night Music*